MW01142235

SAGE was founded in 1965 by Sara Miller McCune to support the dissemination of usable knowledge by publishing innovative and high-quality research and teaching content. Today, we publish over 900 journals, including those of more than 400 learned societies, more than 800 new books per year, and a growing range of library products including archives, data, case studies, reports, and video. SAGE remains majority-owned by our founder, and after Sara's lifetime will become owned by a charitable trust that secures our continued independence.

Los Angeles | London | New Delhi | Singapore | Washington DC | Melbourne

Social Movements in Contemporary India

Thank you for choosing a SAGE product!
If you have any comment, observation or feedback,
I would like to personally hear from you.

Please write to me at **contactceo@sagepub.in**

Vivek Mehra, Managing Director and CEO, SAGE India.

Bulk Sales

SAGE India offers special discounts
for bulk institutional purchases.

For queries/orders/inspection copy requests,
write to **textbooksales@sagepub.in**

Publishing

Would you like to publish a textbook with SAGE?
Please send your proposal to **publishtextbook@sagepub.in**

Subscribe to our mailing list

Write to marketing@sagepub.in

This book is also available as an e-book.

Social Movements in Contemporary India

Krishna Menon

Professor, Gender Studies and Dean, School of Human Studies, Ambedkar University Delhi, New Delhi

Ranjana Subberwal

Senior Faculty, Alternative Learning Systems (ALS), and Chief Functionary, Raahein Development Society, New Delhi

Los Angeles | London | New Delhi
Singapore | Washington DC | Melbourne

First published in 2019 by

SAGE Publications India Pvt Ltd
B1/I-1 Mohan Cooperative Industrial Area
Mathura Road, New Delhi 110 044, India
www.sagepub.in

SAGE Publications Inc
2455 Teller Road
Thousand Oaks, California 91320, USA

SAGE Publications Ltd
1 Oliver's Yard, 55 City Road
London EC1Y 1SP, United Kingdom

SAGE Publications Asia-Pacific Pte Ltd
18 Cross Street #10-10/11/12
China Square Central
Singapore 048423

Published by Vivek Mehra for SAGE Publications India Pvt Ltd. Typeset in 10.5/12.5 pt Baskerville by Zaza Eunice, Hosur, Tamil Nadu, India.

Library of Congress Cataloging-in-Publication Data Available

ISBN: 978-93-532-8321-6 (PB)

SAGE Team: Amit Kumar, Indrani Dutta, Kanika Mathur, Ankit Verma and Sonam Rana

Contents

Detailed Contents

List of Abbreviations

ABVA	AIDS Bhedbhav Virodhi Andolan
ADA	Americans with Disabilities Act of 1990
ADAPT	Able Disabled All People Together
AIMPLB	All India Muslim Personal Law Board
ALS	Amyotrophic Lateral Sclerosis
BAMCEF	All India Backward and Minority Communities Employees Federation
BSP	Bahujan Samaj Party
CAN	Concerned Action Now
CPI(M)	Communist Party of India (Marxist)
DI	Disability Index
DNIS	Disability News and Information Service
DPI	Disabled Peoples' International
DRG	Disability Rights Group
DRM	Disability Rights Movement
DS-4	Dalit Shoshit Samaj Sangharsh Samiti
FCI	Food Corporation of India
IAC	India Against Corruption
ICDS	Integrated Child Development Services
ICF	International Classification of Functioning, Disability and Health
ICIDH	International Classification of Impairment, Disabilities and Handicaps
IDA	Indian Disability Act of 1995
IED	Inclusive Education of Disabled Children
INGO	international non-governmental organization
INP	Indo-Norwegian Project
IUCN	International Union for Conservation of Nature and Natural Resources
JFM	Joint Forest Management
KSMTF	Kerala Swathantra Maistya Thozhilali Federation
KSSP	Kerala Sasthra Sahithya Parishad
LGBT	lesbian, gay, bisexual and transgender
LCFF	Latin Catholic Fishermen's Federation
LPG	liberalization, privatization and globalization
MDM	Midday Meal Scheme
MFPs	minor forest products
MKSS	Mazdoor Kisan Shakti Sangathan
MNREGA	Mahatma Gandhi National Rural Employment Guarantee Act

MSM	Men Who Have Sex with Men
NAFTA	North American Free Trade Agreement
NBA	Narmada Bachao Andolan
NCPEDP	National Centre for Promotion of Employment for Disabled People
NCPRI	National Campaign for People's Rights to Information
NFDW	National Federation of Dalit Women
NFF	National Fishworkers Forum
NFSA	National Food Security Act
NGOs	non-governmental organizations
NSP	Narmada Sagar Project
NSSO	National Sample Survey Organization
NWDTA	Narmada Water Dispute Tribunal Award
PDS	public distribution system
POW	Progressive Organization of Women
Prism	People for the Rights of Indian Sexual Minorities
PUCL	People's Union for Civil Liberties
PUCLDR	People's Union for Civil Liberties and Democratic Rights
PWDs	persons with disabilities
R&R	resettlement and rehabilitation
RPI	Republican Party of India
RSS	Rashtriya Swayamsevak Sangh
RTFC	Right to Food Campaign
RTI	Right to Information
SAP	Structural Adjustment Programme
SEWA	Self-Employed Women's Association
SEZs	special economic zones
SHGs	self-help groups
SP	Samajwadi Party
SSD	Sardar Sarovar Dam
UCC	Uniform Civil Code
UPIAS	Union of the Physically Impaired Against Segregation
USV	Uttarakhand Sangharsh Vahini
VHP	Vishva Hindu Parishad
WTO	World Trade Organization
WWF	World Wildlife Fund

Preface

This book is inspired by the idea of a democratic, diverse and egalitarian India

Beset with deep fissures and ever-increasing zones of conflict, India is witness to a wide variety of social movements in contemporary times. The sheer magnitude and diversity make it impossible for any book to do justice to this vast and challenging field of study. This book is no exception. Although it is true that only few important movements have been included here, an attempt has nevertheless been made to give the readers a comprehensive understanding of the substantive issues and discourses around each movement. As the reader will realize, all the movements included here are ongoing; an attempt has been made to include the latest developments. Further, an effort has been made to relate specific movements to the wider society and the changes which are occurring within it.

The contents of this book were decided keeping in mind the importance of the issues the movements raised for the contemporary Indian society. Whether it is environment, Dalit, women or queer, the issues are clearly both contemporary and significant. An exceptional feature of the book is the inclusion of movements which rarely find a place in books on social movements such as queer, disability and civil society. It is also true that material on these movements was at times scanty and often scattered, and thus difficult to find.

As indicated in the title, the main thrust of the book is on India. However, it also delves into the concept and definition of social movements from different perspectives, general theories regarding their causes and consequences as well as the fundamental debates and treatises on the various issues confronting them (social movements). An effort has been made to incorporate all these facets.

This is an interdisciplinary text which draws upon research and empirical studies from disciplines such as political science and sociology.

The inspiration for this work came from our collective interest in the subject, years of research and an active participation in some of the movements. It was conceived, planned and written collectively by both of us.

ACKNOWLEDGEMENTS

This work is the result of the support and motivation extended to us by many students, friends, family and colleagues. This list would be very long if we name each and every one of them. However, Amit Kumar and Indrani Dutta of SAGE require to be mentioned, especially for their patience and faith in our abilities to deliver the book even when we lost hope.

We benefitted greatly from the insights of the three anonymous reviewers who steered our discussions in meaningful directions.

Media Collective has generously shared photographs that have enlivened the book. We are grateful to them. The photographs for Chapter 5 have been provided by National Centre for Promotion of Employment for Disabled People (NCPEDP), our gratitude to them.

A rich collection of relevant books at the Nehru Memorial Museum & Library, the wonderful and helpful staff and the serene ambience of the place gave impetus to the book.

Our association at different points in time with different movements, offered us an opportunity to learn and sharpen our understanding of the complexities of social movements in contemporary India.

About the Authors

Krishna Menon is Professor, Gender Studies, and currently the Dean, School of Human Studies at Ambedkar University Delhi. Her areas of interest include political theory, Indian politics, and feminist theory and politics. She has published several books, papers and articles on the above fields. Her publications include 'On the Question of Free Speech and Censorship' in *The State of Hurt* (2016), 'Justice' and 'Sovereignty' in *Political Theory: An Introduction* (2008), 'Human Rights—A Theoretical Foray' in *Applied Ethics and Human Rights* (2010), *Human Rights, Gender and the Environment* (2009) and *Gender and Identity: A Case Study of Nurses from Kerala in Delhi* (with Sumangala Damodaran, 2008). She has presented papers in international and national seminars. Dr Menon was awarded the Teacher of Distinction award by the Vice Chancellor of the University of Delhi in 2009. She is the Principal Investigator in a UGC–UKIERI research project with the University of Edinburgh on feminist pedagogy. As a member of a study group, appointed by the Lt Governor of Delhi, she has co-authored a report on women's safety in public spaces in Delhi (2018). She is on the editorial board of the *International Feminist Journal of Politics*.

She is a trained Carnatic musician and a Bharatanatyam dancer with a long record of performances. She was the classical dance critic of *The Indian Express* (New Delhi edition, 1992–1995).

Ranjana Subberwal, a postgraduate in sociology from Delhi School of Economics, University of Delhi, is presently the Chief Functionary of Raahein Development Society, an NGO committed to research, action and advocacy for, by and with the marginalized sections of society. She has also been teaching sociology to civil service aspirants (for Prelims and Mains examinations) for over 30 years, initially at Rau's Study Circle and now at Alternative Learning Systems (ALS). She has participated in and directed grassroots-level projects, research and advocacy on socially relevant issues for over three decades in the spheres of education, income generation, health, family planning and rehabilitation for the marginalized sections of society—including women, children and persons with disabilities—in different parts of India. She has been associated with organizations such as Indian Institute of Mass Communication, Council of Social Development, Centre for the Study of Developing Societies, Concerned Action Now (CAN) and Raahein Development Society.

She has authored and co-authored a number of research reports/articles and one book. These include 'Dilemmas of Democracy' *Mainstream* (vol. 30, no. 46); 'Turmoil and Change in the Western Family' *Mainstream* (vol. 32, no. 28); 'Pride and Prejudice' *Mainstream* (vol. 32, no. 52); 'The New Life Centre', a research report on day care services for the disabled, prepared for the Leprosy Mission of India; 'Project EKJUT: An Action Learning Project to Assess the Impact of the Indian Disability Act' for ActionAid, India; a policy paper on disability issues for OXFAM; 'Disabled People' in *No Foresight...No Follow Up* published by Indian People's Tribunal on Environment and Human Rights; 'Innovative Strategies for Distance Learning for People with Disabilities in an Urban Slum of Delhi' for IGNOU; and *Sociology Dictionary* (2009).

She is a studio potter and has participated in a number of group exhibitions and pottery events.

1

Understanding Social Movements: An Introduction

Every important social movement reconfigures the world in the imagination. What was obscure comes forward, lies are revealed, memory shaken, new delineations drawn over old maps: it is from this new way of seeing the present that hope emerges for the future…. Let us begin to imagine the worlds we would like to inhabit, the long lives we will share, and the many futures in our hands.

—Susan Griffin

The contemporary world has at times been described as the 'social movement's world', as a bewildering array of collectivities of all genres and diversities spread in varied geographical, sociocultural and historical spaces give voice to their concerns. Although social movements have long functioned as a means of articulating grievances or claiming rights, the conspicuous space which they occupy on the world canvas today is truly intriguing. Passionately contested issues around people's concerns for their rights and welfare, including those of women, Dalits, queer, persons with disabilities, farmers, ethnic and religious groups and tribes, provide the adhesive around which they are mobilized, in large numbers, locally, nationally or internationally, for collective action.

As proliferation of social movements is taking place, there is also an upsurge in serious research and theorizing on the subject. The present chapter aims to detail the important social movement writings and theories that have been put forward over the decades, internationally as well as in India, with focus on core fundamental issues and their varied interpretations.

A LATE ENTRANT IN SOCIAL SCIENCES

Although by mid-19th century, intellectuals had started recognizing the role of masses in bringing about social transformation, serious studies on social movements only emerged in the 20th century, especially in its latter half. In India too, major contributions came up in the last few decades, although a number of significant movements such as the SNDP[1] or the DK[2] developed in the early decades of 20th century.

Historians, with their focus on the life cycle approach giving a detailed account of events through a time span, were among the first ones to study social movements. 'But little effort was made to extrapolate from case studies and formulate hypotheses and theories' (Oommen 2010, 1, I).

Psychologists, on the other hand, became involved in social movement studies with the rise of Nazism in Germany and development of concepts like authoritarian personality.[3] They have focused on the needs, frustrations and motives of individual participants which prompt them to participate in social movements.

Political scientists took up this sphere of study much later because, following the Second World War, the structural–functional approach with its focus on stability, harmony and equilibrium rather than on strife, conflict and change became dominant in social sciences. As a result, most studies were engaged with the functioning of political institutions and their role in resolving internal conflicts rather than in discussing anti-establishment conflicts, collective action outside the framework of institutions and the like. It is only in recent years that political scientists have started studying social movements as an important aspect of the political process in the contemporary world.

Sociologists and social anthropologists are the most recent entrants to the study of social movements. Early sociologists, just like early political scientists, followed the vastly popular structural–functional perspective. It is only in the last few decades that significant research and theorizing have been done in this field and conceptual reflections have been integrated with general sociological concepts. Incidentally, social movement studies became a separate subfield, first, in sociology (Fuchs and Linkenbach 2003). Today, it is a vibrant subfield which includes defining the concept and differentiating it from other types of collective action; understanding the conditions which lead to the formation of social movements; identifying factors which motivate people to join in; examining the structures of social movements and their action tactics and lastly, outlining and enumerating their consequences (Wilson 1973, cited in Kuumba 2001, 8).

---

[1] SNDP stands for Sri Narayana Dharma Paripalana movement (movement for propagation of the philosophy of Sri Narayana Guru Swamy) among the Izhavas, a low caste of toddy tappers of Kerala.

[2] DK or the Dravida Kazhagam movement developed in Tamil Nadu as a movement of the non-Brahmins who discarded the Aryan culture and idealized the Dravidian culture.

[3] The concept of authoritarian personality is mainly attributed to Theodor Adorno. It is a particular type of personality which is rigid and authoritarian and it characteristically develops in the family structures of capitalist societies. Such a personality develops due to authoritarian parent–child relationship where parents severely control the child who experiences denial. This situation produces a personality that reveres authority. Authoritarianism can be measured through the F–scale, a classic authoritarian scale. Through this concept, Adorno explained the rise of Nazism and subsequent holocaust.

Hence, although on the one hand, social movement literature started to develop largely in political science and sociology, it is also true that social movements themselves started impacting the concepts and academic deliberations in these and other social sciences. For instance, due to the women's liberation movement, 'academic disciplines and theoretical paradigms have been revisited and transformed in ways that have filled in gaps and corrected sexist biases' (Stacey and Thorne 1985, cited in Kuumba 2001, 9). Increased gender consciousness in sociology has led to more in-depth studies of feminist movement. Similar impact may also be seen in other cases such as Dalits or ethnic groups. Clearly, incorporating movement studies in broad academic research is essential as at times it has even helped in redefining basic concepts such as society and culture (Fuchs and Linkenbach 2003).

As is clear, the last few decades have seen an expansion of serious research and debate on social movements in different social sciences. The definition of social movements, their features and typology, the causes for their emergence and their consequences are some of the important areas of research. This expansion first occurred in the West and some years later in India. Although few Indian writings are closely aligned to specific Western scholarship, there are those which are derived from India-specific studies based on a critical assessment of the Western theories. Given further is an account of the most important theoretical deliberations in the field of social movements.

WHAT ARE SOCIAL MOVEMENTS?

Despite a huge amount of literature on it, a clear and cohesive definition of social movements that would be generally acceptable is still lacking. In the view of Diani, 'even an implicit, empirical "agreement" about the use of the term is largely missing' (Diani 1992, 2). Many attribute it to the basic nature of social movements. Social movements include a wide gamut of social and political phenomena, thus making their definition difficult. Further, they share a resemblance with certain entities that do not qualify as social movements (Wittgenstein 1953). 'Each movement shares some features in common with some other movements, without any feature being both sufficiently inclusive and sufficiently exclusive to demarcate and identify the set' (Crossley 2002, 2). The features which are common to all social movements are also found in entities that do not qualify as social movements and those features which are unique to some are missing in others. Moreover, movements have no clear beginning or end and they may change their basic nature with time, thus making definitions even more difficult. In addition, the terms associated with social movements such as protest, collective action or even social movement itself are commonly used terms and their use often varies according to the context. It is these factors that make defining of social movements an arduous task.

However, it can be said that most social movements 'are based on three or more of the following axes: collective or joint action; change oriented goals or claims; some extra or non-institutional collective action; some degree of organization; and some degree of temporal continuity' (Snow, Soule, and Kriesi 2004, 6). An understanding of these axes is important to comprehend the nature of social movements.

Social movements are one type of collective action. However, there are many other types of collective action. A collective action is any action jointly performed by two or more people to achieve certain common goals. It includes a large variety of human behaviours. A rock star's fans swaying together to his or her music, rioters looting stores, members of Indian Medical Association sending petitions to the authorities in large numbers or gangs indulging in street fights, are all examples of collective action but they are not social movements.

To narrow down to social movements, it will be useful to take up another feature of collective action. There are those collective actions which are within the institutional framework, while following a normative pattern. However, there are others which fall outside the limits of institutions. Social movements are often defined on the basis of their non-institutional character such as sloganeering outside a government office or illegally occupying public spaces to ensure that their demands are met. It should be reiterated here that social movements are not the only collective actions which have non-institutional feature but adding this dimension to the definition helps us to reduce the number of collective actions which have a similarity with social movements.

Another step which will take us closer to the definition of social movement is its relationship with collective behaviour. Generally, collective behaviour refers to 'extra institutional, group-problem solving behaviour that encompasses an array of collective actions, ranging from protest demonstrations, to behaviour in disasters, to mass or diffuse phenomena, such as fads and crazes, to social movements and even revolution' (Snow and Oliver 1995, 571). It is clear then that social movement is not only a collective action, but also a type of collective behaviour. It is, however, different from many other types of collective behaviour or extra-institutional behaviour such as mobs or crowds.

Relating social movements to interest groups is another important step towards their definition. Although social movements share some common characteristics with interest groups, they also differ from them in important ways. The two may be similar in the objectives they pursue but they differ in many other respects. The explanation of interest groups is generally with reference to the government or a political institution; the sphere of social movement goes much further than that to other institutions and authorities. Moreover, even if social movements directly address the political arena, there is a clear difference with interest groups in terms of their standing. Interest groups are entrenched within the political sphere; their members are seen as legitimate entities within them. This is not the case with social movements. They are typically seen as being outside the political hub having an unstable relationship with it. They neither have the access to political authorities the way interest groups have, nor the influence. Further, the interest groups follow their objectives through legal means such as taking donations or campaigning legally; social movements do so by organizing protest marches, blockages and rallies. Even if they agitate within the political sphere, their nature remains extra-institutional and their relationship with the political groups remains precarious. Interest groups and social movements are thus rather similar while their relationship with the state may differ resulting in different kinds of strategies and behaviour (Gamson 1990).

It should be made clear at this juncture that although different from other types of collective behaviours or interest groups, social movements may at times overlap with them. Taking the case of crowds, although they often arise spontaneously and wither away quickly, they may also be the outcome of planning and may even be sponsored by a social movement. Further, a social movement may over time become institutionalized and may transform into an interest group.

As we seek to define social movements, an important feature on which there is a general consensus is that social movements aim to either bring about change or to resist change. However, there are varied views on the type of change and the extent of change. There are those who think that the nature of change is not limited to any particular arena, and there are others who believe that the main arena of change that social movements seek is in the field of policy. The views of Tourraine and McAdam are in line with the latter argument. Tourraine focused on the 'anti-establishment social content' of social movements with orientation to liberty, equality and equity, human rights and dignity (Touraine 1995, 243). McAdam looks at social movement as a variation of 'contentious politics' which refers to 'collective political struggle' that is 'episodic' in the sense of not being regularly scheduled on the political docket, 'public' in the sense of excluding claim making 'that occurs entirely within well-bounded organizations' and 'manifestly political' in the sense that a government is involved as a claimant, target or mediator (McAdam, Tarrow, and Tilly 2001, 5). A more acceptable view with regard to the arena of change brought about by social movement is that both the above approaches are limited, the former being too indistinct and the latter being too narrow. Thus, movements should be seen as disputing or defending the existing order, whether in the field of polity, economy, religion, education or the like (Snow, Soule, and Kriesi 2004).

Another defining feature of social movements on which there is a general agreement is that social movements are not spontaneous uprisings but are essentially organized. Organization would mean having a leader and a working structure based on defined objectives and ideologies. There is, however, a debate regarding the extent of organization. While Lenin held that organization is the key factor in working class movement, Piven and Cloward believed that too much focus on organization is adverse for movements, especially the ones which involve the poor (Piven and Cloward 1977).

For McCarthy and Zald, social movement organization is the key to mobilizing support and achieving the goals of any movement (McCarthy and Zald 1977). Della Porta and Diani have, on the other hand, called social movements 'networks of interaction between actors' which may have formal organization or may not, depending on extraneous circumstances (Porta and Diani

1999, 16). It would be right to say that while most people agree that there is organization in all social movements, they differ on the extent and forms of organization.

Lastly, there is the question on whether movements involve sustained collective action. While most agree that movement action is sustained action, there are some who talk about periods when movement activities are at their peak, followed by an inactive period (Rupp and Taylor 1987), while others believe that most movements are 'clustered temporally within "cycles of protest" that wax and wane historically' (Tarrow 1998). Just like organization, continuity is also a matter of degree. Some sustained action over a period of time is necessary for a social movement.

THE DEFINITION

Keeping the aforementioned dimensions in mind, a fairly comprehensive definition of social movements could be as follows:

> *Collectivities acting with some degree of organization and continuity outside of institutional or organizational channels for the purpose of challenging or defending extant authority, whether it is institutionally or culturally based in the group, organization, society, culture, or world order of which they are a part. (Snow, Soule, and Kriesi 2004, 11)*

Adding to these are features given by Mario Diani: 'Social movements are a distinct social process, consisting of the mechanism through which actors engaged in collective action:

- Are involved in conflictual relations with clearly identified opponents;
- Are linked by dense informal networks;
- Share a distinct collective identity' (Diani 1992, 10–35).

Conflictual relations are formed when different actors get involved in cultural or/and political conflicts in order to bring about or resist change. They make similar claims on political, economic or cultural power, harming the interests of others (Tilly 1978; Touraine 1981, 80–4). It should be noted that merely raising issues of collective concern, whether that of environment or disarmament, do not qualify as social movements unless they are expressed in political and social terms.

Dense informal networks imply that 'both individual and organized actors, while keeping their autonomy and independence, engage in sustained exchanges of resources in pursuit of common goals' (Porta and Diani [1999] 2006, 21).

Collective identity is an essential feature of a social movement. Collective identity implies shared interests, recognition of common membership and commitment to common goals. It is created when actors put together their experiences and weave them into a common discourse (Melucci 1996).

It should be noted that most definitions on social movements generally revolve around the features given earlier, at times to a greater or to a lesser extent. This is true of Indian writers as well. M. S. A. Rao, an early theorist, defined social movement as sustained collective action involving a large number of people. Although it is generally oriented towards bringing about change, it may also be aimed at sustaining a system rather than changing it. Ideology is a crucial feature of a social movement which distinguishes it from other types of collective actions also aimed at bringing about change. Thus, spontaneous protests by students or other groups do not qualify as a social movement since it lacks in an ideology although it is collective action oriented to change. However, unlike most other thinkers, Rao believed that a social movement may or may not have a formal organization (Rao 1978).

In a recent work, T. K. Oommen analysed the definitions of various theorists and came to the conclusion that social movements, 'should be conceptualized as those purposive collective mobilizations, informed of an ideology to promote change or stability, using any means—violent or non-violent—functioning within at least an elementary organizational framework' (cf. Wilkinson 1971, cited in Oommen 2010, 11, I).

Although it seems that there is a kind of broad consensus on the definition of a social movement, it should be clarified that these defining features are neither equally emphasized by all thinkers nor are they equally applicable to all movements. Some features may be accentuated in certain movements while others may be subdued. It should also be noted that features may change as movements evolve.

THEORETICAL APPROACHES TO THE STUDY OF SOCIAL MOVEMENTS

Over a period of time, there has been a perceptible shift in theorizing about social movements on why they emerge, the nature of their organization, their strategies, ideologies and outcomes. This has been due to the dynamic nature of social movements and changes in the social and political milieu in which they occur. The shift is also because of theoretical disputes between well-established perspectives such as functionalism, conflict theory and phenomenology which forced people to think anew about social movements. Further, new theoretical perspectives put forward by a new generation of theoreticians also facilitated fresh research. Moreover, attitudes towards social movements changed over time. Earlier, scholars saw social movements as crowds who were often led by demagogues acting irrationally and emotionally to make their voices heard. In the 1960s, as the civil rights movement progressed in the USA, a better understanding of such movements emerged. It was no longer possible to reject such movements as imprudent and unwise (Goodwin and Jasper 2003).

SOCIAL MOVEMENT THEORIES

At this stage it is important to delineate the main theories of social movements. At the outset we can say that the main theories of social movement emerged in Europe and America although their trajectory was different. In Crossley's words, 'the European trajectory has been more firmly framed by the Marxist/Hegelian tradition of the philosophy of history, while the American tradition, if equally indebted to Marx in certain respects, has adopted a more empirical, scientific and, to a degree, empiricist frame' (Crossley 2002, 10). On one hand, the main thrust of the European thinkers has been on studying social movements in the context of the fundamental conflicts in a society and its history. On the other hand, American theorists study a variety of social movements such as civil rights or feminism through empirical data with less focus on their historical context (Crossley 2002).

Taking 1970 as the cut-off year, Crossley labels social movement theories in Europe and America as shown in Table 1.1.

As is clear, in the pre-1970s era, in Europe, the understanding of social movements was still entrenched in Marxist tradition. In America, on the other hand, the theories were included under the generic term collective behaviour approach. In the years following the 1970s, newer theories of social movement developed in both Europe and America. In Europe, these recent theories were referred to as 'new social movement theories'. They are described thus because they emerged in Europe in the post 1970s when there was serious criticism of Marx's views on capitalism and proletarian revolution and newer issues such as environment, disarmament and child rights became the central focus. Although their inspiration came from Marxist ideas of proletarian revolution, the new social movements represented the newer conflicts in changed times (Crossley 2010).

In America, the shift occurred from 'collective behaviour' to 'resource mobilization approach'. By the 1980s, a new dimension was added to 'resource mobilization', the 'political processes approach'. While the resource mobilization approach looks at how 'costs, rewards and incentives' provided motivation for movements, the political processes approach looks at how opportunities for protest lay within the political system (Crossley 2010, 12).

TABLE 1.1   Social Movement Theories in Europe and America

	USA	Europe
Pre-1970s	Collective behaviour	Marxism
1970s onwards	Resource mobilization/political processes	New social movements

Source: Crossley (2002, 10)

In the late 1980s, more theories emerged in the West. These are the social network theories and theories based on the cultural approach. It should be noted here that in general, theorists have looked for the cause of movements either in features of the protestors or in the wider environment, whether economic, social or political; it is the cultural approaches which have tried to combine the two to understand the origin of movements.

Investigating Social Movements

The first set of questions while studying social movements refers to the relationship between structural change and transformations in patterns of social conflict. Can we see social movements as expressions of conflicts?

Another set of questions has to do with the role of cultural representations in social conflict. How are social problems identified as potential objects of collective action? How do certain social actors come to develop a sense of commonality and to identify with a collective? Where do social movement cultures and values originate from?

A third set of questions addresses the process through which values, interests and ideas get turned into collective action. What forms do organizations take in their attempts to maximize the strength of collective challenges and their outcomes?

Finally, it has frequently been asked how a certain social, political and/or cultural context affects social movements' chances of success and the forms they take. What does explain the varying intensity over time of collective violence and other types of public challenges against power holders? There are of course many variables and political formations that are an important factor that determines the trajectory of any particular social movement.

EARLY THEORIES: COLLECTIVE BEHAVIOUR

As mentioned earlier, a group of early theories (prior to the 1970s) on social movements have been included under the generic term 'collective behaviour'. Social movements were considered as a subtype within collective behaviour just as crowds, riots, panics and crazes were. It came to be widely believed that strain and breakdown produce collective behaviour of all types including social movements. Summarizing these theories, a number of thinkers have identified the following as their central features (Oberschall 1973; Tilly 1978; McAdam 1982). They argue that social movements are a consequence of strain and breakdown, deprivation, anomie and other such hardships which provide the necessary condition and that movements are an irrational, essentially psychological, response to widespread unsettling changes. They also argue that people who participate in them are not properly integrated in the society and are prone to collective hysteria. Collective behaviour theorists tend to club social movements with crazes and panics.

It is widely believed that the foundation of these theories lay in Durkheim's concepts of division of labour and suicide although the term collective behaviour came into use much later. According to Durkheim, the basic condition of social life is that of integration and order. This is visible in simple societies having high collective consciousness and mechanical solidarity. As societies become more complex, collective consciousness declines although they still have solidarity in the form of organic solidarity. Such societies are characterized by anomie and egoism, strain and breakdown which could result in suicide and other forms of deviance. Durkheim's remedy lies in increased moral and normative regulation.

Another and a more direct link to strain and breakdown lies in the theories on crowd behaviour, given by European thinkers around the same time as Durkheim. According to this view, civil violence occurs with breakdown of social control mechanisms because of 'spread of crowd mentality' (Rule 1988, 83). This view was later developed by Robert E. Park, the American sociologist who is said to have been responsible for establishing collective behaviour theory in America. Like the European theorists, he said that collective behaviour is related to breakdown of social controls but unlike them he said this could also be positive and could account for a healthy society.

SYMBOLIC INTERACTIONIST VIEW

Entrenched in symbolic interactionism,[4] a perspective first developed by G. H. Mead, Herbert Blumer recognized collective behaviour as a subfield in sociology. According to Blumer (1951), all types of collective behaviours, whether crowd, panic or social movements, are characterized by social unrest which occurs due to disruptions in everyday life. Social movements emerge as a spontaneous and unstructured reaction against such disruptions. Blumer's view was further developed by Turner and Killian ([1957] 1987) who said that although collective behaviour is initially unstructured, it may promote normative order through interaction and rational communication.

RELATIVE DEPRIVATION VIEW

Relative deprivation theories are a variant within collective behaviour tradition. Unlike the aforementioned theories which focus on structural strain and breakdown, these theories focus on

---

[4] Symbolic interactionism is a perspective associated with George Herbert Mead and his theory of self. It is by interacting with others that a child develops the ability to imagine himself or herself in the role of others and is in a position to act towards himself or herself as others do. The perspective was developed by Herbert Blumer.

socio-psychological strain that people may experience because they assess their present status, in comparison to their reference groups, their past status or in terms of future situations, in a negative way. Relative deprivation is a condition where a person evaluates his/her status with certain reference points as a benchmark. This comparison drives people towards collective behaviour. For Aberle (1966), relative deprivation is the 'negative discrepancy between legitimate expectations and actuality'. This he said is the basis of social movements. Ted Gurr (1980) further elaborated on the concept by defining relative deprivation in terms of expectations as well as 'perceived capabilities'. According to him, 'relative deprivation is a gap between expectations and perceived capabilities involving three sets of values: economic conditions, political power and social status'. In these views, relative deprivation produces strain which encourages collective behaviour.

STRUCTURAL STRAIN VIEW

Neil J. Smelser's view of structural strain is another important view entrenched in the collective behaviour approach. According to Smelser, an incident of any type of collective behaviour, whether panics, riots, reform or revolutionary movements, occurs due to structural strain. Smelser defined structural strain as conflicts, inconsistencies and abstractions in the social structure which provoke irrational and excessive responses which get enlarged by the generalized beliefs. If, at this stage, effective social controls are present, the development of collective behaviour can be prevented. According to Smelser, thus, breakdown in social controls is crucial to the development of an episode of collective behaviour.

MASS SOCIETY VIEW

Inspired by Durkheim's theory of anomie[5] and increasing egoism in modern society, mass society theorists argued (Kornhauser 1959) that there is diminishing significance of small groups and a marked increase in large-scale social structures which account for instances of alienation and isolation among people. These alienated individuals looking for some kind of social support tend to join in collective behaviour.

AN APPRAISAL OF COLLECTIVE BEHAVIOUR THEORIES

It should be noted here that strain and breakdown view of collective behaviour connected a number of diverse approaches to each other. Durkheim's view came to be related to European crowd theorists while Chicago school to structural functionalism. Despite these variants, there is a broad consensus

---

[5] Anomie, as given by Emile Durkheim, is a socio-psychological condition which exists typically in modern complex societies. Such societies change at a fast pace creating a situation of normative turmoil when old norms are still there while new norms come in. As a result, what people want and expect from life is disrupted. Since norms limit desires and expectations, in the state of normative turmoil, they become unlimited leading to unhappiness.

among these collective behaviour theorists. First, collective behaviour occurs due to breakdown or strain in the normal routine life of people. Second, collective behaviour is very different from conventional behaviour in that it is unstructured, spontaneous and expressive. Some thinkers call it irrational, dangerous and disorderly, although Park did talk about its positive side and Turner and Killian ([1957] 1987) focused on rational communication in a crowd. Despite these positive views, the negative criticisms of collective behaviour were responsible for the decline of these theories. In fact, a paradigm shift occurred which led to a near disappearance of theories of collective behaviour. With new generation of sociologists coming in, the emphasis shifted from order and integration to conflict, resistance and change. Moreover, large-scale political and social changes gave impetus to this paradigm shift. Amidst these widespread changes, there was criticism of collective behaviour tradition which came from many quarters, especially from resource mobilization theorists.

In his criticism of collective behaviour tradition, McAdam (1982) put forward a number of points. According to him, while relating social strain to social movements, these theorists have ignored the political milieu in which movements occur. Further, they have related macro-level strain to micro-level behaviour in a linear causal relationship which is problematic. Another problematic area is that collective behaviour tradition relates discontentment at the level of the individual to be the cause of a social movement. They explain social movements through negative psychological profiling of the participants. The explanations they have given are more psychological than political and social movement action as deviant action rather than as political action (McAdam 1982).

Collective behaviour approach (influenced by Durkheim's views on collective psychology and anomie) has been criticized by Charles Tilly (1978). Basing the views on hard data, critics have rejected the notion that increase in objective conditions such as strain and deprivation leads to increase in movement activity. In fact, movement activities increase during reform and economic growth. Further, the critics claim that conflict and strains are a constant factor in a society and they cannot explain movements which occur sporadically and vary in their intensity. For instance, although the strain and conflict between racial groups was there for a long time, the civil rights movement occurred only in the 1960s. According to collective behaviour theorists, individuals who join movements are less integrated in society. On the contrary, it has been found that underlying movements are pre-existing networks which facilitate them. The critics also argue that movement activity is a rational activity and not irrational as reiterated by collective behaviour theorists.

Skolnick in his study of the urban race riots in the 1960s found the explanation given by collective behaviour theorists as deeply flawed. By relating the riots to frustrations and resentment which occur as a consequence of social strain and breakdown of social controls, they considered the behaviour of rioters as destructive and irrational. Skolnick challenged this explanation on many counts such as the vagueness of terms like frustration, the participants being deviants and the explanation being purely psychological. According to Skolnick, these were ordinary people responding to a political situation. Their violence could be better explained in terms of the relationship between the protesters and the authorities.

Hence, the basic assumptions of strain and breakdown theories were questioned and alternate theories were put forward.

LATER THEORIES: RESOURCE MOBILIZATION THEORY

A group of theories which followed the collective behaviour approaches have been included under the generic term 'resource mobilization theories'. They developed in the USA following social movements of the 1960s and 1970s such as civil rights and feminism. Rejecting the psychological orientation of the collective behaviour approach, they focused, instead, on the rational orientation of the participants. According to this approach, it is the financial, organizational and human resources that play a key role in the rise of social movements. The resource mobilization approach looks at how 'costs, rewards and incentives' provided motivation for movements (Crossley 2010, 12). This approach gives an economic explanation of protest. At the core of social movements are formal organizations also called social movement organizations. Being rational organizations, they work just like firms, acquiring resources, recruiting those whose goals and interests match with theirs and advertising their profile to those who can make contributions. There may often be competition between different social movement organizations for contributions. A number of social movement organizations together can be called a 'social movement industry' (Goodwin and Jasper 2003, 6). This approach was called resource mobilization approach as it implied the mobilization of resources by social movement organizations. Important names associated with this approach are Oberschall (1973), Tilly (1978) and McCarthy and Zald (1977).

The basic premises of resource mobilization theories differ from those of the collective behaviour tradition on at least four counts. First, they do not accept that social movements are a sub type of collective behaviour. They are different and ought to be understood in a different way. Second, contrary to the collective behaviour approach which saw social movements as essentially non-institutional behaviour, they consider them as organized and institutionalized, having sustaining pattern of relationships. Third, they work on the premise that people who participate in social movements are rational. Rationality is the basis of their approach. Finally, they have challenged the psychological explanations of social movements and instead have focused on the political aspect detailing on how political challenges are a cause of social movements. Hence, resource mobilization theorists saw social movements as institutionalized collective action based on rational behaviour which occurs in response to political challenges and their success depends on their ability to harness resources. These are rational enterprises based on the costs, possible risks, political advantages and opportunities. For resource mobilization theorists, it is rationality which occupies the centre stage of movements and not emotion. Tilly firmly believed that the world over, collective violence emerges from routine struggle for power (Tilly 1975).

POLITICAL PROCESS APPROACH

By the 1980s, the political dimension took a centre stage in the resource mobilization approach. This later led to the development of a new approach called the political process approach (Jenkins and Perrow 1977; McAdam 1982; Tarrow 1998). According to this approach, economic and political shifts in society facilitate movements. These shifts generally occur independently of the efforts of the protestors. Just like the mobilization theorists, they believe the protestors to be normal, rational people pursuing their interests to the best of their ability. According to this view, 'shifts in the structure of political opportunities and constraints work with organizational resources and subjective perceptions to fuel social insurgency'. The political opportunities 'generally refer to the interplay between external societal conditions and/or institutionalized power relations and the social movement within a given nation-state or territory' (Kuumba 2001, 8). Generally speaking, the external dimensions of political opportunity imply the extent of openness of the political system to allow participation, state structure's capacity for repression and the level of stability. Periods of change in these structures and in power relations create conducive atmosphere for movements. The opportunities for a movement could arise from changes within the political system such as a crisis in the government may be due to losing a war; conflict among the political elites with some members sympathizing with the movement; and lessening of repression by the state. They see the state both as an arbitrator and as a target. Stimulating organizational resources is the other necessary impetus for social movements (McAdam 1982).

An illustration of the process approach can be seen in Rhoda Lois Blumberg's analysis of the civil rights movement in America (Blumberg 1984). She explains how due to migration of African-Americans from rural South, certain changes occurred such as availability of more money, more intense ties, the role of the church and organizational network which facilitated the civil rights movement. This helped in greater mobilization along with higher motivation. As a result, the movement 'won inspiring legal victories' and it grew at a fast pace.

Recent approaches have criticized the political process approach for neglecting socio-psychological factors, issues of identity, sentiment and culture. The political process approach is thus getting transformed keeping in line with these criticisms. It appears that the American theories are coming closer to European theories like the new social movement approach to the study of social movements. There is thus an exchange of ideas between the two. Nick Crossley, however, made an important observation when he said that this shift 'involves a partial return to some of the more fruitful themes and issues of collective behaviour approach' (Crossley 2002, 13).

NEW SOCIAL MOVEMENTS

The concept of 'new social movements' (at times referred to as identity oriented movements) originated in Europe in response to the development of a new genre of movements around new issues. While theorists like Rudolf Abhor tried to modify socialist politics in order to incorporate these new movements, others such as Alain Touraine (1981) and Alberto Melucci (1996) put forward the concept of 'new social movements'. New social movements emerged in the backdrop of the American student movement of the 1960s and include movements on disarmament, animal rights, women, environment and the like. They are diverse ideologically and belong to different social locations. While Marxist ideas of proletarian revolution continued to remain relevant, the new social movements represent the new conflicts of contemporary times.

Broadly, their argument rests on the point that Marxist analysis with its focus on the proletariat–bourgeoisie conflict as the major fault line in capitalist society and as the major cause of social movements is limited. The contemporary world is far more complex, vibrant and varied having a number of fault lines and conflicts. The modern society has created new forms of discontent and alienation. Whether it is the movement of African–Americans for civil rights, of women for equality and equal opportunities, of students against the war in Vietnam or of peace activists against nuclear weapons, all of them dispute the notion that class conflict is the central conflict around which social change occurs.

Moreover, the proletariat have been placated and the labour movement has been incorporated into the society (Crossley 2002). They, however, do not advocate a clean break from Marxist analysis as class relations are still a source of conflict and social movement.

These theories are different from the materialist perception of the resource mobilization and the political process model. They emphasize on the psychosocial and subjective factors in understanding social movements. 'This broad range of theories emphasizes the role of identity formation and symbolic action as central elements of social movement activity and de-emphasizes social structural factors as the basis for resistance activity' (Foweraker 1995, cited in Kuumba 2001, 56). New social movements focus on how collective and oppositional identities are formed and strategically used. They include defining boundaries and symbols which give the collectivity a distinct identity (Kuumba 2001). A central aspect of new social movement theories is the emphasis on collective action frames which imply convergence of individuals' goals and their personal experiences with those of the social movement. These collective frames facilitate mobilization.

Alain Touraine, while analysing movements in contemporary society, held that 'each type of society or "mode of historicity" entails a central movement struggle' (Crossley 2002, 151).

> *Social movements are not a marginal rejection of order, they are the central forces fighting one against the other to control the production of society by itself and the action of classes for the shaping of historicity (i.e., the overall system of meaning which sets dominant rules in a given society. (Touraine 1981, 29)*

Every society, whether agrarian or industrial or the new post-industrial (also called 'programmed' or 'technocratic' society), has been and will be characterized by a 'central movement struggle'.

However, the crucial actors of conflict may change. In industrial society, they were capitalists and workers, in the new 'post-industrial' society there will be new classes.

Claus Offe (1985), a German sociologist, argued that in support of radical democracy, movements develop a basic critique of the democratic system and conservative ways of doing politics. He held that the main feature of new social movements is 'a critical ideology in relation to modernism and progress; decentralized and participatory organizational structures; defence of interpersonal solidarity against the great bureaucracies; and the reclamation of autonomous spaces, rather than material advantages' (Porta and Diani [1999] 2006; 9).

Habermas has characterized the post-1960s movements as 'new' social movements because these movements in the context of late capitalism have moved away from the class labour versus capitalist conflicts such as women's movements and ecology-based movements. This, Habermas suggests, makes possible the consolidation of a rather autonomous space for public debate.[6] Alberto Melucci saw new social movements as collective action to redeem individual's autonomy and identity by opposing the control by systems such as the state or the markets. These movements, unlike others such as worker's movement, neither seek material gain nor some kind of an intervention or concessions from the state. They strive for greater individual autonomy and freedom from state controls.

Although Marxist explanation of social movements still continues to enthuse research, the new social movement approach has added to our understanding in important ways such as by focusing on structural aspects of movements, giving importance to protests which are not related to class, placing the actor in the centre stage as the torch bearer of his action and finally by dissociating movements from production systems and taking their explanation into new arenas.

It should be noted that some of the main theorists have modified their original views. For instance, Claus Offe holds that movement practices have got modified over time. There is the influence of traditional political practices on the way movements run. Melucci tried to understand how representatives of collective identities are created and how they contribute towards the movement (Porta and Diani [1999] 2006, 9). Further, Melucci questioned the newness of 'new social movements'.

In line with Melucci's view, there is a prevalent view today that movements are no longer new. In fact, many of these movements are declining or have become part of the mainstream political system. Some are even reaching their end point. Moreover, as Tarrow had said, further newer movements have emerged which are quite different from new social movements.

Despite these views, many still think that new social movements have a place in understanding movements because of their different perspective. They offer a viable option to understand

---

[6] https://onlinelibrary.wiley.com/doi/pdf/10.1111/j.1467-954X.2004.00476.x

non-class movements. Further, they have brought a paradigm shift in movement theorizing, thus facilitating a deeper analysis of existing theories such as resource mobilization and political process. As mentioned earlier, the political process approach is coming closer to the new social movements as issues of identity and culture are being incorporated in them.

SOCIAL NETWORK APPROACH

In recent years, alongside resource mobilization, political process and new social movements, other approaches have been put forward like the social network approach. The network approach refers to the question of 'who is enlisted in the movement'. It states that the very presence of networks and links between potential recruits gives rise to movements. Presence of a pre-existing formal organization and intense ties are conducive to mobilizing support. Jo Freeman focused on how the existence of social networks play a crucial role in mobilizing support for social movements. They facilitate communication which is vital for a movement. These are movements that benefitted from previously existing networks of activists from the new left and women's movement (Freeman 1973).

The social network approach subscribes to the idea that movements are not isolated but are closely connected entities in which participants and leaders shift from one movement to another. Thus, they share networks. Many movements may emerge at the same time because of similar political conditions. Thus, instead of studying a single movement, this approach started focusing on waves of movements (Tarrow 1998).

CULTURAL APPROACH

In the study of social movements, there has recently been a cultural turn in the form of cultural approaches which developed in the late 1980s. Unlike the mobilization and process approaches that perceive protests in economic and political terms, the cultural approach focuses on the symbols of protest. It also studies the way in which people's consciousness is raised and solidarity created. In this approach, a society's symbols for itself and self-understanding become the subject of study. Elaborating on this view, two cultural components are considered important, 'frame' and 'collective identity'. 'Frame' refers to the way movement organizers frame their issues/demands in order to appeal to the general public and potential protestors. Collective identity, on the other hand, means publicizing and politicizing an already existing identity or creating a new one. Charles Kurzman, in his study of Iranian revolution, showed that cultural perceptions and shifts in state machinery were very important factors for the movement (Goodwin and Jasper 2003). While process theorists emphasized on tangible changes which occurred in the state, independent of the way protestors perceived them, cultural theorists lay emphasis on cultural perceptions.

IMPACT OF GLOBALIZATION ON SOCIAL MOVEMENT THEORIZING

It is important to note here that there are new researches on social movements which are inspired by Immanuel Wallenstein's 'world system theory' (beginning in the 1970s) which focus on global economic restructuring and its widespread impact on social movements. Globalization has led to widespread changes including development of worldwide networks of social relationships, increased interdependence and cultural globalization. It is true that identities, whether national or sub-national, do not disappear but the intermingling of cultures lead to new identities which may compete with them (Porta and Diani [1999] 2006). This is often seen as cultural assault which, thus, leads to protests and movements such as religious fundamentalist movements and ethnic movements. In today's globalized world, movements such as environment, disarmament and feminism have consolidated many separate protests into cohesive entities with a global presence.

Here it might be interesting to take a look at what has come to be described as the alter-globalization movement that can be traced back to a group of indigenous Mexican peasants who, in 1994, rose against the damages inflicted on them by the neoliberal agenda implemented by North American Free Trade Agreement (NAFTA). The movement attacked the consequences of the spread of government-led policies aimed at the liberalization and financialization of the economy, the reduction of social programmes, and privatization of public wealth through both regional and international institutions such as NAFTA and the World Trade Organization (WTO) respectively. This movement has significantly inspired a vast array of social forces comprised in the 'movement of many movements', exemplified by the People's Global Action 'based on a philosophy of decentralization and autonomy, and a clear rejection of "patriarchy, racism, religious fundamentalism and all forms of discrimination and domination"'. In a world dominated by market-oriented policies steered by neoliberal governments based on a utilitarian perspective, these and other similar movements try to encourage creativity and authenticity.

Whereas the alter-globalization movement undertook the task of resisting capitalism in a context of an economic boom throughout neoliberal capitalist societies, the student-led Occupy movement[7] emerged in response to one of the most destructive economic crises since capitalism's inception. Students had been demanding a certain degree of certainty in a world that has come to be increasingly characterized by 'flexibility' and uncertainty.

STUDYING SOCIAL MOVEMENTS IN INDIA

Equipped with the knowledge of the main theories on social movements as put forward by European and American thinkers, it will now be appropriate to focus on Indian scholarship.

---

[7] Occupy movement was an international sociopolitical movement which emerged in response to economic and social inequalities and the dearth of real democracy. It aimed at creating a just and democratic world. The first such protest can be traced to the Occupy Wall Street in New York City in September 2011.

As discussed earlier, scholars (in the 1970s and early 1980s) like M. S. A. Rao and Ghanshyam Shah engaged with older theories such as Marxist and collective behaviour theories. Citing similar trends for movements since the 1980s, T. K. Oommen in his recent book said,

> *Indian scholarship on social movements since 1980s largely falls in line with the existing conceptualizations/theorizations of social movements depending upon the theoretical orientations they adopt—structural-functional or Marxist. Although they do not make or claim any conceptual/theoretical breakthrough, they do make significant contributions towards a clearer understanding of empirical situation in India. (Oommen 2010, 12–13, I)*

It would, however, be more appropriate to say that some Indian theorists in recent years have taken up the challenges of contemporary situation and have gone beyond these recognized

Jashpur Rally Asserting Land Right and against Displacement in March 2009

Source: Media Collective
Photograph Courtesy: The Media Collective. Reproduced with Permission.

NBA Protest

Source: Media Collective and Narmada Archives
Photograph Courtesy: The Media Collective. Reproduced with Permission.

theoretical frameworks into newer arenas. Whether it is new social movements, the role of non-party political formations or ethnographic studies, the trends are towards change.

IMPACT OF EARLY WESTERN THEORIES

As in the West, in India too, early theorists considered Marxist theory as the basis of understanding social movements. However, over time, as in the West, more and more thinkers started realizing the limitations of Marxist theory to explain the highly varied complex fault lines of contemporary Indian society (Fuchs and Linkenbach 2003). An early study which used the Marxist approach to explain social movements was that of M. S. A. Rao, who edited two volumes on

Singur Protest, December 2006

FARM LANDS TO FARMERS ... TA...

CPI (M), DIALOGUE WITH FARMERS NOT TATA...

DOWN with ...te-sponsor ...ties on pea... ...ingur, W...

Singur, Ulaberia...WHAT NEXT?
Stop forceful occupation
Of fertile lands.
"Development" of the TATA,
can't Take place at the co...
the lives of peasants.

Source: Media Collective
Photograph Courtesy: The Media Collective. Reproduced with Permission.

social movements (1978–1979) which included essays on important movements including peasant, tribal, backward classes and the like.

M. S. A. Rao classified movements into three types based on different levels of structural change they usher. These are reform, transformation and revolution. 'Reform movements may be identified with partial changes in the value system and consequential changes in the quality of relationships'. Many such movements occurred over the centuries in India which include the devotional movements. Transformation movements are the ones which bring about structural changes of a middle level and revolutionary movements bring radical social changes like the Naxalite movement. Yet another basis of classification is the extent of conflict within each type of movement. He argued that conflict is mild in reform movements and is more intense in transformation movements, while being an intrinsic feature of revolutionary movements since it is often based on class struggle.

Similarly, in his study of student movement, Ghanshyam Shah analysed the class background of the participants and showed how it influenced their goals and methods. In line with these studies were the works of A. R. Desai, Arvind N. Das, Partha Chatterji, D. N. Dhanagare and Gail Omvedt among others. Shah categorized social movements as revolt, rebellion, reform and revolution on the basis of their objectives or the type of change they are required to realize.

Both Rao and Shah, later, moved away from this structural–functionalist approach which considered equilibrium as the basic state of society and social movements as an interruption to it (Baviskar 2010).

While analysing the theory of relative deprivation, Rao reiterated that it offers an acceptable explanation of social movements. Instead of looking at movements as facilitating functional equilibrium, it looks at social movements as agencies of change. However, the theory of relative deprivation can be improved by omitting psychological and individual deprivations and focusing on the deprivations of collectivities in distribution of rights and privileges in different situations in society. Further, according to him, deprivation can be experienced in different spheres such as economic, educational, political and religious. These may even be interrelated.

A group like the backward classes in India suffer multiple deprivations in all these spheres, thus amounting to discrimination and deep inequalities. Taking the example of backward classes, Rao said that different leaders select different aspects of relative deprivation to formulate an ideology. Ideology is dependent on leaders' perception of deprivation, the extent of actual deprivation and an estimation of their capabilities and resources. Identity formation with regard to other groups is an important feature of ideologies based on relative deprivation. They tend to create a boundary between themselves and the other group. If the group is seen as similar, the boundary tends to be soft and if the group is seen as opposed, the boundary tends to be hard. Rao calls the latter as 'opposite reference groups'. Explaining these opposite reference groups, Rao said that while on the one hand the group imitates the lifestyle and norms of the privileged group, they also at the same time denigrate the group and criticize its domination in various spheres such as education, economic or political. They make efforts to bring them down in the social ladder and at the same time uplift their own standards. Taking the example of Veerasaivas,[8] Rao pointed out that while they adopted Brahminical ways, they also showed aggression towards Brahmins, denigrated them and tried to create parallel institutions. Their approach was clearly confrontationist.

---

[8] Veerashaivism is a subtradition of Shaivism. As followers of the Shaiva tradition, Veerashaivas are followers of the five *peethas* or religious centres called *pancha peetha*. They are distinct from Lingayats, although they have been treated as the same for a long time.

Others who have engaged with collective behaviour theories include T. K. Oommen, when he highlighted the tension between mobilization and institutionalization and Ghanshyam Shah, while attempting a comparative analysis of student's movement in Gujarat and Bihar.

LATER THEORIES

In order to understand the theoretical developments from the 1980s, it is important to see them in the backdrop of the nature of social movements in the 1970s and the 1980s. There was a surge in social movements during this period. A number of movements of different types arose due to the economic crisis triggered by then ruling Congress party's inability to curb corruption and price rise leading to unrest on a large scale. This created a political atmosphere for social movements to rise. A real push came due to a declaration of the state of emergency (Under Article 352 of the Constitution) imposed by Prime Minister Indira Gandhi in 1975. Emergency, which was imposed in the backdrop of student movement which was perceived as a threat to the ruling Congress party, severely compromised people's rights and censored the media. The subsequent lifting of the emergency (1977), the electoral defeat of Congress and the following political surge led to the rise of social movements, mainly aiming to restore political and civil rights of the people. 'All major social movements of this period showed some degree of cross fertilization. As personnel and ideas were exchanged between movements, political ideologies and strategies were contested, and collaboratively produced and refined' (Baviskar 2010, 384).

NEW SOCIAL MOVEMENTS IN INDIA

It became more and more evident in India that the many layered, multifaceted conflicts of the 1970s and the 1980s could not be explained through Marxist theory. For instance, Gail Omvedt revised and modified her understanding of social movements in India especially after her study of Dalit movement. As she put it, contemporary India is witness to many social movements and uprisings which are not the traditional class struggles but revolve around issues of caste, ethnicity, community or gender. These have been popularly called the 'new social movements' (Omvedt 1993). Working class struggles remain important. However, newer issues and methods of articulation have emerged. The issues may vary from debt relief to better price for farm produce. Some struggles may be for implementation of agrarian reforms like giving land to the tiller, but more pressing issues are protecting their lands from being acquired for building dams or other types of infrastructure. Their preference is for 'alternative development'. While class demands have taken a back seat, mobilizing one's community or caste for getting reservation in government jobs is a more important issue.

> *Overwhelmingly, those who work with some kind of 'class' model of Indian politics, indeed any notion*
> *of a "political economy", whether it is Rudolphs, Francine Frankel, other European Marxists, the*

traditional Marxists of the 'mode of production debate', or the new Marxists of the "subaltern studies" group, or for that matter left-identified scholars such as Atul Kohli, define "class" in terms of private property and overlook the relations of exploitation and surplus extraction between toilers and those controlling other conditions of production, the market, or the state itself. (Omvedt 1993, xiii–xiv)

In other words, they may think of the state as supporting exploiters, and do not see the state as exploiter. They do not see the exploitation of marginal farmers, of people who eke out their living through forest produce or of those who produce minor commodities for survival. While subaltern studies made great contribution to our understanding of the colonial period, their work in independent India is wanting as they face a difficulty in defining 'subaltern'. For instance, are women from upper classes subaltern?

According to Omvedt, we have to move beyond the 'historical materialism of the proletariat' to historical materialism of varied sections of the society such as the Dalits, women and peasants. It is not necessary that the analysis of the former may apply to the latter. As Omvedt says, there is a need to redefine revolution. 'Redefining revolution, then, is the need of the time, and the beginning of this process can be seen in India's new social movements' (Omvedt 1993, xvii).

Non-party Political Formations

It was Rajni Kothari and his colleagues at Lokayan[9] who analysed the movements of the 1970s and the 1980s and called them 'non-party political formations'. This includes funded voluntary organizations and civil society groups called people's groups and their movements came to be described as social movements. They were not bound by compulsions of electoral politics and were likely to remain free from corruption. Emergency had shaken people's faith in the state as an agency which could assure them of their democratic rights. Further, the subsequent instability of post-emergency political formations made people wary of the democratically elected governments. Kothari believed that it is non-party political formations which have the promise to oversee the state's policies and actions. These views of Kothari's bear similarity with the analysis of 'new social movements' in Europe in that their space 'is largely a space of non-institutional politics which is not provided for in the doctrines and practices of liberal democracy and the welfare state' (Offe 1985, 826).

In recent years, scholars have debated the relationship of communities, the state and the individual as part of their civil society studies. Baviskar, contrary to Kothari's views, has argued that while it is true that human rights movements have challenged the state, it may not be true of all social movements. There have been times when movements have worked in tandem with

---

[9] Lokayan, meaning dialogue of the people, is a forum of activists, intellectuals and public, established in 1980 under the leadership of Professors Rajni Kothari and D. L. Sheth. Through lectures, workshops, meetings, seminars and the like, Lokayan aims to strengthen democracy through the process of dialogue. It has been a platform for the marginalized and has supported a number of social movements. Lokayan has striven to create a just society and in the process has been critical of the present developmental model.

the state. For instance, within the environment movement, conservationists, while criticizing the state for many of its environmentally degrading policies, have worked closely with the state in pursuance of their goals. In the case of women's movement, a similar situation can be observed where they have been successful in persuading the state to pass women friendly laws (Baviskar 2010).

ETHNOGRAPHIC STUDIES

It was in the 1990s that another transformation occurred in movement studies in India with the work of Ramchandra Guha on Chipko movement in his book *The Unquiet Woods* (1989). He unearthed the many layers of ideological and political consciousness which were woven into a single movement through his intensive fieldwork in the hills of Uttarakhand. While highlighting the limitation of the earlier static systemic approaches, Guha showed how an in-depth under-standing of the internal dynamics of a movement is acquired through ethnographic method like participant observation. Guha through his study revealed that the 'public face' of the Chipko movement was that of an environment movement and the 'private face' was that of a peasant struggle against the state. There is a visible influence of subaltern studies on Guha's work (Baviskar 2010) as he tries to focus on 'history from below'. Ethnographic studies through their holistic and in-depth focus help to look at social movements as dynamic entities where power relations and ideologies are multi-stranded and ever changing.

ISSUES FOR FURTHER RESEARCH

Certain recent developments in social movements in India have highlighted the need for further research on the subject. A number of social movements have developed global links with similar movements and they now have a global presence. The Dalit movement has forged links with movements against racism and tribal movements with international movement of indigenous people. There are not enough studies on the impact of international links on these movements. Such alliances also sometimes exist between rural movements with urban collectivities (Baviskar 2010).

With an unprecedented reach which media has today, it is important to explore the impact of media on social movements. Whether it is for mobilizing support or publicizing movement goals, media has a huge role to play.

Another area in movement research which requires further investigation is the role of non-governmental organizations (NGOs) in giving support through advocacy, organization, publicity, networking, mobilizing, documentation and so on. Formally qualified, professionally efficient and committed NGO personnel play a significant role in the success of a movement. There is a need to look into the role of NGOs in different movements and how it evolves as the movements change. There is also a need to examine more carefully the relationship between social movements and political parties such as Dalit movement and the Bahujan Samaj Party or Ram Janmabhoomi movement and the Bharatiya Janata Party.

CONCLUSION

In conclusion, it may not be inappropriate to say that contemporary societies with their vast complexities, inequalities and diversities are in a constant state of flux, throwing up new issues and conflicts making social movements a core attribute and a central theme for research. Social movements are significant because it is through these movements that collectives are able to give voice to their demands and grievances. It has been argued, perhaps due to the great number of social movements being reported from all parts of the world, that we are living in a 'movement society'. The fact, however, is that social movements are one of the many forms of collective actions that human beings engage in. Social movements, however, are characterized by group action that is not only collective but also bound by a set of common objectives. This action is outside the institutionalized platforms for collective actions—often the action could unfold on streets, town squares and other public spaces.

Sometimes, social movements are confused with interest groups because of their collective nature. The fact is that the two are rather different. Interest groups are generally defined in relation to the government and are more often than not accepted as being part of the polity and the processes of politics. This is not the case with social movements. Social movements may sometimes use the institutionalized methods employed by interest groups like lobbying, but by and large, they make use of other methods such as rallies, demonstrations, boycotts and dharna/gherao. Social movements can often be observed as either seeking or resisting or promoting changes with respect to one or many aspects of the society. This is the raison d'être of social movements.

While social movements might be episodic, it would be incorrect to dismiss them as mere seasonal or fly-by-night occurrences. It is of course undeniable that movements do go through cycles of heightened protests and phases of relative calm. Thus, while social movements have become a part of modern politics, yet these movements are a subject of intense debate and discussion. Some of these debates and perspectives have been examined in this chapter; the subsequent chapters have focused more on specific movements and their role and achievements or limitations in the context of Indian democracy.

POINTS FOR DISCUSSION

- Can social movements be studied? If yes, what are some of the more popular approaches to the study of social movements?

- How has globalization impacted the unfolding of social movements?
- If collective behaviour is one of the key features of a social movement, then is a riot a social movement? When does collective human behaviour become a social movement?
- Why is the book *The Unquiet Woods* very significant with reference to the study of social movements in India?

REFERENCES AND READINGS

Aberle, D. F. 1966. *Viking Fund Publications in Anthropology.* Vol. 42: *The Peyote Religion among the Navaho.* New York: Wenner-Gren Foundation.

Amin, Samir, Giovanni Arrighi, Andre Gunder Frank, and Immanuel Wallerstein, eds. 1990 (2006 in South Asia). *Transforming the Revolution: Social Movements and the World System.* Delhi: Aakar Books.

Baviskar, Amita. 2005. 'Red in Tooth and Claw?'. In *Social Movements in India*, edited by Raka Ray and Mary Fainsod Katzenstein. Lanham, MD: Rowman & Littlefield Publishers.

———. 2010. 'Social Movements'. In *The Oxford Companion to Politics in India*, edited by Niraja Gopal Jayal and Pratap Bhanu Mehta, 381–387. New Delhi: Oxford University Press.

Blumer, Herbert. 1951. 'Social Movements'. In *Principles of Sociology*, edited by A. McClung Lee, 199–220. New York, NY: Barnes and Nobles.

Blumberg, Rhoda Lois. 1984. *Civil Rights: The 1960s Freedom Struggle.* Boston, MA: Twayne Publishers.

Cooper, Davina. 2004. *Challenging Diversity: Rethinking Equality and the Value of Difference.* Cambridge: Cambridge University Press.

Crossley, Nick. 2002. *Making Sense of Social Movements.* Jaipur: Rawat Publications.

Das, Veena, ed. 2003. *The Oxford Companion to Sociology and Social Anthropology.* New Delhi: Oxford University Press.

Diani, Mario. 1992. 'Analysing Social Movement Networks'. In *Studying Collective Action*, edited by M. Diani and R. Eyerman, 107–35. London: SAGE Publications.

Escobar, Arturo, and Sonia E. Alvarez, eds. 1992. *The Making of Social Movements in Latin America: Identity, Strategy, and Democracy.* Boulder: Westview Press.

Foweraker, Joe. 1995. *Theorizing Social Movements.* London: Pluto Press.

Freeman, Jo. 1973. 'The Origins of the Women's Liberation Movement'. *American Journal of Sociology* 78 (4): 22–31.

Fuchs, Martin, and Antje Linkenbach. 2003. 'Social Movements'. In *The Oxford India Companion to Sociology and Social Anthropology*, edited by Veena Das, 1524–1552. New Delhi: Oxford University Press.

Gamson, William A. 1990. *The Strategy of Social Protest.* Second edition. Belmont, CA: Wadsworth.

Goodwin, Jeff, and James M. Jasper, eds. 2003. *The Social Movements Reader: Cases and Concepts.* Malden, MA: Blackwell Publishing.

Gurr, T. R. 1970. *Why Men Rebel.* Princeton, NJ: Princeton University Press.

Gurr, Ted, ed. 1980. *Handbook of Political Conflict: Theory and Research.* New York, NY: The Free Press: A Division of Macmillan Publishing Co.

Ibarra, Pedro. 2003. *Social Movements and Democracy.* New York, NY: Palgrave Macmillan.

Jenkins, Craig J., and Charles Perrow. 1977. 'Insurgency of the Powerless: Farm Worker Movements (1946–72)'. *American Sociological Review* 42 (2): 249–68.

Kornhauser, William. 1959. *The Politics of Mass Society.* Glencoe, IL: The Free Press.

Kuumba, M. Bahati. 2001. *Gender and Social Movements.* CA: ALTAMIRA Press.

Lee, Su H. 2007 (Indian reprint 2010). *Debating New Social Movements: Culture, Identity and Social Fragmentation.* Jaipur: Rawat Publications.

Maheu, Louis, ed. 1995. *Social Movements and Social Classes: The Future of Collective Action.* London: SAGE Publications.

McAdam, D. 1982. *Political Process and the Development of Black Insurgency.* Chicago, IL: University of Chicago Press.

———. 1983. 'Tactical Innovation and the Pace of Insurgency'. *American Sociological Review* 48: 735–54.

McAdam, Doug, Sidney Tarrow, and Charles Tilly. 2001. *Dynamics of Contention.* New York, NY: Cambridge University Press.

McCarthy, John D., and Mayer N. Zald. 1977. 'Resource Mobilization and Social Movements: A Partial Theory'. *American Journal of Sociology* 82: 1212–41.

Melucci, Alberto. 1996. *Challenging Codes.* Cambridge/New York, NY: Cambridge University Press.

Moghadam, Valentine M., 2009. *Globalization and Social Movements: Islamism, Feminism and the Global Justice Movement.* Lanham, MD: Rowman & Littlefield.

Nash, June, ed. 2005. *Social Movements: An Anthropological Reader.* Malden, MA: Blackwell Publishing.

Oberschall, A. 1973. *Social Conflict and Social Movement.* Englewood Cliffs, NJ: Prentice-Hall.

Offe, Claus. 1985. 'New Social Movements: Challenging the Boundaries of Institutional Politics'. *Social Research* 52 (4): 817–68.

Omvedt, Gail. 1993. *Reinventing Revolution: New Social Movements and the Socialist Tradition in India.* New York, NY: An East Gate Book.

Oommen, T. K., ed. 2010. *Social Movements I: Issues of Identity.* New Delhi: Oxford University Press.

———, ed. 2010. *Social Movements II: Concerns of Equity and Security.* New Delhi: Oxford University Press.

Opp, Karl-Dieter. 2009. *Theories of Political Protest and Social Movements: A Multidisciplinary Introduction, Critique and Synthesis.* London/New York, NY: Routledge, Taylor and Francis Group.

Petras, James, and Henry Veltmeyer. 2005 (Pluto Press, 2009 Indian edition). *Social Movements and State Power: Argentina, Brazil, Bolivia, Ecuador.* Kolkata: Update Publications.

Piven, Francis Fox, and Richard A. Cloward. 1977. *Poor People's Movements.* New York, NY: Vintage.

Porta, Donatella Della, and Mario Diani. (1999) 2006. *Social Movements: An Introduction.* Malden, MA: Blackwell Publishing.

Rao, M. S. A, Ed. 1978. *Social Movements in India* (Vols. I–II). New Delhi: Manohar Publications.

Rule, James R. 1988. *Theories of Civil Violence.* Berkley, MI: University of California Press.

Rupp, Leila, and Verta Taylor. 1987. *Survival in Doldrums: The American Women's Rights Movement, 1945 to the 1960s.* Columbus, OH: Ohio State University Press.

Sahoo, Ajaya Kumar. June 2005. 'Social Movements in India: A Select Bibliography'. *Social Change,* 35: 167–83.

Shah, Ghanshyam, ed. 2002. *Social Movements and the State: Readings in Indian Government and Politics – 4.* New Delhi/Thousand Oaks, CA/London: SAGE Publications.

———. (2004) 2005. *Social Movements in India: A Review of Literature.* Second edition. New Delhi: SAGE Publications.

Singh, Rajendra. 2001. *Social Movements, Old and New: A Post-Modernist Critique.* New Delhi: SAGE Publications.

Snow, David, and Pamela Oliver. 1995. 'Social Movements and Collective Behaviour: Social Psychological Dimensions and Considerations'. In *Sociological Perspectives on Social Psychology,* edited by K. Cook, G. Fine, and J. House, 571–99. Boston, MA: Allyn and Bacon.

Snow, David A., Sarah A. Soule, and Hanspeter Kriesi, eds. 2004. *The Blackwell Companion to Social Movements.* Malden, MA: Blackwell Publishing MA.

Stacey, Judith, and Barrie Thorne. 1985. 'The Missing Feminist Revolution in Sociology'. *Social Problems* 32 (4): 301–16.

Tarrow, Sidney. 1998. *Power in Movement: Social Movement and Contentious Politics*. Second edition. New York, NY: Cambridge University Press.

Tilly, Charles. 1978. *From Mobilization to Revolution*. Reading, MA: Addison-Wesley

———. 2003. *The Politics of Collective Violence*. Cambridge: Cambridge University Press.

Tilly, Charles, Louise Tilly, and Richard Tilly. 1975. *The Rebellious Century 1830–1930*. Cambridge, MA: Harvard University Press.

Touraine, Alain. 1981. *The Voice and the Eye: An Analysis of Social Movements*. Cambridge: Cambridge University Press.

———. 1995. *Critique of Modernity*. Oxford: Blackwell.

Turner, Ralph, and Lewis Killian. (1957) 1987. *Collective Behaviour*. Englewood Cliffs, NJ: Prentice-Hall.

Wilkinson, P. 1971. *Social Movements*. London: Macmillan.

Wilson, John. 1973. *Introduction to Social Movements*. New York, NY: Basic Books.

Wittegenstein, L. 1953. *Philosophical Investigations*. Oxford: Blackwell.

2

The Quest for Dignity: Dalit Movement

Ours is a battle not for wealth or for power.

It is a battle for freedom.

It is a battle for the reclamation of human personality.

—Dr B. R. Ambedkar

The term Dalit[1] refers to the most oppressed and marginalized castes in India, earlier referred to as the 'untouchables' or the *asprushya*. The word Dalit literally means the 'wretched' and refers to the large mass of exploited people who belong to lower castes and other marginal groups. Over the years, however, it has come to be associated with 'untouchables' who are variously described as scheduled castes, depressed castes, *bahishkrit*, Ati-Shudras, Harijans and so on. Treated as the lowest, most subjugated castes, forced to live demeaning lives away from so-called purer spaces, engaging in those occupations that are considered polluting, excluded socially and culturally, deprived and discriminated on all counts, Dalits have suffered from absolute inequality or what has often been referred to as cumulative inequality.[2] It is the social movement of this group (referred to as Dalit hereafter) that forms the central theme in this chapter.

Spread over different geographical areas and time periods, led by diverse, at times, conflicting personalities and driven by various social, economic and political forces, Dalit movements have developed along many directions. However, in independent India, there has been a certain level of confluence of ideas and action among Dalit activists around the charismatic personality of B. R. Ambedkar, often eulogized in popular imagery as the Sun. This is not to undermine the many tensions and controversies that have plagued the Dalit movements at different points of time, thus sometimes, preventing a unified platform from developing.

---

[1] The term Dalit was first coined by Jyotirao Phule to refer to all those labelled as lower castes and untouchables by Brahmins.
[2] Cumulative and dispersed inequality concept was given by Andre Beteille. When caste and class are linked with each other, that is, upper castes are also upper classes, it is cumulative inequality. When the link between the two breaks, that is, upper castes are not necessarily upper classes, it is dispersed inequality.

AS A 'NEW SOCIAL MOVEMENT'

Placing the post-Independence Dalit movements in a theoretical framework, a number of theorists have characterized them as a new social movement, distinct from class-based politics, in terms of their agenda, issues and methods.

Elaborating on the limitations of traditional Marxist understanding to explain caste movements, Omvedt, drawing from Godelier, demonstrates that caste is part of the base and not the superstructure. In an agrarian society like India, material factors are intensely interwoven with caste. Thus, any approach which looks at caste as a part of the social milieu and class as the base is inaccurate. A similar sentiment was conveyed by Oommen when he said that unlike the consciousness of the proletariat which is entrenched in material factors, the consciousness of Dalits is highly complex as it emanates from 'inhuman conditions of material existence, powerlessness and ideological hegemony' (Oommen 1990, 256). At a time when traditional socialism has come into disrepute, these new movements are faced with the task of 'reinventing' revolution (Omvedt 1993).

CHALLENGES AND OPPORTUNITIES: SOCIO-RELIGIOUS REFORM MOVEMENTS, SANSKRITIZATION AND CONVERSIONS

The socio-religious reform movements spearheaded by many Dalits and others form the backdrop for the articulation of the political agenda of B. R. Ambedkar in a modern milieu. The achievements of the socio-religious movements were largely symbolic. Their aim was to ameliorate the sociocultural status of vulnerable groups. 'It is logical to expect that a collectivity subjected to multiple deprivations will protest first against those disabilities which it perceives to be the most inhuman and unbearable...Therefore, it is no accident that Dalit protest in India first crystallized against socio-cultural oppression' (Oommen 1990, 256).

For Oommen, caste-based movements are 'primordial' (based on ascription) movements which, to begin with, had 'symbolic' goals like upliftment of their status and prestige but over time they developed 'instrumental' goals as well such as political representation and economic amelioration. This transition is clearly visible as one moves on from the early precursors of the Dalit movement to its later manifestations.

The socio-religious reform movements have often been delineated along a number of criteria, such as their time period, nature of leadership and so on. The following sections contain an account of the various streams of socio-religious reform movements keeping these criteria in perspective including bhakti, neo-vedantic, Phule and Periyar's movements, Adi movements, sanskritization and conversion movements.

BHAKTI MOVEMENTS

Among the early reform movements that addressed the question of caste were the bhakti movements (between the 12th and 18th centuries). Charismatic saints (such as Raidas, Ramanand and Kabir in the north, Ramanuja and Basava in the south, Tukaram and Narsinh Mehta in the west and Chaitanya in the east) sought to reform existing social practices based on caste without seeking abolition of caste system. The movements did not have a socio-economic agenda, thus their appeal was limited. The promises of equality remained illusionary. These movements could not outlive their charismatic leaders.

NEO-VEDANTIC MOVEMENTS

A number of religious and reform movements began in the latter part of the 19th century or early 20th century which came to be known as neo-vedantic movements. Most of these were initiated by upper caste leaders, for example, the Arya Samaj movement started by Dayanand Saraswati and the Ramakrishna movement launched by Vivekananda. These have often been named as neo-vedantic movements. Although these movements separated untouchability from Hinduism, calling it an aberration, they supported division of society into occupational categories of the Varna system and *varnashrama dharma* as essential ingredients of a harmonious society. Some of the principles that these movements advocated include inter-caste marriages, commensality and temple entry for lower castes along with education, legislations and economic upliftment. The neo-vedantic movements in retrospect have a rather limited set of achievements with regard to challenging caste structures (Oommen 2010).

PHULE AND PERIYAR

It was in the late 19th and early 20th centuries that two movements challenging the caste system were initiated by Jyotirao Govindrao Phule (1827–1890) and Savitri Bai Phule (1831–1897) in the former Bombay province and the other in erstwhile Madras by Periyar E. V. Ramasamy Naicker (1879–1973). These came to be known as the non-Brahmin movements which became an important inspiration and precursor of the Dalit movement of the 20th century. Both movements organized their communities against the caste system and its oppression. They assimilated Shudras and Ati-Shudras (a term given by Phule to refer to Dalits) and fought against the practice of untouchability. However,

> they could not sustain this unity for long in the face of the caste contradiction within these groups. Unable to accommodate the untouchables' yearning for emancipation, these organizations ultimately splintered into various factions. Phule's Satyashodhak Samaj,[3]...disintegrated after his death in 1890

---

[3] Jyotirao Govindrao Phule was a 19th century social reformer and a philosopher who was a pioneer for education of girls, lower castes and peasants. In 1873, he set up Satyashodhak Samaj (Society of Seekers of Truth). The purpose of this society was to purify the society from the influence of caste and caste discrimination.

with one coterie merging with the Indian National Congress and the other ultimately with the communists. Ramaswamy's Dravidar Kazhagam[4] similarly disintegrated by 1949, having been transformed into a ruling-class lobby that ignored the caste question altogether. (Teltumbde 2010, 23)

ADI MOVEMENTS

Yet another stream of reform movements was the Adi[5] movements of the 1910s and 1920s. Adi movements were inspired by Jyotiba Phule's reiteration that Brahmins were Aryans who conquered the original inhabitants. Spread across India (Adi Dravida in Tamil Nadu, Adi Andhra, Adi Karnataka, Ad Dharma in Punjab and Adi Hindu in Uttar Pradesh), these were the first major endeavour on the part of Dalits to break away from Hinduism. According to the activists of Adi movements, their ancestors were the original inhabitants when the Aryans invaded India. Hence, they were the lawful owners of this country. As noted by Juergensmeyer, these ideas were first formulated by the Adi Dravida movement of South India but the first claimant of the use of the concept of 'Adi' was the Ad Dharma movement of Punjab. In Hyderabad, the Adi Hindu movement started under the leadership of Bhagya Reddy Varma and Arigay Ramaswami.

Although there is no evidence that there was contact between the Adi movements of north and south, there is however proof that there was communication between Ad Dharma and Adi Hindu movement in the north. In fact, Swami Achyutanand, a leader of Adi Hindu movement, called for a meeting in Delhi in 1926 with an aim to create a joint front among the activists of Delhi, Punjab and Uttar Pradesh. His aim was to mobilize these earliest inhabitants thus:

> Sing the song of Adi Hindus.
> Awaken the community from deep slumber.
> Aryans, Sakas, Huns, Muslims and Christians
> All came from outside.
> They are all foreigners
> Who have captured our land.
> Tell these facts to everyone.
> (Upadhyay, in Imtiaz Ahmed and Shashi Bhushan Upadhyay [2010, 5])

To put it in perspective, it is important to note that the 1920s was a period of change in India with the Indian National Congress on the rise, formulation of separate identities for Hindus and Muslims and the growth of Hindu nationalism. It was in this environment that attempts were made to give the depressed castes a distinct identity and character from the Hindus by the leaders of Adi movements.

---

[4] Dravidar Kazhagam or Dravida Kazhgam is one of the first Dravidian parties in India. It was founded by Periyar E. V. Ramasamy Naicker in 1944. Its original goal was to eradicate caste system and to carve out a new nation from Madras Presidency for Dravidian people called 'Dravida Nadu'.

[5] The terms Ad or Adi mean the original or ancient.

Ad Dharma and Ravi Das

The Ad Dharma was inspired by Ravi Das, a 16th century Bhakti poet (a *sant*) and was established among 'Chamars', an 'untouchable' caste of leather workers in Punjab in 1926 with Mangoo Ram as the president of the executive committee. In line with the Bhakti tradition, Ravi Das had conveyed his anti-caste sentiments through popular poetry. Ad Dharma not only popularized Ravi Das's poetry but also his anti-caste sentiments through various texts, posters and pamphlets. A poster of Ad Dharma in 1927 read,

> *We are the original people of this country and our religion is Ad Dharma. The Hindu qaum came from outside and enslaved us. When the original conch was sounded, all the brothers came together—chamar, churha, sainsi, bhanrje, bhil, all the untouchables—to make their problems known. Brothers, there are seventy million of us listed as Hindus, separate us and make us free…There was a time when we ruled India, brothers, and the land belonged to us…Come together to form a better life. (Juergensmeyer 1982, 86)*

There was also a demand for a separate homeland, Achhutistan, the land for untouchables, although the idea was rather tentative.[6]

Although the Adi movement gave Dalits a distinct identity, separate from Hindus, there were inherent dilemmas in this reiteration. First, the Adi movements took their inspiration from the bhakti movement which was essentially within the Hindu fold. To then declare themselves to be separate from Hindus posed a problem. Reflecting on another aspect of the dilemma, it is said that the arguments put forward by the Adi movements were not only that the 'untouchables' lived prior to Hindus and separate from them but 'it could, albeit exceptionally mean that the Adi Hindus were the very first and the "true" Hindus' (Omvedt 1994, 122).

SANSKRITIZATION[7]

Some sociologists have suggested that at times certain Dalit groups employed sanskritization as a strategy for social mobility while some others rejected this path and steered clear of any upper

---

[6] Many decades later, a similar demand was made by Jagdish Mahato, a poor school teacher from Bihar, who organized Dalit upsurge from 1967–1971 for a separate land, Harijanistan.

[7] Sanskritization is the specific case of universal drive to imitate a higher group for the sake of achieving mobility. Based on his study of Coorgs of South India, M. N. Srinivas gave the concept of Sanskritization as a process whereby lower castes imitate the ways of life of generally a dominant caste for the sake of achieving mobility. Dominant caste is characterized by numerical strength, owns the maximum land in the area and has the maximum power.

caste influences. Those who took to sanskritization imitated ritually or culturally higher castes in order to achieve mobility as recorded in the studies by Rudolph and Rudolph (1987) (the case of Shanas who claimed to be Nadars in Tamil Nadu) and Owen M. Lynch (1974) (the case of Chamars who claimed to be Jatavs in Agra). It was, however, apparent that achieving mobility through sanskritization was extremely difficult for the lowest castes as the resistance by caste Hindus, at times resulting in violence, was immense.

CONVERSIONS

Yet another strategy adopted by some Dalit groups for mobility was through religious conversion. Conversions among Dalits were to Islam, Christianity, Sikhism and Buddhism. Dalits were attracted to these religions as they did not espouse caste system. It is ironical that Dalits continued to be discriminated since the caste system had penetrated into these religions.

> *Hutton sounds convincing when he says that when Muslims and Christians came to India, caste was in the air and the followers of even these egalitarian ideologies could not escape the infection of caste.*
> *(Husnain 2005, 207–08)*

Recent studies have shown that, by and large, lower caste converts to Christianity have remained within their caste group, followed their caste dictions and married within their caste. Often known as neo-Christians, they face discrimination at the hands of upper caste Christians. They are at times even allotted separate seats in the church. It is quite clear that Dalit Christians face twofold discrimination. One, they are exploited by both upper caste Christians and Hindus. Second, unlike other Dalits, they are not entitled to reservations in jobs and educational institutions.

It is widely believed that majority of Indian Muslims adopted Islam through conversion. In medieval times, it was common for a whole local caste group to convert instead of an individual. It was a gradual process, sometimes extending through generations, in which Islamic rituals, beliefs and customs were incorporated into local caste ethos while replacing Hindu features. Thus, the local caste group retained its identity and its basic features like endogamy even after Islamization.

> *It was thus not the influence of Hinduism among a previously 'pure', 'uncontaminated' Muslim community as such, but, rather, the continued impact of Hindu beliefs and practices, that explains the continued hold of caste-related practices and assumptions among large sections of the Indian Muslim community. (Sikand 2010, 256)*

Another case in point is that of Dalit Sikhs who embraced Sikhism to escape discrimination but found themselves socially excluded by economically affluent and politically powerful Jat Sikhs.

Dalit Sikhs is by no means a homogeneous category. It comprises Ramdasia Sikhs who consider themselves as superior to Mazhabi and Rangreta Sikhs. Dalit Sikhs have been all along discriminated against and kept apart by other Sikhs, although in their practices and mannerisms, they were similar to Jat Sikhs. They found themselves on the wrong side of the contradiction between egalitarian ideology of Sikhism and a reality that was entrenched in inequality and discrimination. This situation has, over the years, pushed a substantial population of Dalits to join non-Sikh deras who promise them dignity, social inclusion and economic upliftment denied by the rich landowning Jat Sikhs. In contemporary Punjab, these alternative organizations like Deras (Radha Soamis, Sacha Sauda, Namdharis and Nirankaris are some examples) have become centres for Dalit mobilization. The confrontation between the deras and mainstream Sikhism does not augur well for the relationship between Dalits and Jat Sikhs (Ronki Ram in Ahmed and Upadhyay 2010).

Conversions to Buddhism began in the latter part of the 19th century in Tamil Nadu. However, Buddhism became a religion of preference for Dalits when Ambedkar along with his supporters, the Mahars, converted in 1956 as has been explained in detail in the following section.

Another path of conversion for Dalits was to set up their own *panths*, inspired by saints of the Bhakti movement such as Kabir and Raidas. Some examples include Sivnarayni Sant Sampradaya which started in Allahabad and Satnami sect movement of 'Chamars' in Madhya Pradesh. The Satnami sect put forward their own religion which was different from Hinduism and the 'Chamar' identity. 'As Satnamis, they were no longer Hindus and no longer Chamars' (Vivek Kumar 2010, 119). Dube in his study of the history of the Satnami sect locates the movement lasted from 1780 to 1950 (Dube 2001).

Looking at the aforementioned account of socio-religious reform movements, one can conclude that while most of them belong to history and had ceased to exist at different points of time, some like sanskritization or conversions to Buddhism are trends that continue. 'The process of sanskritization though invisible still remains as one of the most important means of status enhancement by the Dalits…Conversions to Buddhism is gaining in momentum both among literate and illiterate Dalits' (Vivek Kumar 2010, 120).

A NEW BEGINNING: BHIMRAO RAMJI AMBEDKAR

It is in this context that, there emerged the towering personality of Bhimrao Ramji Ambedkar, a man of exceptional merit who was responsible for the development of a Dalit identity and movement (the term Dalit, however, came into popular use only after Ambedkar's death). His iconic status did not only mesmerize his followers but also gave a new meaning to Dalit identity and movement. He came to be affectionately called Babasaheb, meaning 'respected father'.

Bhimrao Ramji Ambedkar

Ambedkar (1891–1956) was from an *asprushya* caste, 'Mahar', from Maharashtra. Unlike others of his caste who were obliged to perform menial jobs, his father was working for the British army. Ambedkar was a brilliant student, and seeing this, Maharaja Sayajirao III of Baroda helped him to pursue his studies at Columbia University and London School of Economics. These achievements were rare and remarkable and truly outstanding.

GANDHI AND AMBEDKAR

Ambedkar's basic ideas, philosophy and activities developed in the milieu of an emerging nationalist movement for Independence. In his early years, he was influenced by Congress, and especially, Mahatma Gandhi and his form of protest. He came closest to Gandhi during Vaikom Satyagraha (1924–1925) which focused on the issue of rites of passage of Ezhavas, a low caste in Kerala and the question of temple entry for backward castes. In later years, however, the distance between the two only grew and at times their relationship became bitter. The disagreement between them, however, played a crucial role in building an anti-caste discourse (Hardtmann 2009). Although both Gandhi and Ambedkar were equally engaged in the fight against untouchability, their approach as to how this can be achieved differed fundamentally. While Gandhi advocated caste reforms and change of heart of caste Hindus, Ambedkar worked for Dalits writing their own destiny by changing their circumstances through their own efforts.

The differences between Gandhi and Ambedkar were on two major counts, 'political' and 'religious' (Hardtmann 2009). The political breakdown between the two occurred in 1932 when the communal award was announced by the British Government on Ambedkar's demand according to which special electoral benefits were given to the 'depressed classes' (the term for Dalits, in use at that time), the benefit of two votes in elections for their political gain. The arrangement was to be valid for 20 years. According to this provision, depressed classes were eligible for two votes, one in their separate electorate and the other in some of the constituencies in the general electorate. For Ambedkar, this was politically significant and had the potential to empower depressed castes. Gandhi opposed these provisions by going on a fast unto death. He strongly believed that the above provision was like poison for Hinduism and would do no good for the depressed classes. The controversy ended with a withdrawal of the communal award and the signing of the Poona Pact (1932), increasing the reserved seats for depressed castes.

Ambedkar believed that inequality was central to Hinduism and that Dalits would never get equal status as long as they remained in Hindu fold. Gandhi, on the other hand, believed that the Varna system was capable of reform and hence argued that the law of Varna had nothing to do with the inequalities of caste system. Instead, he believed that varnas are about earning one's living in accordance with ancestral calling. He was of the view that varnas define duties and not rights. For Ambedkar, the Varna system could not be the basis for equality in society. Although both Gandhi and Ambedkar rejected untouchability, Gandhi believed it to be an aberration of Hinduism while Ambedkar thought that it was its inherent feature.

The profound differences between Gandhi and Ambedkar could not be resolved but it can be said that they laid the foundation for a strong social movement among Dalits and led to the rise of Ambedkar as a leader of great stature, who came to be accepted internationally as a champion of equality and democracy. He boldly represented Dalits in international and national conferences. He became the first law minister of free India,[8] the main architect of the Constitution of India and a member of the constituent assembly.

AMBEDKAR: THE LIBERAL DEMOCRAT

Liberal democratic institutions greatly influenced Ambedkar. He had, it is often said, a strong faith in these institutions and their capability to bring about social justice. He, thus, believed in the constitutional method and the instrument of law to bring about fundamental social changes. Often questions are asked whether Ambedkar had any other options but to follow the parliamentary politics, given the resources and the unfavourable circumstances (Chatterjee 2004). Irrespective of what his reasons were, Ambedkar greatly relied on the democratic State to uplift the oppressed people of India, especially the 'untouchables'. It was due to this that he feared that in independent democratic India, the State might get hijacked by narrow interests of the powerful castes.

Although, as is clear from above, Ambedkar had great confidence in the Western liberal traditions, he was also influenced in his economic thought by Marxism. In the initial years, he accepted the basic ideas of Marx regarding class and even aligned with communists to mobilize Mahars and Kunbis along class lines against the landlords. Ambedkar, however, diagnosed a dual system of exploitation in our society; one is Brahminism, to be fought through caste struggle, and the other is capitalism, to be fought through class struggle. His weekly publication *Janata* carried articles on this. It was, however, in his *States and Minorities*[9] that, one, Ambedkar's differences with the communists and two, the inherent contradiction of the dual system emerged. Focusing on the former, while he criticized capitalism, he called for 'State socialism' with nationalization of land and basic industries instead of a working class revolution. With regard to the latter, he reflected on the tenuous connection between caste and class. In fact 'the dual systems of capitalism and brahminism provided a useful rhetoric....but it left the question of connection between the two completely unresolved'. Further,

---

[8] He later resigned from the post of the law minister over a controversy on the Hindu Code Bill.
[9] *States and Minorities* by B. R. Ambedkar was published in 1947. He wrote it on request of Scheduled Caste Federation who wanted the Constituent Assembly to take their interests into account. For many, it was like a mini-constitution complete with a Preamble.

there are other systems of exploitation such as patriarchy or national oppression which are likely to create a difficult blend of different types of exploitations. Ambedkar did find it difficult to form a consolidated approach through the dual system view (Omvedt 1993).

Ambedkar likened the condition of Dalits to slavery that ought to be fought. He called upon Dalits to reject Hindu scriptures and practices that advocated untouchability and to unite and fight for their own upliftment. He was clear that only Dalits could understand their own problems and they alone could fight for their rights. Education and politics were identified by Ambedkar as the two ways to achieve equality. Ambedkar encouraged Dalit women to participate in the movement as well, and women enthusiastically joined in the rallies, satyagrahas and meetings on various issues such as temple entry, separate electorates and conversions.

Like Jyotirao Phule, who gave a call for the unity of Shudras and Ati-Shudras (Dalits) in creating 'alternate socialism' in India, Ambedkar consistently worked to bring an alliance between them. For him, Dalits, Shudras and tribals were natural allies who needed to fight oppression together. He, thus, tried to bring Dalits and Kunbis together in his Independent Labour Party and tried to incorporate Shudra interests. However, over time he became disillusioned and started believing that Dalits would have to fight their battles alone. He feared that caste Hindus would never allow such a unity to develop. His movement, thus remained confined to the Dalits. Ambedkar, however, did not attach oppressed identity to any region. He saw Dalits as a minority group. This was in contrast to Periyar who attached Shudras to Dravidian identity and demanded for a separate Tamil land.

BUDDHISM AND AMBEDKAR

Although his efforts to achieve political power for Dalits continued throughout, there was a visible shift in Ambedkar's views with regard to ameliorating Dalits socially and culturally. It began with efforts at sankritization and temple entry but as his ideas became more radical, he advocated religious conversion to Buddhism. He believed that for a moral order, religion is necessary. In his search for alternatives, he started moving away from communism towards Buddhism. In his *Buddha or Karl Marx*, he said that communism can give us only equality but not liberty and fraternity. To get all the three, we must follow the ways of Buddha.

Hence, in later years, Ambedkar tried to uplift Dalits in two ways—spiritually and politically. For their spiritual upliftment, he chose the path of Buddhism by establishing *prabuddha bharata*, his vision of achieving cultural renaissance in India through Buddhism. For him Buddhism represented a secular, rationalistic ideology for change. In order to strengthen Dalits politically, he established a political party, the Republican Party of India (RPI), which replaced the earlier organizations formed under his leadership, Independent Labour Party (1936) and All India Scheduled Castes Federation (1942). Things, however, did not go in the way Ambedkar had anticipated.

Although it is true that just before he passed away in 1956, Ambedkar along with his followers numbering thousands embraced Buddhism as he saw no hope of removal of the stigma against the lower castes within Hinduism, he could not establish the organizational form of Buddhism. The main Buddhist organization, the Maha Bodhi Society, was at that time staffed by Sinhalese Buddhists and headed by a Hindu Brahmin, Shyama Prasad Mukherjee, a situation totally unacceptable to Ambedkar. However, soon after his death, a Trailokya Bauddh Mahasangh was formed. This came to be controlled by certain dominant Dalit castes such as the 'Mahars' in Maharashtra and 'Chamars' in Uttar Pradesh.

> Buddhism, it is believed 'did not produce much of a change in their social identity…. Almost no caste Hindus followed them in converting and the result was that Buddhism itself became rather untouchable in India'. (Gail Omvedt in Shah 2002, p. 300)

Regarding political upliftment of Dalits, Ambedkar could not really establish the RPI along the lines he wanted to due to his untimely death. He was keen on setting up a reformed version of All India Scheduled Castes Federation which would achieve great goals for Dalits and Indian society.

AFTER AMBEDKAR

Ambedkar's death slowly led to a decline in the Dalit movement, both in his native Maharashtra and at the national level. The movement so passionately nurtured by Ambedkar had lost its sheen. At the political level, the RPI split into various factions, some of these groups aligned with major political parties. This was due to personality politics, electoral opportunism and various other factors. There were, however, some like Dadasaheb Gaikwad who energized the party by joining the communists in *land satyagrahas* of 1956 and 1965 aimed at the right of Dalits to use common lands for cultivation as well as the use of forest lands. However, Gaikwad's efforts only brought temporary reprieve. The party, dominated by only few Dalit castes, stagnated once again. Ambedkar's death, thus brought a lull in the Dalit movement.

DALIT SAHITYA AND DALIT PANTHERS

This calm, however, was not to last for long. In the 1960s and the 1970s, powerful literary protest movements emerged in Maharashtra, Dalit Sahitya and Dalit Panthers. These movements expressed, in strongest terms, the plight of Dalits, despite the constitutional provisions and positive legislations, and their resolve to fight for their dignity. They became the precursors of Dalit literature in the form of poetry, autobiographies and fiction, which was to develop in later decades of the 20th and early 21st centuries. In the 1960s, Dalit Sahitya, with contributions from various prolific Dalit writers and poets, had achieved the status of a school of literature. Keshav Meshram's (1978) 'one day I cursed that mother-f****r God…' became an important symbol of revolutionary Dalit writing.

In the year 1972 came the Dalit Panthers, a new generation of Dalit activists. Closely linked to and at times fused with Dalit Sahitya, they were openly defiant of the establishment, radical in their approach and ready to go that extra mile to fight caste atrocities and humiliation meted out to them and their families for generations. They were inspired by Black Panthers. They came from poor illiterate families who had left their home and hearth in their villages to escape poverty, unemployment and a life of humiliation and violence. They were young writers and poets, the first educated generation in their families, who grew up in Mumbai slums amidst a sea of humanity and an overarching stench of poverty. Their sense of pride at Ambedkar's achievements had long been doused due to the cruel reality of slum life and opportunistic politics which led to a decline in the Dalit movement. Coming out of universities in the latter part of the 1960s, they faced a blank future. The Constitutional provisions appeared like a mirage.

It was in this milieu that Dalit Panthers formulated their identity and their counter culture more on lines with Eva-Maria Hardtmann's 'alternative counterpublic'[10] (Hardtmann 2009). Whether it was their name, strategy or agenda, Panthers defined it all on the streets of Mumbai, in tea houses, public libraries and from homes. Theirs was a paradigm shift from the kind of stance taken by Dalit activists before them. Clearly militant, they expressed their anger through poetry, articles and speeches as well as through revolts. As the Panthers emerged to the centre stage of Dalit politics, with massive rallies and a new genre of writings, they attracted Dalit youth and progressive liberals alike.

Founded by Namdeo Dhasal along with three other Dalit youths—J. V. Pawar, Raja Dhale and Arjun Dangle—Dalit Panthers fought for Dalit dignity as passionately as Ambedkar, only their methods to achieve this were very different. Incidentally, Namdeo Dhasal, like Ambedkar was a 'Mahar' from Maharashtra, committed to fight against Dalit atrocities but while Ambedkar believed in achieving it through legal procedures, Dhasal, who was a follower of Marx, chose a fiery and uncompromising path.

DALIT PANTHERS AND NAXALITES

It is often said that the Panthers were the urban counterpart of Naxalites who were active in parts of Indian countryside in the 1960s and 1970s. Although both aimed to get power, their method and underlying ideology were different. The focus of Naxalites was on class revolt and armed struggle, the thrust of the Panthers was on a cultural revolt to do away with caste system and its inherent inequalities. While Naxalites organized armed struggle to build a power base at the local level, the Panthers had higher designs of achieving power to rule the country. This was clearly expressed in their manifesto which reads thus, 'We do not want a little place in the Brahamin alley. We want to rule the whole country....'. Further, as against the 'armed revolt' of

---

[10] It basically refers to the formation and spread of counter discourse by Dalit activists in order to create and recreate a Dalit identity according to their interests and needs.

the Naxalites, Panthers' revolt was more at a symbolic level, although they did organize protests as well (Omvedt 1993). Unlike Naxalites, Dalit Panthers were fighting on various fronts, for Dalit dignity and self-respect, against sexual exploitation of Dalit women by upper caste men, violence against Dalits and poverty. Despite these differences, there were similarities in their rhetoric and method. It is not surprising that Naxalites and Panthers at times found themselves on the same side of the fence, fighting caste wars in class terms or vice versa (Omvedt 1993).

NAMDEO DHASAL'S *GOLPITHA*

A poet of some repute, Namdeo's poetry depicted the living reality around him in a most poignant style. The poetry is such that the reader would always feel that the poet is a performer, giving a live performance on the most profound issues concerning human species. *Golpitha*, published in 1972, was his first collection of poems. It 'is written in an idiolect[11] fashioned in the streets of the red light district of central Mumbai, and from the Mahar dialect spoken in Maval region of the Pune district in Maharashtra—his native language' (Chitre 2007, 9). It is widely believed that Namdeo always had the strength to deal with literature on his own terms.

In *Golpitha*, Namdeo depicted the deep-set stigma and loathing towards a Dalit by portraying the female prostitute. 'Her status is that of the ultimate untouchable, serving other humans by allowing them to degrade one-self'. Through his poetry, Namdeo 'seems to be launching from the very start—single-handedly—a guerrilla war against the effete middle class and sanitized world of literary readers, among them many professors of literature, critics and ideologues of the Left' (Chitre 2007, 11–12).

Dalit Panthers came into prominence with the publication of a number of their articles and poems, often controversial, at times scandalous, in a socialist magazine, *Sadhana*. The publications not only aroused the interest of the Marathi intellectuals but also established Panthers as the bastion of the Dalit movement. An incident which took a scandalous turn was related to Raja Dhale and his two pieces of writing published in *Sadhana*. One was an article which compared the fines levied by the government on insulting the national flag and on molesting a Dalit woman. For the former it was ₹300 and for the latter only ₹50. The second writing comprised his views on comments made by Durgabai Bhagwat, a well-known Marathi littérateur at the publication ceremony of *Golpitha*. Bhagwat had said that 'since prostitutes performed a necessary function for society, they should be treated with respect'. This, according to many Dalits, was similar to the Gandhian view of letting the Dalits perform their traditional occupation but to give respect to all occupations. Dhale reacted thus, 'Bhagwatbai wants to keep prostitutes as prostitutes but give them honour. If she thinks this is the way to uplift the downtrodden, why doesn't she take up the occupation herself?' (Omvedt 1993, 48). This scandalized many and

---

[11] Idiolect refers to an individual's unique and distinct way of speaking and writing.

that issue of *Sadhana* was banned. Marches were held by Dalits defending Dhale's comments followed by adoption of a Panther 'red on black' flag and a reiteration of their name (Omvedt 1993).

In the following year, the Panthers formulated a passionate manifesto calling for nothing less than a revolution. The manifesto reflected the deep anguish that was felt by every Dalit, the anguish of living on the edge in which the overwhelming theme was violence against their person and their dignity. The Panthers' revolt was against the pure/impure dichotomy of the Brahminical and patriarchal order. Their poetry and writings were an attack on its intrinsic underlying beliefs and the institutions thus created. 'The burning to death of dalit labourers in villages like Kilvenmani, the tearing out of eyes of assertive men, the rape and molestation of women all expressed the horror of what was happening to their people after twenty five years of independence' (Omvedt 1993, 49).

The Panthers regularly organized protests against atrocities on Dalits by caste Hindus which were frequent in the 1970s. The protests were also fuelled by government's inaction and insensitivity towards Dalits. As part of Dalit assertion, the Panthers erected statues of Phule and Ambedkar at many places. They changed names of neighbourhoods to Samata Nagar, Jai Bheem Nagar, Ambedkar Nagar, Kabir Nagar and the like. Soon the Panthers became notorious for 'disturbing peace', were in and out of jail where they were often beaten brutally. Namdeo was even branded as Naxalite in police records. By 1975, there were 360 charge sheets against the Panthers in Maharashtra (Chatterjee 2004). It was in 1975 itself that the national emergency was declared by Indira Gandhi. Namdeo Dhasal went to meet her presenting the case of Dalits which she heard sympathetically and ordered dropping of all cases against the Panthers. Many branded this as a sell out to Congress.

It is often said that the Panthers did not have a broad vision nor an organizational framework to take the movement forward. By the 1980s, differences started emerging among the Panthers. 'The major contentious issues were, *inter alia*, whether or not to include non-Dalit poor and non-Buddhist Dalits; whether to give primacy to cultural or economic struggles' (Chatterjee 2004, 158–59). Then there were personality and ideological clashes, especially between Namdeo Dhasal, a Marxist, and Raja Dhale, an Ambedkarite. The Ambedkaites won in the end as the attraction of caste was immense and so was the fear of Brahmins holding positions of authority in Naxalite groups. As the cracks started developing, some of the factions aligned with mainstream parties like the Congress.

> *The villagers never forgot nor did they let us forget, that we were untouchables. High caste children sat inside the school; the Bauri children…about twenty of us, sat outside on the veranda and listened. The two teachers, a Brahman outsider, and a temple servant, refused to touch us even with a stick. To beat us, they threw bamboo canes. The higher caste children threw mud at us. Fearing severe beatings, we dared not fight back. (Freeman, 1979)*

POST PANTHERS

Although the Panthers weakened, they left indelible marks on the socialist politics in India and the Dalit movement as well as on other movements of the day including that of women, environment, peasant and tribal. One, the discourse of revolutionary movements expanded to include class, caste, social and economic concerns and two, the symbols changed. Mythology, for instance, came to be reinterpreted.

As the influence of Panthers was declining, the Dalit movement was evolving through literature and through political action in various streams along different paths, sometimes radical and at other times moderate. While poetry as a medium of expression for the Dalits, which started in the 1960s, continued to remain a weapon for their cause, new genre of writings started emerging in the 1980s, such as autobiographies, novels, short stories, essays and so on. Autobiographical writings began with men but soon women started narrating their inhuman experiences. Some well-known Dalit autobiographies are Daya Pawar's *Baluta*, Vasant Moon's *Growing Up Untouchable in India* and Omprakash Valmiki's *Joothan*.

BAHUJAN SAMAJ PARTY (BSP)

In 1984, Kanshi Ram launched a political party, the BSP. The party emerged from an earlier organization of government employees formed in 1974—All India Backward and Minority Communities Employees Federation (BAMCEF) in Pune with a functioning office in Delhi. They looked into the issues of discrimination and related matters concerning Dalit employees. BAMCEF started in Maharashtra and then spread to Madhya Pradesh, Delhi, Haryana, Punjab and Uttar Pradesh. A very important programme of BAMCEF was 'Ambedkar Mela on Wheels' (first organized between April 1980 and June 1980, in a number of towns and cities). This was a pictorial and oral depiction of Ambedkar's ideas and works along with a portrayal of atrocities against Dalits, their poverty and oppression. Overtime, BAMCEF organized a cadre of highly disciplined Dalits who had attained education and employment through reservations. In the terminology of BAMCEF, they helped the Dalit movement in creation of 'Man, Money and Mind Power', a slogan around which Kanshi Ram and his organization mobilized support for the movement.

Despite its widespread success, BAMCEF needed a political platform for pursuing its interests. Kanshi Ram, thus set up a partial political organization called DS-4 (Dalit Shoshit Samaj Sangharsh Samiti) in 1981, which by 1984 became a full-fledged political party—the BSP. BSP was set up to reflect the political aspirations of 'Bahujan' which includes not just Dalits but also other lower castes and religious minorities. Kanshi Ram strongly believed in a united front for all these groups. The launch of BSP signified a more formal engagement of Bahujans in politics.

Kanshi Ram strongly believed that while Dalit politics had its roots in Maharashtra, it was nurtured and honed in Uttar Pradesh. The coming of BSP, however, did not mean the fading away of BMACEF which is now the biggest organization of Dalit employees. Under the leadership of people like B. D. Borker, the organization has carried out multifarious activities such as publishing, producing audio and video materials, organizing conferences and national conventions to create awareness about Dalits and other marginalized sections.

It is often emphasized that BSP developed under the aegis of RPI (it has taken the elephant symbol of RPI) which was founded and inspired by Ambedkar and still exists as different factions in Maharashtra. It was the legacy of RPI that led to the formation of BSP. Both, RPI and BSP were founded by people who belonged to the scheduled castes to escape upper caste dominance within the Congress. It drew upon on Muslim support and won elections where there was dominance of Dalits and minorities. BSP achieved certain level of electoral success in 1985 when it polled 4 per cent of the votes. Political pundits had predicted only a brief period of success for BSP. Its success has proved them wrong. BSP has ruled the largest state of India, Uttar Pradesh, three times, earlier in coalition and then on its own. BSP's main objective has been to achieve political success along the constitutional path, initially under Kanshi Ram and now under Mayawati.

AMBEDKAR AND KANSHI RAM

After Ambedkar, the coming of Kanshi Ram and his achievement in successfully mobilizing Dalits of Uttar Pradesh is believed to be an important development in the Dalit movement. However, Badri Narayan believes that the success of Kanshi Ram has also created anomalies within the Dalit movement. While on the one hand there is the ideological stand of Ambedkar, on the other, there is the down to earth and practical approach of Kanshi Ram (Narayan 2011). The two had contrasting backgrounds which reflected in their approach and strategy. While Ambedkar had western education as mentioned earlier, Kanshi Ram was born and brought up in a small village in Punjab. Ambedkar's understanding of Dalits was more historical, whereas Kanshi Ram's approach was inspired by folk culture.

Slogans of BSP

Babasaheb Ka Dusra Nam, Kanshi Ram, Kanshi Ram

(Kanshi Ram is the second name for Babasaheb Ambedkar)

Baba Tera Mission Adhura, Kanshi Ram Karega Pura

(Babasaheb Ambedkar, Kanshi Ram will complete your unfulfilled mission)

(Ram 2008)

As has been explained earlier, Ambedkar's fight was for Dalits as his efforts at bringing Shudras and Dalits together had failed. On the other hand, Kanshi Ram preferred to term it the 'Bahujan[12] movement' avoiding the use of the word 'Dalit'. Thus, Kanshi Ram grouped Dalits of Uttar Pradesh with the broader category of Bahujan.

While Ambedkar's approach was entrenched in ethics, Kanshi Ram's was more practical. For him, the end was to achieve political power, the means mattered little. Ambedkar advocated the eventual annihilation of the caste system, whereas Kanshi Ram and then Mayawati, felt that Dalits, in fact Bahujans, should deploy the caste identity for emancipation. Brahminical hegemony was challenged through an attack on what has come to be known as *Manuwad*. Unlike Ambedkar who thought the right path is to get separate electorates, Kanshi Ram wanted the society to change into *Samta Muluk*, an equal society, where each would have their separate identity. This idea of *Samta Muluk* became the underlying philosophy of BSP.

Kanshi Ram often said that Ambedkar learnt from books, whereas his own laboratory was the people. According to Badri Narayan, to have a successful Dalit movement, there is a need to combine the value-based approach of Ambedkar with the practical methodology of Kanshi Ram (Narayan 2011).

MOBILIZING DALITS IN UTTAR PRADESH

On moving to Uttar Pradesh, Kanshi Ram initially used the symbols and political language he had used in Maharashtra but he soon understood that it was not effective in mobilizing Dalits. In the distinct environment of Uttar Pradesh, there was a need to explore and highlight the local histories, indigenous folk culture and legendary tales and fables to mobilize each Dalit caste. Local historians from each block were deputed to collect case studies depicting stories of oppression and courage among different Dalit castes and their glorious leaders which were then woven into a colossal discourse on their subjugation. A pyramid like symbolic structure of the various leaders was then formed. In the lower most echelon were local heroes such as Mahavir Bhangi, Jhalkari Bai and Uda Devi, followed by Dalit kings in the next echelon such as Baldeo, Bijli Pasi and Daldev. The third echelon was that of the saints of Bhakti movement such as Ravi Das and Kabir as well as the idols from the epics Ramayana and Mahabharata such as Shambook and Eklavya. In the top rung were Ambedkar and Periyar, the great leaders of the Dalit identity and movement. The images of BSP leaders were built around these figures. They became the symbol of Dalit unity for BSP (Narayan 2011).

---

[12] The term Bahujan literally means the majority.

SUBMERGED IDENTITIES

In this quest for building a grand homogeneous identity of Dalits, the individual identity and history of many Dalit castes have got submerged. Taking the case of Uttar Pradesh, Badri Narayan has pointed out that smaller castes such as Jogi (monkey, bear owners) Rangrej (people who dye clothes) and Nat (street performers) have been sidelined. He has argued that the top most echelon of Dalit leadership and their castes became most important, sidelining the rest. This has led to tensions among Dalits. Even among the major Dalit castes such as 'Chamar' and 'Pasi', there is competition to take a larger share of the pie. Each caste has, to an extent, a distinct history of exploitation. In an effort to bring about grand unity, these different identities have somewhere got submerged. Further, it is clear that the castes which succeeded in developing their identity through their heroes and history have also got political representation, whereas those who have not been able to do so have got left behind in the political race as well (Narayan 2011).

In Uttar Pradesh assembly elections of February 2012, different political parties such as the Congress and BJP tried to take advantage of these discrepancies within BSP and focused on mobilizing the more marginalized Dalit castes by honouring their heroes, highlighting their histories and promising to develop their traditional crafts. Congress organized *ati pichhra* (most backward caste) rallies and honoured their heroes of the 1857 rebellion such as Samadhan Nishad, Lochan Mallah and Ahilyabai Holker. BJP also promised to put up statues of leaders like Bijli Pasi, a pre-medieval Dalit hero (Narayan 2011).

DALIT WOMEN

Exploited on account of their caste, class and gender, Dalit women and their issues remained largely invisible both from the women's and the Dalit movement. The representation of Dalit women in the women's movement has remained negligible. Women's movement groups have not focused enough on the sexual and physical exploitation and oppression of Dalit women by the upper caste men, the Dalit men and the State machinery like the police. A reason for this can be that the women's groups are dominated by upper caste women who ignored the issues (Subramaniam 2006). Although Dalit groups and individuals have written and talked about Dalit women, they too have not focused enough on the harsh reality of the their lives (for further details see Chapter 3).

However, Dalit women have been involved in the Dalit movement from the beginning of the 20th century. For instance, Dalit women in 1909, protested in a year-long strike which was spearheaded by the famed Dalit leader Ayyankali at Venganur to claim the right to education (Yasudasan 1999). Markers of caste identity such as distinctive jewellery and clothes became the further basis for Dalit mobilization (e.g., many Dalit women insisted on wearing upper cloth against prevailing caste norms). Such incidents of resistance often resulted in violence. In Maharashtra, Dalit women challenged the Devdasi system and the stigma of 'prostitution'.

In the 1930s, large numbers joined in Satyagraha at Kalaram temple in Nasik. They conducted meetings and conferences to press for the demand for separate electorates. Some women joined the 'Scheduled Caste Federation' in 1942. Shantabai Dani led Dalit women in Maharashtra on several occasions during the 1940s and 1950s.

The participation of Dalit women in later years increased with the setting up of Dalit Stri Samwadini (Dalit Women's Dialogue) in 1986 and the National Federation of Dalit Women (NFDW) in 1994. Over time, NFDW has organized and participated in several national and international conferences like the one on 'Racial Discrimination, Xenophobia and Related Intolerance' organized by the United Nations Human Rights Commission at Durban in 2001 representing this most vulnerable section.

In recent years, a number of Dalit women writers had produced poetry, fiction, autobiographies and other works of literature to take their cause further. These include Sumitra Bhave's *Pan on Fire* (Marathi, 1988) (it is a collection of eight illiterate Dalit women's life stories); Kumud Pawade's *Antasphot* (Marathi, 1981); Bama's *Karukku* (Tamil Nadu, 1992) and Urmila Pawar's *Amhihi Itihas Ghadawala* (Marathi, 1998) (Raj Kumar 2010). The autobiographies of women generally portray the exploitation they face at home due to entrenched patriarchy and the one they face outside by upper caste men who treat them as easy sexual prey. Of late, Dalit women's literature is proliferating, thus impacting the discourse in the Dalit movement and society at large. It is important to note that as this most vulnerable section of our society becomes visible, there is at times backlash against these groups and the families that they belong to.

INTERNATIONALIZING DALIT ISSUES

Since the 1990s, efforts have been made to internationalize the Dalit problem. It began with the World Conference on Human Rights at Vienna in 1993 and the World Summit on Social Development held at Copenhagen in 1995 where caste-based discrimination was discussed and analysed. However, an exclusive Dalit convention (World Dalit Convention) was held in Kuala Lumpur in 1998 under the aegis of Dalit International Organization. Here, a resolution was passed to push for appointment of 'special rapporteurs' by the United Nations in order to investigate human rights violation and also take appropriate measures to effect the implementation of fundamental human rights instrument for Dalits in India and other parts of the world.

Following this convention, there were others—International Conference on Dalit Human Rights, London, 2000; Global Conference Against Racism and Caste-Based Discrimination, New Delhi, 2001; The Durban Conference on Racism, 2001; United Nations Committee on the Elimination of Racial Discrimination, 2002 and International Dalit Conference, Vancouver, 2003.

In the year 2000, Martin Macwan, a Dalit human rights activist was the recipient of the Robert F. Kennedy Human Rights Award in recognition of his outstanding work for the Dalits nationally and in Gujarat through his organization Navsarjan Trust (Sommer 2001, 51–52).

The issues raised in international forums have varied from implementation of present laws to formulation of new laws to protect Dalits against discrimination and get them their rightful place in society. In the year 2002 (12 and 13 January), Dalit leaders, activists and intellectuals met at Bhopal to reflect on issues of concern and to find ways to address them. A 21-Point Action Agenda was unanimously adopted as Bhopal Declaration. The mainstay of the Declaration was that Dalits should initiate efforts to align with other human rights and liberation movements internationally.

PRESENT TRENDS

In today's India, one can see many tangible achievements of the movement. There is the powerful Dalit mobilization on myriad issues such as reservations, atrocities meted out at the hands of upper castes, formulation of new legislations and desecration of the statues of their leaders. This is clearly visible in various pro-reservation protests. There is then the success story of political parties like BSP with its formidable presence in some of the North Indian states as well as the Dalit lobby in mainstream parties making Dalits the new key players in politics. An ever expanding new and educated middle class among Dalits which is both aware and vocal is today the new face of Dalit groups. Then there is the vibrant portrayal of Dalit issues through recent writings and theatre. Whether it is poetry, autobiographies, short stories, novels, critical essays or street plays, Dalits are actively challenging caste domination. A number of Dalit playwrights, both women and men, have successfully depicted the contradictions and dilemmas of being Dalit through theatre and street plays. Of late, Dalit literature is not only increasing but it is emerging from many other states as well such as Punjab, Odisha and Tamil Nadu apart from Maharashtra, Andhra Pradesh, Gujarat and Karnataka. Dalit Rangabhoomi, founded by B. S. Shinde in 1979 has put up a number of meaningful performances over the years.

However, unity between the various streams of the movement is still elusive. Any efforts at bringing the scattered groups together have failed. In the 1990s in Maharashtra, the grandson of Ambedkar, Prakash Ambedkar made an effort to bring all shades of Dalit activists, leaders and organizations under one umbrella. A massive rally was organized in Mumbai in which around 500,000 people participated. However, the unity was short lived as they soon got divided into various dissenting groups, undermining the whole effort.

Further, while there is a widespread realization that if Dalits and other backward groups like Shudras come together, they can become a very powerful force with immense political potential. As has been pointed out earlier, this unity has had a turbulent history. In present times also, they are together in one instance and bitter enemies in another. The BSP and SP (Samajwadi Party) relationship in Uttar Pradesh is an example of this.

Direction of Bahujan Movement in Recent Years

Recent incidents in North India have given a new direction and meaning to the Dalit movement. Since 2016, there has been a rise of young leaders such as Jignesh Mevani in Gujarat and Chandrashekhar Azad in Uttar Pradesh (founder of Bhim Army) who are bringing a shift in Dalit movement which was dominated by Kanshi Ram/Mayawati run BSP for nearly the last three decades. Although BSP in its early years used aggressive symbolism to create a discourse of 'us and they', it has over the years shed that symbolism for a more inclusive stance. These young leaders, on the other hand, have brought a new assertiveness to the Dalit movement and have jumped into the political foray head on.

Chandrashekhar, who set up the Bhim Army has been jailed for his alleged involvement in caste riots of Saharanpur and Shabbirpur. His release recently has led to widespread speculations on whether he will support the ruling BJP or the Mahagathbandhan of the opposition. Many believe that he may take support of the Congress party like Jignesh Mevani is believed to have done. Another question that is of importance is the role of BSP and Mayawati towards these young leaders. Till now her stance has been evasive. Will they be absorbed in BSP to create a larger Bahujan movement? Answers to these questions, as of now, remain in the sphere of conjecture (Narayan 2018).

CONCLUSION

This chapter has focused on different phases of the Dalit movement. During this journey, the movement has frequently reinvented itself due to its internal dynamics and extraneous factors which include the type of leadership, the aspirations of the movement at that point of time, the sociocultural and legal factors, the political milieu and the intellectual environment. At times the focus was on constitutional means as under the leadership of Ambedkar, at other times far more radical means were employed as under the Dalit Panthers. The objectives too are varied from demanding concessions to eradication of untouchability, to complete abolition of the caste system, to separate electorates, to reservations and the like.

When we look at the Dalit movement as it has unfolded over the centuries and decades, and place it in the contemporary Indian society, one can see a progressive trend from 'untouchable' to 'Dalit' implying a transition from the oppressed and the dehumanized to the awakened and the assertive. Dalits have a significant presence in the polity and a voice to reckon with. There is an increase in educated and employed Dalits today who form the middle class. There are Dalit entrepreneurs. There is a vast Dalit literature which is ever increasing. It can be said that the reality of being a Dalit in contemporary India is very different from what it was at the time of Ambedkar. However, at the ground level, Dalits are still stigmatized, isolated and exploited. The tide, no doubt, seems to be turning in favour of equality and dignity, although the path is still very long and arduous.

POINTS FOR DISCUSSION

- Do you think the attempts of contemporary Dalit leaders are less focused on the eradication of the caste system and more focused on questions of identity?
- There is a widespread belief that the Dalit movement today is scattered across leaders, political parties and regions, presenting little possibility of a consolidated agenda. Discuss.
- The Dalit movement has mainly benefitted the more dominant groups, thus leaving the smaller, less visible groups behind. This has created a new hierarchy which has kept the large more marginalized sections untouched by the changes that are taking place. Discuss.

REFERENCES AND READINGS

Ambedkar, B. R. 1989. 'What Congress and Gandhi Have Done to Untouchables'. In *Dr Babasaheb Ambedkar: Writings and Speeches* (vol. 5). Bombay: Education Department, Government of Maharashtra.

Chatterjee, Debi. 2004. *Up Against Caste: Comparative Study of Ambedkar and Periyar*. Jaipur: Rawat Publications.

Dhasal, Namdeo. 2007. *Poet of the Underworld*. Selected, introduced and translated from Marathi by Dilip Chitre. Chennai: Navayana Publishing.

Dube, Saurabh. 2001. *Untouchable Pasts: Religion, Identity and Power among a Central Indian Community, 1780–1950*. New Delhi: Vistaar Publications.

Freeman, James. 1979. *Untouchable: An Indian Life History*, 67. Translated from stories on Muli's life, originally in Oriya. Stanford, CA: Stanford University Press.

Hardtmann, Eva-Maria. 2009. *The Dalit Movement in India: Local Practices, Global Connections*. New Delhi: Oxford University Press.

Hasan, Zoya. 2009. *Politics of Inclusion: Castes, Minorities and Affirmative Action*. New Delhi: Oxford University Press.

Husnain, Nadeem. 2005. 'Muslims in India: Caste Affinity and Social Boundaries of Backwardness'. In *The OBCs and the Ruling Classes in India*, edited by H. S. Verma, 84–97. Jaipur: Rawat Publications.

Joe, Arun C. 2007. *Constructing Dalit Identity*. Jaipur: Rawat Publications.

Juergensmeyer, Mark. 1982. *Religion as Social Vision: The Movement against Untouchability in 20th Century Punjab*. Berkeley, CA: University of California Press.

Kumar, Raj. 2010. *Dalit Personal Narratives: Reading Caste, Nation and Identity*. New Delhi: Orient BlackSwan.

Kumar, Vivek. 2010. 'Different Shades of Dalit Mobilization'. In *Social Movements I: Issues of Identity*, edited by T. K. Oommen, 116–34. New Delhi: Oxford University Press.

Lynch, Owen M. 1974. *The Politics of Untouchability*. Delhi: National Publishing House.

Meshram, Keshav. 1978. *Vidrohi Kavita (Poetry of Protest)*. Translated by Jayant Karve and Eleanor Zelliot with Pam Espeland. Pune: Continental Prakashan.

Narayan, Badri. 2011. *The Making of Dalit Public in North India: Uttar Pradesh, 1950–Present*. New Delhi: Oxford University Press.

———. 2018. 'The Battle for the Bahujan'. *Indian Express*, December 4.

Omvedt, Gail. 1993. *Reinventing Revolution: New Social Movements and the Socialist Tradition in India*. New York, NY: An East Gate Book.

———. 1994. *Dalits and Democratic Revolution: Dr Ambedkar and the Dalit Movement in Colonial India*. New Delhi/ Thousand Oaks, CA/London: SAGE Publications.

———. 2003. 'Ambedkar and After: The Dalit Movement in India'. In *Social Movements and the State: Readings in Indian Government and Politics-4*, edited by Ghanshyam Shah, 293–309. New Delhi: SAGE Publications.

Oommen, T. K. 1990. *Protest and Change: Studies in Social Movements*. New Delhi: SAGE Publications.

———, ed. 2010. *Social Movements I: Issues of Identity*. New Delhi: Oxford University Press.

———, ed. 2010. *Social Movements II: Concerns of Equity and Security*. New Delhi: Oxford University Press.

Pawar, Daya. 1974. *Kondwada*. Translated by Eleanor Zelliot and Jayant Karve with A. K. Ramanujan. Pune: Mehta Publishing House.

Ram, Nandu, ed. 2008. *Dalits in Contemporary India: Discrimination and Discontent* (vol. I). New Delhi: Siddhant Publications.

Ram, Ronki. 2010. 'Social Exclusion, Resistance and Deras: Exploring the Myth of Casteless Sikh Society in Punjab'. In *Dalit Assertion in Society, Literature and History*, edited by Imtiaz Ahmed and Shashi Bhushan Upadhyay, 273–97 New Delhi: Orient BlackSwan in association with Deshkal Society.

Rao, M. S. A., ed. 1979. *Social Movements in India*. New Delhi: Manohar Publications.

Rudolph, Lloyd, and Susanne Rudolph. 1987. *The Modernity of Tradition: Political Development in India*. New Delhi: Orient Longman.

Sahu, D. R., ed. 2012. *Sociology of Social Movement*. New Delhi: SAGE Publications.

Shah, Ghanshyam. (2004) 2005. *Social Movements in India: A Review of Literature*. Second edition. New Delhi: SAGE Publications.

Sikand, Yoginder. 2010. 'Islam and Caste Inequalities among Indian Muslims'. In *Dalit Assertion in Society, Literature and History*, edited by Imtiaz Ahmed and Shashi Bhushan Upadhyay, 254–72. New Delhi: Orient BlackSwan in association with Deshkal Society.

Singh, Rajendra. 2001. *Social Movements, Old and New: A Post-Modernist Critique*. New Delhi: SAGE Publications.

Sommer, John G. 2001. *Empowering the Oppressed: Grassroots Advocacy Movements in India*. New Delhi/Thousand Oaks, CA/London: SAGE Publications.

Subramaniam, Mangala. 2006. *The Power of Women's Organizing: Gender, Caste and Class in India*. Lanham, MD: Lexington Books.

Teltumbde, Anand. 2010. *The Persistence of Caste: The Khairlanji Murders and India's Hidden Apartheid*. New Delhi: Navayana Publishing.

Upadhyay, Shashi Bhushan. 2010. 'Introduction'. In *Dalit Assertion in Society, Literature and History*, edited by Imtiaz Ahmed and Shashi Bhushan Upadhyay, 1–14. New Delhi: Orient BlackSwan in association with Deshkal Society.

Yasudasan, T. M. 1999. 'Caste, Gender and Knowledge: Towards a Dalit Feminist Perspective'. In *Dalits and Peasants: The Emerging Caste-Class Dynamics*, edited by Ashish Ghosh, 334–5. New Delhi: Gyan Sagar Publication.

3

Towards Equality: Women's Movement

You may write me down in history

With your bitter, twisted lies,

You may tread me in the very dirt

But still like dust, I'll rise.

—Maya Angelou

The account of the women's movement in India is long and inspiring. Before narrating the history of the Indian women's movement, it is pertinent to point out that the term 'Indian women's movement' is itself today highly contested. The discomfort stems from the belief that the term Indian obscures all other politically relevant divisions such as caste, class or religion. For instance, a Dalit woman in rural Bihar would have very different concerns from an urban upper caste Hindu woman living in Delhi.

Radha Kumar in her book *The History of Doing* suggests that while colonialism and the struggle against it was very significant on the women's movement in the pre-Independence period, in the post-Independence period, democratic politics and institutional structures have been the most important influences. This obviously does not mean that the two phases are unrelated.

PRE-INDEPENDENCE PERIOD

During the pre-Independence period, questions of women's freedom and equality were often projected not as political questions but as social questions. It was placed by leading historians as part of the so-called 'social reform movement'. It was in the 19th century that women's issues became important. The so-called 'woman question' was posited as something that would be resolved within the domestic sphere; it was not seen as being linked with the other struggles of the anti-imperialist movements. Women were seen as occupants of the domestic sphere, and hence, their concerns would have to be resolved within the domestic sphere. There was a great deal of reluctance to engage politically with the colonial state over the question of women's freedom. The nationalist patriarchy believed that it was eminently qualified to resolve the woman question with no interference from the colonial state.

There seemed to be a belief that the status of women determined the claims of modernity and indeed of nationhood itself. In the context of the anti-colonial struggle, therefore, this issue gained momentum and added relevance. The emerging new Indian elite educated in Western ways sought to remedy the worst aspects of the existing patriarchal structures. In this enterprise, they sometimes sought the help of the British government. These efforts were also guided by the desire on the part of the westernized Indian elite to create a new Indian woman who would be able to share her sensibilities and approach to life. It is perhaps because of this desire that education for women became such an important issue within the reform movement. The other big issue was of course the campaign against Sati.

There were two kinds of opinion within this newly emergent Indian elite; one that sought the intervention of the government and the other that resisted it. Lata Mani argues interestingly that both sides were of course not prepared to grant women agency, they merely used the woman question as the site on which to carry on their discourse and definition of Indian identity and tradition.

A small group of elite women benefited from the efforts of the male social reformers and the changes brought about by the British government. Most of these efforts were however located within the language and understanding of upper caste men. This not only glossed over the experiences of women belonging to marginalized groups and castes but indeed took away from them their traditional freedoms and rights. Ironically, the very steps taken by colonial modernity to empower a certain section of the Indian women became the foundation for the disempowerment of the poor, low caste and minority women.

A stock taking of the results of the 'social reform movement' would show that the changes brought about as a result of these efforts converged with the interests of the colonial state, capitalist employers and indigenous elite men. Thus, a new kind of patriarchy was being created to replace the existing one. By the end of the 19th century, the social reform movement began to bear fruit, women's education came to be accepted and many women made independent evaluation and took initiative to ameliorate the status of women. Women in Bengal pioneered most of these efforts, although similar efforts were being made elsewhere also. Women's role as mothers came to be glorified. An educated mother's ability to train and nurture her sons and support her husband in the task of nation-building came to be emphasized. Indian women, it was hoped, would be mothers of the Indian nation and not mothers of the British Indian Empire.

By the end of the 19th century, a few women emerged from within the reformed families who formed organizations of their own. One of the first to do so was Swarnakumari Devi, daughter of Debendranath Tagore, a Brahmo leader, and sister of the poet Rabindranath Tagore, who formed the Ladies Society in Calcutta in 1882 for educating and imparting skills to widows and other poor women to make them economically self-reliant. She edited a women's journal, *Bharati*, thus earning herself the distinction of being the first Indian woman editor. In the same year, Ramabai Saraswati formed the Arya Mahila Samaj in Pune and a few years later started the Sharada Sadan in Bombay.

Saroj Nalini Dutt

Saroj Nalini Dutt (1887–1925) was a social reformer and a feminist who was a pioneer of mahila samitis (women's institutes) in Bengal. She set up the first mahila samiti in 1913 in Pabna district with the objective to encourage cooperation among women.

The early 20th century witnessed acceleration in the pace of women's participation in nationalist politics. One of the most well-known organizations set up for this purpose was the All India Women's Conference, established in 1927. This and many similar organizations were concerned with eradication of social problems affecting women and made many attempts towards popular-izing women's education. Although they began with a commitment towards these issues, it was not before long that nationalist politics engulfed them. In the inter-war years, between 1917 and 1945, there were two main issues that the women's movement took up—political rights for women and reform of personal laws.

Women in pre-Independence India were actively involved with labour politics as well. As early as 1917, Anasuya Sarabhai had led the Ahmedabad textile workers' strike and in 1920 under her leadership the Majoor Mahajan—the Ahmedabad textile mill workers union—was established. By the late 1920s, the presence of women in the workers' movement was noticeable. There were several prominent women unionists, and women workers who were consciously organized and a special role was given to them in the workers' movement. Bombay was the centre of this development and Maniben Kara emerged as the socialist leader of railway workers and Ushabai Dange and Parvati Bhore as communist leaders of textile workers. In the 1928–1929 Bombay textile mill workers' strike, women played a leading role, as they did in the Calcutta strike during the same years.

From the 1920s, nationalist politics began to make a conscious effort to address women. This is also the time Mahatma Gandhi became part of the national movement. By the 1920s, Radha Kumar identified two distinctive rationales for women's rights. The first was based on women's socially useful role as mothers. The second was based on the belief that men and women had same desires and needs, and hence need the same kind of rights.

The Salt Satyagraha in 1930 marked a new high in the numbers of women who participated in the national movement. Very soon, separate organizations were set up to mobilize greater women's participation in the national movement. This helped most of the upper class women activists to come out of their elitist moorings, and this in turn, had an impact on the organization and working of the women's organizations.

Gandhi's influence is acknowledged as one of the most important reasons for increasing women's participation in the national movement. From his experience in South Africa, Gandhi concluded that women have an extraordinary capacity for self-sacrifice. His appeal to Indian women was based on this conclusion. He argued that women have a great ability to tolerate suffering, and hence were ideally suited to carry out the politics of non-violence. This idea was derived from his understanding of women's role as mothers. Because of this mothering capability, Gandhi argued that women are preceptors for men. He subscribed to the position that men and women are biologically different, and hence have different roles to play.

There is no doubt thus, that Gandhi legitimized women's participation in public activities and politics. But the basis of his understanding was firmly located within traditional upper caste Hindu patriarchy. He hesitated to acknowledge the need for expanding the role women played in politics, he argued instead that the home is an important arena with far reaching impact on the world outside. It was the woman's job to bring about change in that domain. However, he remained unconvinced about expanding their role in the world outside. The compulsions of politics made him change his stand in later years. Gandhi's support of the women's cause led the already liberal sections of the Congress to commit themselves to the cause of women's equality.

It is this commitment that led the Congress party to draft the Fundamental Rights Resolution at the Karachi Session of the Congress party in 1931. The basic principle of equality between sexes was accepted. After Independence, therefore, the Constitution makers unhesitatingly accepted this idea. A committee set up by the Congress to map out the future of planning in independent India had a subcommittee to investigate and recommend measures addressing women, specifically headed by Lakshmibai Rajwade and assisted by secretaries, Mridula Sarabhai and Mrs Purvis N. Dubash. This committee made many bold and radical recommendations, especially about the exploitative nature of the household labour performed by women. It made many radical suggestions for the restructuring of work and wages to facilitate women's participation in the public sphere as well. It recognized very clearly the fact that women's work and labour in the public and private sphere is interlinked and would have to be addressed as such (Shah 1947).

Women in pre-Independence India became active participants in the communist as well as the other revolutionary organizations. They were actively involved in working class struggles, peasant movements and Adivasi uprisings. Of course, the domination of the Congress ideology meant that most of these efforts were overlooked.

WOMEN'S MOVEMENT IN INDIA: POST INDEPENDENCE

Independence came in 1947 with the promise of a new beginning. The hope was that within the democratic framework guaranteed by the new Constitution, Indian women would find greater autonomy and freedom. The economic and social changes, it was hoped, would ameliorate the conditions of the poor and marginalized sections of the society and empower women. The immediate years following Independence were thus marked by hope.

By the mid-1960s, however, the consensus put together under Jawaharlal Nehru's leadership was beginning to crack. Indian defeat in the war with China, an adverse economic scenario and finally Nehru's death led the Congress that had been the undisputed party of power to experience dissent and finally electoral defeat, albeit in State assembly elections. There was a growing realization of the fact that the Congress party was unable to fulfil all the promises that it had made during the national struggle. Economic development was taking place but there was no place in this for the vast majority. The resultant discontent was channelized through various political forces and groups, and thus women became a prominent part of these movements. Ilina Sen (2004) has in her writings brought out the essential difference in the mobilization of women in politics in this phase from the mobilization that happened earlier. She contends that in this phase, the accent was not solely on mobilizing women but on introspection of how and why women continued to be subordinated. Thus, the women's movement was being revived after a lull in the 1950s and 1960s. Interestingly, the movement this time round was unfolding in the context of contemporaneous radical movements.

The left parties that had been the beacon of radical politics were now getting fragmented. Many adherents of left politics left the formal political party organization and became part of other radical movements that were asking fundamental questions. The women's movement benefited from this general mood of investigation and became a part of this new political ethos. Women became a big and important part of landmark campaigns such as the Shahada, Dhulia, Self-Employed Women's Association (SEWA) and Nav Nirman.

The Shahada movement emerged in the Adivasi areas of Maharashtra in the 1970s. Harassment by the local landlords and conditions of famine and drought led the Adivasi people to organize themselves into the Shramik Sangathana in 1972. They directed their efforts in the direction of famine relief and reclaimed land for cultivation. The movement, thus became very popular among the labourers, specially the women. It was the women who mobilized the men to join the movement and remained steadfast in their negotiations with the landlords. As women's militancy and participation grew within the movement, concerns specific to women's lives were raised. These women were far removed from the negative stereotypes of feminists in India, namely westernized, university educated and urban.

Radha Kumar discerns a pattern in the development of the Shahada movement that went from being a social reform movement to a Sarvodaya movement and finally a far left one. Thus, with the development of militancy in the movement, the scope for raising questions related to gender concerns became possible. She points out that whenever a community becomes conscious of its own oppression, and is actually able to express it through a large scale movement with active involvement of women, there is bound to be an examination by women of their subordination. In the Shahada movement this examination centred on the issues of wife-beating and alcoholism. Women organized themselves into groups that would raid liquor dens and come to the assistance of any woman who was beaten by her husband. In this the activists were guided by a clear feminist understanding that alcohol was only a subsidiary problem, the main issue was wife-beating which was unacceptable. Thus, a clear anti-patriarchal sentiment imbued the Shahada movement

Ela Bhatt pioneered the SEWA. Formed in 1972, in Ahmedabad, Gujarat, this was an effort guided largely by Gandhian principles. SEWA focused upon the exploitation and low wages of the women in the informal sector. These women faced harassment by the civic authorities and their work was not recognized as socially useful. After a long struggle, SEWA was able to get recognition as a trade union. This was indeed a tremendous achievement since its members did not work either in a factory or for a particular employer.

SEWA remained within the Gandhian framework and focused upon reformist efforts. The Shahada movement was thus closer to the feminist political sensibilities than the SEWA, which too kept its distance from the feminist movement.

The anti-price agitation that spread throughout Gujarat and Maharashtra in the 1970s is noteworthy from the point of view of the number of women participants it was able to attract. A United Women's Anti-Price Rise Front was formed to mobilize women against inflation. Women from the communist and socialist parties were involved in its organization. From Mumbai, the movement spread to Gujarat and became the foundation of the Nav Nirman movement that started in 1974. This movement against price rise soon became a movement that questioned the very basis of the Indian State. Their critique of the Indian State and parliamentary democracy were inspired by Jai Prakash Narayan's concept of 'total revolution' that was beginning to gain popularity in Bihar.

Both the anti-price and the Nav Nirman movement involved many women but did not necessarily raise questions related to women's subordination. For instance, the most obvious question would have been to examine why was it that only women were concerned about the rise in domestic expenditure? In fact, the movement through many of its actions seemed to reinforce traditional norms of contempt for women, as when they offered bangles to those in power suggesting that they were not manly enough to be in power.

The call for 'total revolution' on the other hand raised far more difficult questions. The movement involving many women and students questioned the existing power structures in the State and society. They challenged the institution of the family and the role of women within this structure. Apart from unequal property rights for men and women, the movement even re-examined the whole nature of male–female relationships and even the issue of female sexuality. The main proponents of this feminist critique of patriarchy were the young men and women who were part of the Chhatra Yuva Sangharsh Vahini, the vanguard of Jai Prakash Narayan's movement.

One of the most important struggles that they were involved with was the Bodh Gaya Math struggle. The Math controlled the lives and lands of the poor peasants of this area. Interestingly, when the poor began to ask for land rights, there was a clear recognition of women's rights to ownership of property. While most of these landmark political developments were unfolding in rural India, urban India too witnessed the strengthening of feminist activism and politics.

It was in this context that the autonomous women's movement emerged in India. One of the first groups to be formed was the Progressive Organization of Women (POW) in 1974, in Hyderabad. Most of the women who were part of the POW were drawn from the Maoists groups that were very popular in Andhra Pradesh. The POW identified the sexual division of labour and the cultural justification of this division on which women's subordination is based as its main adversaries. They saw the need to challenge the existing economic system based on capitalism, and sought its replacement by socialism which they argued would bring in a culture of equality.

In the year 1975, many new organizations and efforts that were beginning to ask fundamental questions about women's subordination began to emerge, especially in Maharashtra. This was a significant year because internationally the UN had declared it as Women's Year. For the first time, International Women's Day was celebrated in India on 8 March. Most of these efforts came from women within Maoist groups. Radha Kumar finds the gradual realization of the connection between patriarchy and caste; especially the coming closer of the anti-caste Dalit movements with feminist groups, a very significant development in this period.

These groups were different from the ones in the earlier phase in that they stressed on the sexual oppression of all women and not just of certain categories of women like sex workers. Of course, within them there were different explanations for women's subordination, some groups attributed women's sexual oppression to their economic dependence on men, whereas others argued that women's enslavement was a consequence of their reproductive functions. Thus, it was a clear divide between those who held biological differences to be the root cause of women's oppression and others who did not wish to predicate women's oppression upon these biological differences. This latter group argued that women's subordination was not a consequence of their biological differences but was based on an unequal sexual division of labour that was centuries old.

It was also in the year 1975 that Mrs Indira Gandhi (Prime Minister of India) declared the Emergency. The two year period till 1977 saw most political activists either behind bars or engaging in underground political activities. This became the context for a serious and complete re-examination of the foundations of Indian democracy and the nature of the Indian State. The new women's groups that were coming together at this time were engaged in a re-examination of one of the fundamental assumptions of the Indian society—the sexual division of labour and the subordination of women. Hence, they declared themselves to be feminist, although many of these women belonged to the traditional left groups. Left parties have, by and large, been sceptical of feminist ideology and politics seeing them as divisive and more seriously as bourgeois. Perhaps it is because of this that these women's groups decided to be autonomous and not affiliated to any big political party. Soon these groups, formed all over the country, began to come together to share their ideas and strategies and form networks.

This is not to suggest that there was complete uniformity in the understanding, politics or strategies of these diverse groups despite the fact that most of them belonged to far left groups. In the 1970s, the most important questions for these groups were of self-definition and of representation. Radha Kumar explains the dilemma these groups faced vis-à-vis the question of organization and representation. Not all groups felt confident of being effective organizers or representatives. Most of the activists in these groups were drawn from urban, educated, middle class backgrounds. This, they believed, created a wide gap between them and the peasant and working class women they were seeking to organize and hoping to represent. Still others believed that although the issue of women's subordination was very important, it however had to be linked with other mass movements. They sought space within existing mass organizations such as trade unions and peasant bodies for raising feminist issues. Still others hoped that with the gradual spread of their ideals, organizations would spontaneously be formed. This last group obviously was not very hopeful of arousing feminist sensibilities within the existing organizations. These differences often led to sharp disagreements.

Most groups were, however, agreed upon the desirability of autonomy. Existing political parties were seen as hierarchical and entrenched within the power structures of the society. Some groups believed that it was possible to transform them, whereas others believed that the institution of the political party would never lend itself to the radical and democratic political vision that feminism espouses. It was in 1977 with the end of the Emergency that a group of women in Delhi came together and set up a journal called *Manushi* that was to be published both in Hindi and in English. Many such initiatives were taken elsewhere, apart from setting up documentation centres.

WOMEN'S MOVEMENT AND THE CAMPAIGN AGAINST DOWRY AND RAPE

Two issues towards the end of the 1970s, and through the 1980s, galvanized women's groups further. The forceful campaign against rape and the highly charged and emotional campaign against dowry brought in new energy into the movement. As early as 1975, the POW in Hyderabad launched a campaign against dowry. But the overall political climate, thanks to the Emergency, was not conducive to the campaign taking off in a big way. However, soon after the lifting of the Emergency, Delhi became the centre of a forceful campaign against dowry. In the democratic upsurge following the defeat of Indira Gandhi's government, the movement found many supporters. Delhi spearheaded the campaign also because it had the dubious distinction of a very high number of deaths of young brides that everyone suspected was related to unfulfilled dowry demands, but were reported as either accidental deaths or suicides. These deaths were seen as private affairs and not open to the State for investigation. Feminists insisted that the disproportionately large numbers of women who died in fire accidents were definitely related to harassment due to unfulfilled dowry demands and were thus murders. The movement gained in popularity. Public campaigns, protest marches and street plays and posters were all employed to arouse consciousness against dowry. They systematically recorded the last statement of the dying woman, assisted the woman's family in reporting the death to the police (this was not being done till now) and collected evidence from friends and family. Under pressure from the massive success of the anti-dowry campaign, the government in 1980 passed a law against dowry-related crimes. Like all legislations, this too has its limitations and loopholes.

The next big issue that feminists took up in the 1980s was the issue of rape. Women's groups had been consistently protesting against rape by landlords and employers in various parts of the country, but two incidents of custodial rape by the police sparked off an agitation that marked a new phase in the feminist movement in India. Rape has been an important issue in the feminist discourse internationally. The issue of rape and how it is discussed tells us a great deal about how societies and communities perceive a woman's body. It is common to use rape to establish power and authority over an individual as in the case of landlord raping women workers employed by him, or the wives of the workers employed by him. It is almost seen as a right that the landlord has over his workers. Rape is often used to establish the superiority of caste groups or to prove the vulnerability of the minority community. It is also used to 'humiliate' the vanquished in war. A young 17-year-old woman called Mathura was raped by policemen (1972), the courts acquitted the policemen on the grounds that since she had a boyfriend, she was of dubious moral character, and hence, cannot allege rape. This and later in 1980, the rape of a woman called Maya Tyagi, once again by policemen in Haryana, made the issue of custodial rape central to feminist concerns. The Forum against Rape was established in Mumbai in 1981, which later came to be known as the Forum against Oppression of Women. Their forceful campaign resulted in the government responding with an extremely radical piece of legislation that shifted the onus of proof onto the accused among many other provisions such as 10 years imprisonment and *in camera* trial.

Subsequent judgements in many rape cases disappointed the feminists who discovered that the quick response from the government was little more than political opportunism. The attitude towards rape, the problem of marshalling medical evidence, especially in rural and small town India, all made the legislation rather redundant. The courts continued to look at past conduct of the woman to condone rape. Feminists continued to protest against this, and the National Front government in power in the early 1990s promised changes. The painful realization, however, was that despite the enactment of radical legislations, it was the terrain of implementation and interpretation of the law that was difficult to negotiate. Feminists also drew attention to the fact that the technical definition of rape itself was problematic because it did not recognize the basically violent nature of rape, since it recognized only the forceful penetration by the penis of the vagina as rape. By the end of the 1980s, the number of rape cases that were registered by the police had more than doubled as a consequence of the changing social attitudes that emboldened more women to report rape.

The issue of violence against women and rape remains relevant to the women's movement even today. The brutal gang rape and murder of a young woman in Delhi in the winter of 2012 resulted in a huge public outcry and series of protests across the country drawing people from diverse sections of society. This resulted in the setting up of the Justice Verma Committee that invited various sections of citizens to share their observations on rape and related issues. The committee's report with a section on bill of rights for women makes this a landmark in the struggles against rape and violence against women in India. The report addresses a wide variety of issues including child sexual abuse and sexual harassment at the workplace.[1]

With the experience of two successful mass campaigns against dowry deaths and rape behind them, feminist groups began to diversify their activities to include running of legal aid centres, media monitoring groups and so on. They began setting up counselling centres and health care facilities. These new efforts differed from the somewhat similar efforts in the past. The guiding principle now was the interrelated nature of the problems that beset women, and their origins in women's subordinate position in society. Thus, a feminist and not a social welfare approach began to guide these efforts. In doing this, there was a conscious effort to translate into reality the feminist ideal of sisterhood, it was hoped that the existence of organizations run by women for other women would create this sentiment and create avenues for women to come together outside of the approved familial context.

The Sati that took place in Rajasthan in 1987 was yet another issue that became the focus of the feminist campaign in the 1980s. At the heart of the campaign was not only the act itself, but also the subsequent glorification of Sati and the half-hearted attempts by the State to control this. More worrying was the sight of women who enthusiastically marched through the streets of Jaipur and other cities to demonstrate their support for the practice. A section of the intellectuals argued that being alienated from their traditions and culture, feminists and others who opposed Sati were unable to understand the discourse and the logic of Sati as an example of self-sacrifice.

The support for Sati that came from within the Rajput community spoke of Sati as being one of the distinguishing features of their community's identity. This practice they argued was part of the personal laws of the Hindus and should be kept beyond the purview of the State. In the context of the Muslim Women's Protection Bill, they demanded that the State should show the same discretion with respect to the family laws of the Hindus. The issue of Sati became the site on which the secular credentials of the Indian State were to be evaluated. The Indian State was repeatedly being accused of accommodating interests of the minority community, while interfering

---

[1] See http://www.prsindia.org/uploads/media/Justice%20verma%20committee/js%20verma%20committe%20report.pdf

with matters of personal law of the majority community. This, they argued, made the secular claims of the Indian State rather suspect.

The pro-Sati campaign posited the traditional Hindu woman against the alienated, westernized, feminist woman who could not share the sentiments and understanding of her sisters. Of course, closer examination did reveal that most women perhaps wholeheartedly supported the worship of Sati, while being unsure of the desirability of its practice. However, facing women who were pro-Sati forced the feminist movement in India to take up issues of culture and tradition as well as communities and representation. The legislation (Commission of Sati [Prevention] Bill) that followed the feminist campaign against Sati did not bring much consolation because it had far too many loopholes and considered the woman who commits Sati also an offender. This would let the family members of the woman to go scot-free, despite the fact that they aid and abet the act.

Culture became the new focus of research and analysis. The attempt was to take a close look at traditions and identify possible allies within the tradition. For this it became necessary to re-interpret traditions and redefine them wherever necessary. One of the favourite figures that lend itself to such attempts was that of the Mother Goddess Kali. The attempt was to present Kali as a symbol of power and energy, a feminist icon, far removed from the docile, domesticated goddesses of the traditional Hindu pantheon. There were other efforts made to identify the spaces that were already available to ordinary women in the traditional context. Radha Kumar discusses the example of pregnant women in traditional contexts, often using their condition to extract concessions for themselves as a possible space that women used for negotiation.

Much research was focused on trying to find precursors of the contemporary feminist movement. History, therefore, became a very important arena of research. It is in this context that the Chipko movement of the early 1970s, which was hitherto seen as an environmental movement to save the trees and forests of Uttarakhand, gradually made an appearance as an illustration of women's special bond with environment. This eco-feminist reconstruction has not been without its critics. The obvious criticism emerges out of a discomfort with the essentialist nature of the eco-feminist assumptions that defines women's nature in an eternal and unchanging sort of way (for further details see Chapter 6).

Meanwhile, academia and research institutes in the 1980s incorporated women's studies as the focus of their research and eventually teaching. Feminist issues and movements began to show a clear impact on media as well as medicine. Health care and related issues became very important points of reference. Malnutrition has been recognized as a major health hazard for women. But it is common to justify women's intake of nutritionally less healthy food on the basis of the supposedly less amount of work that women do. Shah and Gandhi point out that it is not a specific kind of work but the overwork that women engage in that becomes a health hazard (Gandhi and Shah 1992). The double burden of work both in the public and the private sphere is the problem. Time spent in collecting fuel, food or water is not recognized as work. Breathing the smoke in the kitchens that use traditional fuel such as cattle dung and agricultural waste is very harmful because of its carcinogenic character. Feminist health campaigns have pointed out that health policies of the State must have a more holistic and non-sexist attitude towards women's health. The guiding principle should not be to see women as potential child bearers and mothers but as people who have a quintessential right to health care. It is in this context that one of the big feminist campaigns of the 1980s unfolded on the issue of contraceptives. After a storm of protest against injectable contraceptives in the West, it was tried out in India in the 1980s. Apex medical bodies began to try these drugs on women who had no information about the negative side effects of using these injectable contraceptives. Activists stormed meetings that were being held to study the feasibility of this injectable contraceptive called Net-EN and soon realized that a ban on this alone would not be of much consequence.

The next big campaign was against high-dose oestrogen progesterone formulations, popularly referred to as EP drugs. This drug came to be used for a variety of gynaecological conditions, but the fact that it could create congenital heart conditions in the foetus was not revealed. A high voltage campaign by women activists in the field of health care and sustained discussions with government health authorities resulted in the banning of this drug in the tablet form.

A medical diagnostic test called amniocentesis has been the other issue that feminists interested in health issues have taken up. This test that analyses the amniotic fluid surrounding the foetus is meant to detect over 70 genetic diseases. It is also capable of revealing the sex of the unborn child. Health activists have campaigned against this test because in our country this test is used primarily for the latter purpose and if the foetus is found to be female, an abortion follows. This abortion itself being carried out in the second trimester of the pregnancy has chances of turning fatal, besides resulting in physical dislocations in the foetus. It was a difficult campaign to take off given the son-loving cultural context. Subsequently, legislations not banning but 'regulating' the tests have been passed. Maharashtra passed the first law in this regard in 1986, but among the many other dissatisfactory provisions, it held the woman undergoing the test also guilty.

The year 1997 is a crucial year in the history of women's movement in India, as the Supreme Court in response to pressure from women's groups announced the Vishakha Guidelines to address the issue of sexual harassment at the workplace. The gang rape of a government employee Bhanwari Devi and her fight for justice have now acquired an iconic status and resulted in the guidelines that made the setting up of mechanisms to address and enquire into instances of sexual harassment at the workplace.[2]

In 1994, the Pre-Natal Diagnostic Techniques (Regulations and Prevention of Misuses) Act was passed. The Act permits the test only under certain specific conditions and only for the detection of a limited number of abnormalities in the foetus. Revealing the sex of the foetus is, however, prohibited. Several loopholes in the proposed law were identified only to be ignored.

---

[2] http://www.iitg.ac.in/iitgicc/docs/Vishaka_Guidelines.pdf

For instance, the information regarding the sex of the foetus is not to be revealed to the woman or her relatives but does not prevent such information being shared with non-relative. It also treats the woman as an offender unless she can prove that she has been coerced. It is indeed strange that in a cultural context where women seldom make autonomous decisions, they should be thought of as being capable of taking decisions on this issue. The fact is that the law obviously has not had much effect. The 2011 Census figures show a further decline in sex ratio, especially in the 0–6 years of age group, suggesting a large-scale femicide of foetuses and children.

Nivedita Menon has raised the issue of femicide of foetuses as being distinct from the issue of abortion (Menon 2004). Steering clear of the use of the word foeticide, she implies that the use of this word does not leave much room for feminists to defend abortion on the one hand, and ask for a ban on selective abortions based on the sex of the foetuses on the other. The point that she makes is that people have rights not in an abstract, ahistorical sense but within a particular context. Given the son-loving and misogynist context of our country and the fact of the alarmingly disproportionate sex ratios, it is perfectly possible for feminists to argue both for the woman's right to abortions as well as a ban on femicide of foetuses. Patriarchy creates specific kinds of constraints because of which abortion must be made accessible to women. It is these constraints that produce a society that seeks femicide. As a consequence, the numbers of women would shrink even further and the world over it has been seen that societies with fewer women than men are invariably more sexist. Hence, selective abortion of female foetuses should be prevented. This insightful line of argument frees feminists from the seemingly contradictory stand they took on the issue of abortion on the one hand and femicide on the other. This understanding would free feminists, as Nivedita Menon has argued, from being forced to choose between the rights of future women to be born and the rights of existing women over their bodies.

CHALLENGES TO THE WOMEN'S MOVEMENT: IS THERE AN INDIAN WOMAN?

Towards the end of the 1980s, feminists began to realize that the category of woman is far too universal and undifferentiated. In the context of caste, community and class among many other differences, it was no longer possible to talk in terms of undifferentiated women. This made a shift away from the unmarked nature of the definition of citizenship essential. If differences were to be acknowledged, then the traditional terms of discourse seemed to be faltering.

COMMUNITY, RELIGION AND WOMANHOOD

The closing years of the 1980s and the 1990s saw a new kind of political contest gaining importance. Politics of backward caste, Dalit and minorities claiming democratic rights has been offset by the attempts of the Hindu right-wing to redefine the nation itself. The latter have tried repeatedly to present a monolithic picture of the Hindu society that is united by its hoary past. This vision glosses over all kinds of internal differences, specially the ones based on caste and in its own unique way gender. This political perspective does perceive caste and to a certain extent gender politics to be potentially divisive forces. The spectre of minorities and backward castes cornering all the benefits that the State has to offer has driven many sections of upper caste India into the arms of Hindu right-wing politics.

Feminists, to their dismay, discovered that upper caste women were enthusiastic supporters of a meritocratic worldview oblivious to the inequalities of caste, as well as extended support to a new and more militant Hindutva campaign. As Tanika Sarkar and Urvashi Butalia (1995) has shown, a new kind of woman activist was thus being created who consciously wished to distance herself from the feminist activist. Their activism often had the blessings of the family and was seen as an extension of their nurturing role in the family. The new breed of women activists have been described as being not home breakers but as torchbearers of Hindu tradition. Their activism in most cases has not involved or permitted any challenges to traditional family structures and practices. Women's roles are accepted as pre-given and immutable. These women activists of the Hindu right-wing clearly show that women could come together and even be engaged in politics without necessarily challenging patriarchy. On the contrary, the way they come together and their manner of working wins approval from patriarchal structures (Sarkar 1995).

Community politics, especially majoritarian politics in the Indian context has posed one of the biggest challenges to the women's movement. The enthusiastic support offered by some sections of women to a majoritarian politics has made feminists rethink the whole issue of community and politics. This process undoubtedly began in the context of the Shah Bano case. In the 1980s, this issue became very controversial. Shah Bano's appeal for maintenance was upheld by the court (1985), this was immediately seen by a certain section of the Muslim community as a threat to their community's identity, for in their opinion, Islamic law had provisions for the protection of the rights of the divorced woman and any interference by the law courts would be tantamount to interference in their personal laws. Earlier in the 1950s, Hindu men had expressed similar reservation regarding the Hindu Code Bill that was intended to empower the women within the Hindu community. The conservatives within the Muslim community alleged that the judgment endangered Islam and took away the rights of the Muslim community to their unique identity that was in part derived from their special family laws.

Shah and Gandhi have argued that the judgment itself in the Shah Bano case pronounced by the Supreme Court was not problematic, but it was the manner in which it was worded that stirred a controversy finally leading to the passage of the Muslim Women (Protection of Rights on Divorce) Act, 1986. This Act supposedly protected Islam and, as Shah and Gandhi have said, gave to the Muslim man more control over his wife. Thus, in the guise of religious freedom, women of the Muslim community were denied basic constitutional rights (Gandhi and Shah 1992).

It was in this context that the debate on uniform civil code (UCC) became central to feminist politics of the 1980s and 1990s. The code has a long and controversial history. Even while the Constitution was being framed, this issue was raised only to be set aside, given the heterogeneous nature of the Indian society. The debate on this issue continues. Surprisingly, the pro-code position is occupied by a certain section of the liberal opinion that shares the platform with the Hindu right-wing. The latter argues that a separate code for members of different religious communities is a violation of the secular principle. The growing strength of majoritarian politics and its vociferous support for a UCC has forced feminists to re-think their earlier support to this idea. In the guise of equality, the Hindu right-wing seems to be suggesting a homogenized code based largely on the practices and assumptions of the upper caste Hindus. Feminist groups have in this new context adopted a nuanced position on the issue of UCC. Equality and dignity and not necessarily uniformity would be the guiding principles of the code that they would support.

The Supreme Court of India and the Practice of Triple Talaq

On 22 August 2017, the honourable Supreme Court of India adjudicated that instantaneous triple talaq will not be acknowledged by the law on a 3–2 majority in a five bench trial while maintaining the ethos of equality as enshrined in the Indian Constitution. This judgment is 'historic' in terms that it gives a legal acknowledgement to the demands of Muslim activists across the country and also occult the self-styled 'authentic' representatives of the community—All India Muslim Personal Law Board (AIMPLB). This judgment is a result of sustained campaign by women's groups such as the Bebaak Collective and others in support of Shayara Bano's petition who challenged the validity of unilateral triple talaq in the Court. After failing to push the Triple Talaq Bill or the Muslim Women (Protection of Rights on Marriage) Bill, 2017 in the Rajya Sabha during the Monsoon Session, the Union cabinet proceeded to approve an ordinance in September 2018, making instant triple talaq (divorce) a punishable offence. A law against triple talaq is the need of the hour. However, it would have been ideal if both houses of parliament had passed the Bill unanimously. Zakia Soman (founder of Bharatiya Muslim Mahila Andolan) has pointed out that the ordinance is flawed on many counts; it is only on the rarest of rare occasions that a woman wants to see her ex-husband behind bars. She and other Muslim women activists like her have been asking for the law to lay down a procedure for divorce that would be fair, just and transparent. Ideally, they have been demanding a codified Muslim personal law governing all aspects of marriage and family. Yet she and others like her welcome this initiative as something that has been a result of the arduous and lonely trek by Muslim women for gender justice.

Thus, essentially an issue about the rights of women became the peg on which to conduct the entire debate on secularism in India. The 1980s had witnessed increasing communal assertions by the majority community. The anti-Sikh riots following Indira Gandhi's assassination in 1984, and the general mood of distrust and animosity towards the minority communities characterized the 1980s. The aggressive campaign for the temple in Ayodhya that followed soon after seemed to have the tacit approval of the State.

The middle class, upper caste Hindu male had convinced himself of being besieged by the frightening forces of minority politics, Dalit and backward caste movements and feminist women. The fear stemmed from the belief that old and familiar structures of authority and power would be pulled down. This fear is the basis to a great extent of Hindu right-wing politics that grew in strength in the 1980s.

Sections of the minority communities were in the meanwhile swamped by the fear of the State's attempts to homogenize their distinctive identities. The agitation for the temple and the judgment that supposedly challenged Islam came to be linked and seen as an onslaught on the minorities, specially the Muslims. Feminists learnt many lessons through the course of these years. One important lesson was that the 'community in danger' argument is very appealing and as part of protecting the community, one of the demands is regulation and control over the woman of 'our community'. They also learnt that the State very easily succumbs to such demands, even at the cost of withdrawing basic constitutional rights to women (in this case of the Muslim community). These lessons among many others forced the feminist movement to re-think the whole issue of an undifferentiated, UCC not based on specific religious laws that they had been campaigning for. The campaign stemmed from the conviction that all existing family laws based on specific religious codes and practices were discriminatory to women. However, in the highly charged and communal milieu of the 1980s and the 1990s, any demand for such a code has become politically suspect. Flavia Agnes has been quoted as saying that with the rise of majority communalism, it is not possible to any longer discuss the UCC as a non-sexist code. Equal citizenship in the context of attempts made by politicized religious groups to gain hegemony over the State can hardly be discussed.

Is the choice for women then between the State's control and regulation on the one hand, and the community's on the other hand? Kumkum Sangari (2015) has argued that posing the choice, thus obscures the possibility of feminist agency. In her opinion, women should not be in a position where they need to choose between patriarchy regulated by the State or by the community. Rather their struggle should be for the recognition of gender justice as a principle and a social horizon.

The Hyderabad-based women's group Anveshi has words of caution that deserve to be mentioned here. Although the discourse of citizenship based on universal ideal of equality and justice has an emancipatory potential, it also tends to homogenize and marginalize other understandings of justice. Women are perceived as a universal category, based on biological differences from men. What about different understandings of rights and justice that are emerging out of movements based on caste, class or religion, they ask. Hence, they suggest that any demand for a singular conception of gender justice is problematic. Does that however mean surrender to relativism? Their answer is no. What they suggest is a re-examination of dominant meanings of terms such as justice, equality and rights.

In this complex context, hence there is no consensus possible within the feminist movement on the issue of UCC. The fear of the Hindu right-wing inscribing its agenda over the UCC has unnerved those who were at the forefront of the demand.

CASTE AND THE WOMEN'S MOVEMENT

Caste is an issue that the women's movement had not paid much attention to in the past. By the end of the 1980s, it became clear that it was no longer possible to talk of the Indian woman as a universal and undifferentiated category. The autonomous women's movement, in Sharmila Rege's opinion, did not constitute a challenge to *Brahminism*. She recognizes the fact that although the autonomous women's movement did raise issues concerning Dalit and Adivasi women, it did not allow for the emergence of a feminist politics centred on the experiences and problems of women from the most marginalized sections of our society. Although the movement did raise issues of sexuality, but in her opinion they remained within the framework of lifestyle choices, missing the essential linkage between caste and sexuality.

The consolidation of Hindu right-wing politics along with the assertion by backward and Dalit castes has fractured the romantic notion of an Indian sisterhood. This happened almost simultaneously with the collapse of the idea of global sisterhood.

The tabling of the Mandal Commission's recommendations by the V. P. Singh government announcing the extension of the policy of reservation to the Other Backward Classes in 1990, unleashed upper caste fury in many parts of North India. It seemed as though caste that had been 'forgotten' had somehow reared its ugly head again.

To the builders of modern India, caste seemed like an embarrassment that was best sidestepped in the hope that by not talking about it, it would go away. This was the way in which the Nehruvian elite in the early decades after Independence conducted its affairs. This was the dignified, secular, modern civil society, but unfolding away from the watchful eyes of this civil society was the daily and unrelenting drama of the political society from where caste had never gone away (Chatterjee 1995). By the end of the 1980s, the Nehruvian consensus was well and truly over, caste was out in the open and its continued presence after nearly four decades of Independence and 'development' had to be explained.

It is in this context that the feminist movement in India began to address the question of difference. Smarting under the criticism of universalism, feminist theory and politics in India had to respond to the charges. It became clear that theorizing gender is no easy enterprise anywhere, and most certainly not in India, given the number of differences among Indian women. The task is clearly political, for these differences spell hierarchy, power, marginalization and oppression.

Although the impact of caste ideology and notions of womanhood found in the upper caste religious and mythological texts have received a considerable amount of attention from feminist scholars, the same could not be said about Dalit women's voices and struggles.

Mandalization of Indian politics has, however, made it imperative for the feminist movement in India to grapple with the issue of caste and explain the contours of the feminist movement as shaped by the caste question. It became clear that all women in India cannot come together on an undifferentiated platform because women's experiences are vastly different. One of the primary differences is based on caste. The complex relationship between gender and caste is one of the most important questions facing the women's movement in India.

The resolution offered to address the caste question was to quietly sweep it into the inner recesses of the private sphere, and thereby, create a caste-free public sphere. This manner of resolving the caste question was challenged by Ambedkar, Phule and a host of others who saw the possibility of a new and free India emerging only on the debris of the caste system.

Opposition to caste was thus restricted to pious platitudes against caste in the public sphere, and a retreat into the secure caste marked private sphere. This fractured modernity (Sanjay Joshi's book *Fractured Modernity: Making of a Middle Class in Colonial India* [2001] looks at this phenomenon) was understood rightly by Ambedkar and others as nothing but an attempt to continue with caste-based privileges in the private sphere, while denouncing it in public. Viewed from this vantage point, Dalit–Bahujan[3] activists who insist on raising the bogey of caste in public appear casteist, non-modern and sectarian. Ambedkar, on the other hand, posited a different kind of modernity, a modernity that would be characterized by its challenge to caste-based exploitation and oppression.

Very early on in his political journey, Ambedkar established an insightful relationship between independence for India, the overthrow of the oppressive caste system based on closely regulated marriage norms and eventually freedom for women. He identified the domination and control of women through the practice of the foundational principle of caste and its perpetuation. Hence, he advocated inter-caste marriage as the only way out to challenge caste and in the process free women (Ambedkar 2015) (for further details see Chapter 2).

---

[3] The Dalit–Bahujans make up what are known as the Scheduled Castes, the Scheduled Tribes and the Backward Castes. 'Scheduled' means they are listed in a special 'index' appended to the Constitution. 'Backward Castes' are those whose rank and occupational status are above that of Dalits, but who still remain socially and economically depressed. The Scheduled Castes were until recently also known as the 'Untouchables' because they were deemed literally untouchable by the upper castes. The word 'Dalit' means 'broken' or 'crushed' and the word 'Bahujan' indicates membership in the majority people or the larger population. Combined, these groups make up 67 per cent of the population of India.

By 1995, the NFDW had been formed. The basis for the formation of the NFDW and many similar organizations was the sentiment that Indian feminism had been unable to address the issues of caste and its inseparable links with patriarchy. Feminist theorization, they suggested, was unable to see the caste-based inequality. Indian feminism was seen as hegemonic and the formation of the NFDW was a challenge to what came to be described as 'Brahminical feminism' (Rao 2003). The reluctance of the existing Dalit groups to address issues specific to Dalit women and the feminist movement's Brahminical orientation were the reasons cited for setting up the NFDW.

Today, Dalit–Bahujan feminists are re-thinking feminism based on the unmarked Indian woman as the ideal subject of feminist theory and politics. In the process, Dalit–Bahujan feminists are keen to demonstrate the limited nature of the feminist enterprise as it has existed in India. Dalit–Bahujan feminism states forcefully that caste is not just a matter of identity or difference but indeed it is an entire matrix of power and privilege on the one hand, and exploitation and humiliation on the other hand.

The specific nature of patriarchy experienced by Dalit women consists of two distinct strands, on the one hand, Brahminical patriarchy that considered Dalit women as unclean and polluting, and a more intimate form of patriarchal control over work and sexuality exercised by the Dalit men on 'their' women, on the other. This view is echoed by an emerging body of academic and political insight that expresses its discomfort with mainstream Indian feminism. The claims of 'Indian feminism' to speak on behalf of 'Indian' women came to be questioned aggressively. Gopal Guru's argument is that social location determines the perception of reality, and hence, any attempt by non-Dalit women to represent Dalit women's lives appears less authentic and valid, indeed it appears to be homogenizing (Rao 2005).

The caste-mediated nature of patriarchy produces different worlds for different women depending upon their caste. Gopal Guru illustrates this argument with the example of rape. Instances of rape are typically explained by feminists as the expression of male aggression, and or as a symbol of patriarchal control and regulation of women. Such an explanation misses out on a very important dimension of most incidents of rape in India. The woman's body is seen as marked by caste and the instance of rape is a message to her caste, it cannot be understood fully by describing it as merely an exercise of male power. The caste calculus lends to the account of rape a completely different dimension.

The other big challenge to the feminist movement comes from the forces and ideology of globalization. Efficiency is valued above everything else. Poor women, especially in countries of the global south, are seen as efficient managers of limited resources, and hence, good subjects for governance, while their men are seen as unruly and unmanageable. This is the reason for global agencies' and lending bodies' willingness to align with women. The nation-state is, especially in the countries of the global south, no longer the most important economic or even political actor. The pride in the nationalist market has been replaced by the frenzied worshipping at the altar of global consumerism. This encourages unbridled individualism that is clearly inimical to any organized political activity. The lure of the global market, the focus on efficiency above everything else and the marginalization of the nation-state are indeed very challenging developments for the women's movement in India. International aid and 'development' agencies have, in a surprising turn of events, incorporated a concern and commitment to the 'grass roots' and to gender in particular. They look at women as ideal subjects amenable to efficient governance. In such a context, the women's movement has to be very careful about who it aligns with.

From the 1990s, the deepening of globalization and the proliferation of new information and communication technology (blogs, websites and other internet-based groups and petitions) have meant greater opportunities for feminists to learn and engage in action together. This has enabled the women's movement to question not only their immediate localities, but also cross-border relations and to question the claims of uncontested sovereignty of the nation-state.

Globalization is characterized by two divergent trends—one is the expansion of neoliberal economic politics, including integrated financial markets, and an increased role of the WTO and transnational capitalist class. Neoliberalism attaches singular significance to the individual and his/her achievement, whereas feminist politics that inspires the women's movement in India invokes the group. It is undeniable that neoliberalism has tremendous seductive appeal because of its consumerist options—consumerism comes to replace human rights and justice.

These movements are characterized by groups working across local and global contexts. They are committed to shared values and solidarity across differences and are keen on evolving a common discourse through dialogue and action. They aim to change structural inequalities and address the deepening impact of globalization on gender, class, race and ethnic relations.

The contemporary phase of women's movement is witnessing a sharper focus on issues of sexuality and questions of body and disability. The mobilization by lesbian and bisexual women as well as trans-women has posited a strong challenge to the women's movement in India. It is rather clear that a composite Indian woman who is readily available as a subject of feminist study or mobilization does not exist. What this means is that each of the subject positions that women occupy produces widely differing understanding and knowledge of the India that we live in. A woman with physical or mental disabilities posits herself differently and from her unique vantage point the knowledge generated about Indian society and political questions that would be raised need to be acknowledged specifically and not collapsed under an umbrella term of 'Indian women'. Questions raised by lesbian women have been an equally challenging set of concerns for the women's movement in India, this has been discussed in the chapter on queer movement. Women's movement today in India is committed to the idea that universal and homogenous categories of analysis and mobilization cover the cracks and fissures and privilege the powerful (for further details see Chapters 5 and 7).

CONCLUSION

This has been a very brief survey of the contemporary women's movement in India, there are many more issues and campaigns beyond what has been presented here. But even this brief examination reveals the complex and interrelated nature of most of the issues and campaigns raised by the women's movement in India. It has addressed issues of work, wages, education, health, family laws, culture and aesthetics, history, law, participation in contemporary politics, environment and sexuality. The sheer diversity of issues raised by the women's movement makes it vibrant and dynamic and somewhat difficult to define. A vast number of organizations and groups would like to be included in this collective called the Indian women's movement. Groups affiliated to various political parties as well as autonomous groups are both present.

One of the biggest challenges to the women's movement in India undoubtedly comes from the Hindu right-wing efforts to mobilize and organize women politically. Other kinds of criticisms also need to be taken stock of. Conventional left groups were for a long time suspicious of the women's movement dismissing it as essentially a bourgeois movement that talks of waging war on men, thus weakening chances of worker's unity. Today, however, most political parties have appropriated the issues and demands of the Indian women's movement with not very happy consequences. A major dilemma faced by many of the groups is the question of funding which either comes from international donors or from the government; this does place certain constraints upon their working. The problems faced by Indian women are complex and diverse, and hence, the response also has been diverse. Women are located in different cultural contexts and no uniform answers would be satisfactory. The search, however, should be able to strike a balance between respecting diversity, while creating a just and egalitarian society.

POINTS FOR DISCUSSION

- Discuss the coverage given to the contemporary women's movement in India by the press. Is it possible to discern any patterns?
- The International Women's Day was celebrated in India for the first time in 1975. Try and look at the newspaper coverage of the event back then, and how different is it today?

REFERENCES AND READINGS

Ambedkar, B. R. 2015. *Annihilation of Caste: The Annotated Critical Edition*. Delhi: Navayana.

Chaudhuri, Maitrayee. 2004. *Feminism in India*, 187–210. New Delhi: Kali for Women.

Gandhi, Nandita, and Nandita Shah. 1992. *The Issues at Stake: Theory and Practice in the Contemporary Women's Movement in India*. New Delhi: Kali for Women.

Kapadia, Karin, ed. 2002. *The Violence of Development*. New Delhi: Kali for Women.

Kumar, Radha. 1997. *The History of Doing*. New Delhi: Kali for Women.

Menon, Nivedita. 2004. *Recovering Subversion: Feminist Politics beyond the Law*. Delhi: Permanent Black.

Menon, Nivedita, and Aditya Nigam. 2007. *Power and Contestation in India since 1989*. Delhi: Zed Books.

Nanda, Bijayalaxmi. 2018. *Sex Selective Abortion and the State: Policies, Laws and Institutions in India*. Delhi: Har Anand Publishers.

Rao, Anupama. 2005. *Gender and Caste (Issues in Contemporary Indian Feminism)*. Delhi: Zed Books.

Sangari, Kumkum. 2015. *Recasting Women: Essays in Colonial History*. Delhi: Zubaan.

Sarkar, Tanika, and Urvashi Butalia, eds. 1995. *Women and the Hindu Right: A Collection of Essays*. New Delhi: Kali for Women.

Shah, K. T. 1947. *Woman's Role in Planned Economy, Report of the Sub-Committee*. Mumbai: Vora Publishers.

4

The Land and the Tiller: Farmer's Movement

Before independence it was the British government which took their raw materials for a song, processed the raw materials in London and Manchester and then sold the finished product at enormous profit. Today, Pune, Calcutta and Bombay are the London and Manchester. And our current rulers have replaced the British in grabbing the wealth of the country. I do not believe in sophisticated terms like 'class struggle'. You may call this whatever you like. But I call this struggle between Bharat and India, the fight for liberation by Bharat from India.

—Sharad Joshi

INTRODUCTION

Agriculture has a central role in the economic organization of India. Land and labour, ownership and prices, subsidies and finance—these are some of the more important issues around which various segments of people connected with this activity have organized themselves politically. It is difficult to describe these movements as a singular and homogenous group because there is much diversity to contend with. Farmers are divided by caste, gender and of course the nature of land ownership among many other categories. Movements have sought redress for specific grievances or sometimes they seek more radical and revolutionary changes. Farmers' movements have generally sought redress from the State.

Often the movements protest some specific change in the agricultural policies of the State. The State for long has been an important organizing principle in the agrarian sector. Changes in the principles of organizing agriculture (more and more capitalist direction) have resulted in greater class differentiation, and hence, new kinds of class conflicts. Sudha Pai has created a fivefold typology to understand the diverse nature of agrarian movements in India (Pai 2010). First, the basis of this typology is the pattern of land ownership that determines the mode of production, class structure and agrarian relations. Second, it would also take on board State policies; this is very significant because many of the movements have been in response to the changing nature of State policies on agriculture. The third criterion would be the role of technology in creating disquiet among the farming classes of India. Technological changes have brought about diverse kinds of changes; they impact the soil, productivity, ecological systems and the nature of social relations very differently, both in terms of geography as well as in terms of classes. In other words, the same technological initiative could impact different groups in diverse ways. This results in various political consequences, resulting in different articulation of political demands. The basis of the mobilization, that is, caste or class or any other social criterion, would be yet another ground on which to categorize famers' movements. Last but not least, the nature of leadership and the manner of conducting the movement itself would be a very significant basis for the study of the various kinds of farmers' movements in India.

THREE BROAD TYPES OF FARMER'S MOVEMENTS

Based on the aforementioned typology, farmers' movements in post-Independence India could be clubbed under three broad categories—anti-feudal movements, rich peasants and capitalist farmers' movements, especially following the Green Revolution which was introduced as a technological intervention in the 1960s, and finally those movements that are a consequence of the overall slackening and decline of the agrarian sector, especially after the introduction of the structural adjustment programme (SAP) in the early 1990s.

The study of social movements has always focused a great deal on peasant movements. Skocpol's analysis of the State and social revolutions revealed that there is a conjunction of two key factors— agrarian sociopolitical structures and political crisis—that give rise to widespread peasant discontent and facilitate insurrection against landlords (Kriesi 2006). It has been observed that peasant revolts become uncontrollable at the moment when elites begin to lose social control. Hence, even for the State, a feel of the agrarian sector and especially its discontent is politically very significant. The role of the peasantry and its influence in the possibilities of change in any given society are very crucial and have been studied very closely by scholars. Peasant revolts and agrarian unrest are significant from sociological as well as political perspectives. The nature and role of this segment in colonial states is significantly different and many scholars have paid close attention to the role of the peasantry and landlords vis-à-vis colonial states. It is in this context that the works of Dhanagare, Desai and others might be placed as far as the study of farmers' movements in India is concerned. (Pai 2010). These studies were mostly inspired by a Marxist framework and argued that the commercialization of agriculture in colonial India had resulted in differentiation within the peasant groups and often the peasantry did develop a radical and progressive worldview. The subaltern approach led to a greater focus on the history of the common people, and therefore undertook a study of peasant struggles not just as a consequence of class interests, but rather as a form of expression of collective community interests and identity. The nationalist approach to the peasant question placed farmers' movements within the overarching framework of anti-colonial struggles, which too incidentally were politically and ideologically of various types. Some were more radical than others, while others settled for parliamentary forms of working and solutions.

In the immediate period following Independence, many peasant groups did feel let down by the Indian State and this resulted in some radical political initiatives such as the land grab movement in some parts of India, often led by leaders who had a socialist or communist leanings. Most of these movements raised the issues of land redistribution, for example, the Naxalite uprisings. However, these radical demands were eventually made redundant by the various institutional mechanisms introduced to absorb some of the unrest. Following the Green Revolution in the 1960s, agriculture got increasingly commercialized, and thus class differentiation resulted. Rich farmers soon began to act as pressure groups that came to be seen as the new power holders in rural India. Often this group tried to align with other peasant groups, excluding the small tenants and landless labourers. These groups in some instances do invoke caste-based ties to consolidate their support base as can be expected. Post the introduction of structural reforms in the early 1990s, the focus has largely been against the changes in the agrarian policies of the State and often of the state governments with which the farmers are in direct contact. This has led to the neglect of the issues of the small and marginal farmers. On the other hand, there have been struggles that are spearheaded by small landholders against the spate of land acquisition attempts sponsored by the state governments in a bid to attract industrial investment like in Nandigram, West Bengal.[1]

It is in the 1960s that rich-farmers-led protests began to emerge in India, following the introduction of the technology-driven (biochemical and mechanical interventions) initiative called the Green Revolution. This period also indicates the quickening dissolution of the earlier Congress consensus carrying around diverse social interests together and was the beginning of various social groups moving away from the Congress, one by one. The Green Revolution followed the failure and the lack of the Indian State's committed pursuit of an institutional attempt to reform land ownership. Food supplies undoubtedly increased as a result of the Green Revolution and this led the Indian State to lose interest in the agrarian issue. The concentration of new technology and irrigation facilities led inevitably to the consolidation of the class inequalities. Modern large-scale farming favoured big farm sizes and intensive investment, this in turn promoted the possibilities of big farmers further consolidating their interests and monopolizing the scarce resources, which were earlier spread thinly over a larger cross section of farmers. It also resulted in regional imbalances, since only certain states and districts were part of this new intervention (Frankel 2016).

Although there is considerable academic debate around the use of the terms rich peasants and capitalist farmers, but all scholars agree that what set them apart from the rest was their ability to produce agricultural surplus. In this context, it might be pertinent to point out that the scholars Rudolph and Rudolph preferred to use the term 'bullock capitalists' to capture the complexity of agrarian class formation in India (Rudolph 1987). This was done to reflect the mix of capitalist, pre-industrial and non-capitalist features of many sections of the so-called capitalist farmers. Scholars do agree that one of the challenges while describing the farmers' movements in India is that of tremendous diversity in terms of the class character, the mode of production and, of

---

[1] See https://kafila.online/2008/09/06/mediotics-industrialization-and-the-angel-of-history/#more-670

course, the historical background. The nature of land relations and tenurial arrangements varied, much of it being the legacy of the colonial administration.

It is this disparity that resulted in only a small section of the farmers being in a position to take advantage of the Green Revolution with its heavy focus on technology and biochemical interventions. Those with small land sizes remained sealed out of these initiatives. The big farmers were able to consolidate their economic position by the 1970s, leading to political mobilization of this section of the agrarian classes in Punjab, Maharashtra and Karnataka and some parts of Andhra Pradesh and Tamil Nadu. New political groups like the Bharatiya Kisan Union in western Uttar Pradesh, Punjab and Haryana emerged at this stage.

Mahendra Singh Tikait

Mahendra Singh Tikait (6 October 1935–15 May 2011) was the president of Bharatiya Kisan Union, a farmer's movement having its base mainly in Uttar Pradesh. He has often been referred to as the second most important farmer leader after the then Prime Minister Chaudhary Charan Singh.

The Karnataka Rajya Ryot Sangha became prominent in Karnataka, whereas the Shetkari Sanghatana became an important force in Maharashtra. These movements were primarily like powerful lobbies and pressure groups that were trying to negotiate with the Indian State and not the landlord that was the focus of the earlier phase of peasant movements. These movements of big farmers sought concessions in policies, subsidises, prices and taxes and were not raising issues of ownership or wages. Issues of prices, fertilizer availability, diesel supplies, access to the banks and so on became crucial issues and not ideological issues. Much smaller union-like organizations formed out of these large movements that bargained with state governments for subsidies and tax cuts and have been described as rural unions. These movements were very different from the earlier phase of peasant movements in that they were no longer characterized by a certain social insularity or pre-political backwardness. These groups were politically alert and were prepared to employ the methods of modern liberal democracies.

Shetkari Sanghatana

Shetkari Sanghatana, a farmer's organization in Maharashtra, was founded by Sharad Anantrao Joshi (3 September 1935–12 December 2015). Sharad Joshi is known for coining the slogan *Bharat vs India* to highlight the exploitation of rural masses by urban elites. The organization has led many mass agitations in different parts of Maharashtra on agricultural issues such as prices offered to farmers, electricity tariffs or on waiving off of loans.

The development story in India is characterized by extreme unevenness between regions as well as between sectors, for example, service versus agricultural sector. The impact of the British policies related to land revenue, irrigation, plantations and so on led to a great degree of differentiation within the agricultural sector. The colonial rulers ignored the traditional proprietary patterns and created a complex web of non-cultivating intermediaries all of whom were in a position to stake a claim on the meagre surplus that was being produced (Ravi Srivastava 1994). This was more common in the permanent settlement areas of eastern India rather than the Ryotwari areas of the south. This combined with demographic and other economic factors led to diverse kinds of agrarian issues being raised and mobilization being undertaken. Thus, it is very difficult to create a universal account of farmers' movements in India. Areas that were able to generate greater revenue, got more State support in the form of investment by the British government in terms of irrigation facilities and so on, thus widening the differences even further.

THE EARLY YEARS AFTER INDEPENDENCE

It is well known that in the years following Independence, a two-pronged approach was followed by the Indian State. First were the attempts to re-organize the agrarian structure to make it more conducive to growth and equity through schemes such as the land reforms. The outcome of these initiatives was not even, as can be imagined. The second thrust of the initiatives was to increase yield through adopting modern agricultural technology, high-yielding seeds, irrigation initiatives and so on. Of course, the Green Revolution introduced in the 1960s, in some parts of north, south and western India, brought in a new set of variables. A central aspect of this change was the drawing of new groups in hitherto backward areas into the process of capitalist production and accumulation. This increased the trend towards proletarianization in the agrarian sector. New social groups and classes emerged in the agrarian context, giving rise to political equations and possibilities offering opportunities for novel political mobilization.

The agricultural landscape in India changed from rent-based to owner-based cultivation resulting in increasing proletarianization of the peasantry. This led to greater polarization of classes in agrarian India. It resulted in a spate of left-led land and wage struggles. These left-inspired movements were met with stiff repression from the government. It is a fact that till the 1970s, the agrarian movements were politically sharper than their counterparts in the later years.

THE TURBULENT 1970S

From the 1970s onwards, there has been a considerable change in the nature of agrarian politics in India. Farmers have made use of kinship and caste alliances as well to forge ahead with their political demands. Very often the farmer politics of the post 1970s led by the new cultivating classes has tried to maintain a non-political party character as well. This phase is characterized by the emergence of rich farmers and rich peasants and their increasing influence on political and institutional structures and processes in areas of capitalist agriculture. The late 1970s was characterized by the striking fact of consolidation of powers by the newly emergent dominant landholders/rich farmers and rich peasants who belonged to intermediate castes. Thus, the voice of the new group of agricultural capitalists began to make an impact on the agrarian scene in India and thereby on farmers' movements.

THE LOCALIZED MOVEMENTS OF THE 1980S

The 1980s came to be characterized not by large farmers' movements, but smaller geographically concentrated and intensely issue-specific mobilization of farmers that became the norm. This is not to deny the importance of certain ideological and philosophical issues that were raised by these groups, one of which came to be captured in the pithy phrase of *Bharat vs India*. This was meant to suggest that rural India was being exploited by its urban counterpart and that there was a sociocultural divide that was growing between the rural and the urban. Many of these groups were able to appropriate the entire political space in agrarian India and claimed to speak on behalf of all sections of the agrarian classes, while not offering anything in particular to the smallest and the weakest sections of the farming groups. Caste too played an important role in this mobilization, for example, in Northwest India, largely the Jats, Gujjars and Tyagis found themselves consolidating their economic, political and sociocultural interests. Some of these groups did try to extend their roles into formal parliamentary party based politics only to find that the going was not very easy. Some individual leaders, no doubt, caught the national imagination, for instance Mahendra Singh Tikait. However, by the end of the 1980s, the agrarian issues lost their immediacy.

LIBERALIZATION, PRIVATIZATION, GLOBALIZATION AND FARMERS' MOVEMENT

The 1990s witnessed many new and very bold initiatives and changes in the economic policies popularly referred to as the liberalization, privatization and globalization (LPG). Agriculture was to be freed from State regulatory controls as per the SAP. This meant greater dependence on market forces and less protection from the turbulence of the international markets. Market-oriented policies have resulted in several state governments across India withdrawing the protectionist policies that were earlier guaranteed to farmers. A very crucial announcement of the Government of India came in 2000 when the then ruling coalition led by the Bharatiya Janata Party decided to confer upon agriculture the status of industry. Fragmentation of land holdings has increased steadily and large holdings have systematically declined in numbers. Inputs for farming have become more and more expensive, thus rendering it economically less attractive to big farmers and unaffordable to small farmers. Agricultural growth has as a result slowed down considerably and it is languishing behind the other sectors of the economy. This has led to a worsening of the incomes and status of farmer households. Water management, river health and a new imagination, in short, to boost agriculture even in the hitherto star states would have to be conjured for agrarian sector to perform better. The fact is that new political economy regime inaugurated in the 1990s, created robust growth, but the agricultural sector has been experiencing a sharp decline.

The Karnataka Rajya Ryot Sangha in the 1990s raised some very important issues. It was one of the first to question and challenge the new economic policies of the government. It was weary of the withdrawal of subsidies to agriculture, warned against the introduction of seed manufacturing multinational companies like Monsanto. This group warned against the stringent patent regime that they feared would lead to unequal knowledge transfer, and finally they opposed genetically modified food on the grounds that it would lead to complete destruction of indigenous crop varieties and diversity.[2]

One of the big issues from the 1990s with reference to farmers' movements would have to be the alarming increase in the numbers of farmers' suicide. Most of these suicides are linked to the inability of small farmers to repay the loans that they take for buying expensive inputs, payment for water charges and so on. There has been an attempt to brush these suicides away as a localized or sociological phenomenon; rather it is a consequence of structural challenges faced by the agricultural sector and the inequalities that beset it.[3]

The agricultural landscape in India is witnessing further fragmentation of the farming classes. A small but powerful class of farmers attracted by the new policies have shifted to agribusiness in a big way—moving away from growing food to growing flowers and exotic fruits and so on. This class is able to access the benefits of urban India such as education and travel. They are thus disconnected from the lives and travails of smaller farmers. These farmers are able to benefit from the processes of globalization and hence are not very enthusiastic with regard to campaigns against global agricultural businesses and multinationals. In fact, some members of this class have openly supported globalization as offering freedom from the regulatory mechanisms of the Indian State. Sharad Joshi in Maharashtra has been a leader associated with this point of view.[4]

Farmers' suicides have continued to attract attention, however in recent years, there have been no large-scale farmers' movements. Tribals and other small farmers have begun to organize and agitate around the issue of land acquisition for mining and other industrial purposes. Odisha has been witness to some of the better organized agitations on these issues.[5]

---

[2] See https://viacampesina.org/en/wp-content/uploads/sites/2/2013/05/EN-05.pdf
[3] See https://psainath.org/category/the-agrarian-crisis/farmer-suicides/
[4] See http://www.isec.ac.in/JSED/JSED_V4_I1_42-54.pdf
[5] See http://www.environmentportal.in/files/Kalinga%20Nagar.pdf

LAND ACQUISITION AND FARMERS' MOVEMENT

Land acquisition is in contemporary India one of the biggest political challenges. Metropolitan India, as suggested by Shrivastava and Kothari (2012), continues to live off the countryside. A range of compensation schemes for farmers are announced by governments periodically who take over farm lands to be converted into real estate projects, shopping and other commercial purposes. The assurance to the peasantry that they would have land to till, made at the time of Independence, has almost been wiped off. Instead, what we see is a creeping change in land legislations to gradually remove land ceiling limits and make land available to industrial and housing needs. Sometimes, land is acquired as part of 'land banking' to be converted into special economic zones (SEZs). Estimates tell us that around 114,000 farming households and an additional 82,000 farm worker families would have been displaced by now due to land acquisition for SEZs. This suggests that close to 1 million people who depended on agriculture for their survival will face eviction. This loss of farming land would potentially adversely affect India's food security as well. As discussed in Chapter 6, farmers have also had to contend with agricultural land being taken away for the construction of big dams.

There is little doubt that very big movements and struggles by peasants and farmers that characterized Indian politics in its early decades now seem to be a thing of the past. However, the downturn in agriculture, the deepening economic crisis, the growing challenge from globalization, and last but not least, forcible land acquisition by the states create the grounds for unrest and disquiet in the agricultural sector. The nature of political mobilization of these issues and the response of the Indian State to these demands would determine the character of farmers' movement in the years to come.

CONCLUSION

Farmers' mobilization in the decades following the introduction of the new economic policies (LPG) have been in the nature of responses to these challenges. Many of the movements in the last two decades may be characterized as responses to the exigencies of a globalized neoliberal capitalism and, in particular, the effects on peasant farmers. This period has seen cutbacks in wages and social welfare, on the one hand, and capitalist completion has increased, on the other hand. Neo-populist mobilization ideologies with chauvinistic undertones have come to characterize farmers' movements in the contemporary phase.

Emerging from the late 1970s, the most important of them are: the Shetkari Sanghatana in Maharashtra, led by Sharad Joshi; the Bharatiya Kisan Union, led by M. S. Tikait in Uttar Pradesh; and the Karnataka State Farmers' Association (Karnataka Rajya Ryota Sangha) in Karnataka, led by M. D. Nanjundaswamy. It is impossible to ignore or underestimate the powerful effect the farmers' movements have had on local, regional and national politics in India throughout the past decades.

An interesting issue to be considered is whether the farmers' movements in more recent times in India are similar to forms of (urban) mobilization elsewhere in the world during the 1980s. Scholars have suggested that the contemporary farmers' movements in India are the response of a mass-based, commodity-producing peasantry to a State whose control over input/output prices affects rich, middle and (to a lesser extent) poor peasants. These movements draw on a plurality of traditions, are organizationally anarchic or postmodern, and lack a set of fixed criteria for membership. Traditional practices (such as bonded labour, atrocities against backward castes, tribals and women) continue but resistance is also sharp (Brass 1994).

The contemporary farmers' movements in northern India may largely be attributed to the decline in this area of the prosperity generated by the Green Revolution. Increasing market integration and smallholding made the peasants vulnerable to price fluctuations. The farmer's demands in this area are, thus, rather similar to the other areas including lower input prices, crop insurance schemes, the ending of bureaucratic corruption and the imposition of rural quotas for entry into higher education and government employment. In Gujarat, the impetus for farmers' movements maybe attributed to a different dynamic, where the inter-penetration of the urban and the rural is producing unique social dynamics. Some farmers' groups, for instance, in Karnataka have invoked the need for a 'khadi curtain' to keep at bay the influences of global markets and financial volatility. Other groups like Shetkari Sanghatana and leaders like Sharad Joshi are looking for a greater integration with the neoliberal market arrangements, in the hope that farmers would be able to get better prices.

The new farmers' movements in India are often projected just as conduits for the interests solely of rich peasants or kulaks, this is a view strongly upheld by scholars like Gail Omvedt. Other scholars such as Banaji and Hasan strongly differ from this point of view (Brass 1994).

On the question of the ideological framework of the contemporary farmers' movements, it has been suggested that populism on which most farmers' movements are based, is not a class ideology per se but rather a discursive form which enables a dominant class to establish and reproduce its hegemony over the farmers' movement as a whole.

The current phase in the farmers' movement is located within the large-scale global changes on the one hand, and the immediate local context of precarious price support, on the other. This makes the nature of issues and mobilization that follows rather complex and diverse.

POINTS FOR DISCUSSION

- The initial section of this chapter discusses the fivefold typology of understanding farmers' movements. Within this typology how would you place a study of the Naxalbari movement?

- What do you think the Rudolphs were suggesting when they employed the term 'bullock capitalists'?
- What do you think is the significance of conferring the title of industry on agriculture?

REFERENCES AND READINGS

Brass, Tom. 1994. 'Introduction: The New Farmers' Movements in India'. *The Journal of Peasant Studies* 21(3–4): 3–26. doi:10.1080/03066159408438553.

Frankel, F. R. 2016. *India's Green Revolution: Economic Gains and Political Costs.* New Jersey, NJ: Princeton University Press.

Kriesi, H. 2006. 'Political Context and Opportunity'. In *Routledge Handbook of Social Movements*, edited by S. A. David and A. Snow, 67–90. Massachusetts, MA: Routledge.

Pai, S. 2010. 'Farmer's Movements'. In *Oxford Companion to Indian Politics*, edited by P. B. Mehta and Niraja Gopal Jayal, 391–405. New Delhi: OUP.

Rudolph, L. I. 1987. *In Pursuit of Lakshmi: The Political Economy of the Indian State.* Chicago, IL: University of Chicago Press.

Shrivastava, Assem, and Ashish Kothari. 2012. *Churning the Earth: The Making of Global India.* New Delhi: Penguin/Viking.

Srivastava, Ravi. 1994. In *Social Change and Political Discourse in India*, edited by T. V. Sathyamurthy 219–47. New Delhi: OUP.

5

Struggle for Rights: Disability Movement

My advice to other disabled people would be, concentrate on things your disability doesn't prevent you doing well, and don't regret the things it interferes with. Don't be disabled in spirit as well as physically.

—Stephen Hawking[1]

The year was 1995 and the setting, New Delhi. A large crowd had gathered to press for their demand for a unique legislation which had the promise to hurl them out of wilderness into a life of dignity and freedom. Amidst the chaos and excitement, slogans like 'we want justice' and 'nothing about us without us' could be heard, loud and clear. It was a declaration by persons with disabilities (PWDs) of their inalienable right to chalk out a future life of dignity, equality and freedom. These slogans resonated in the corridors of power and had an electrifying impact on hundreds and thousands of people, many with disabilities. This was a special time in the history of disability movement in India. Disability as an issue became a part of the discourse of the academia and the activists like never before. PWDs started to come out of exclusion to form groups across disabilities and the Persons with Disabilities (Equal Opportunities, Protection of Rights and Full Participation) Act, 1995 became a reality.

Many years later, scholars and activists look back at that time as the start of a new era of struggle and hope which awakened India from its slumber to look at PWDs in a new light. While the year 1995 was a culmination of a number of changes which occurred from the 1960s onwards, it also proved to be a landmark year which set the ball rolling for more profound changes in the

---

[1] Stephen Hawking was a theoretical physicist, cosmologist, author and director of research at the Centre for Theoretical Cosmology at the University of Cambridge. His outstanding achievements overshadowed his acute disability, amyotrophic lateral sclerosis (ALS), a rare, early onset, slow progressing condition which had gradually paralyzed him over the years. He used to communicate through a single cheek muscle which was attached to a speech generating device.

future. Thus, an analysis of the movement advocating rights of PWDs in India could be taken up around the episodic changes that took place prior to and following the magical year of 1995.

THE BEGINNINGS

The campaign for the rights of PWDs in India is closely related to a similar movement in the West. Hence, any understanding of the Indian scenario will have to explore its development in the wider international context and its influence therein. The civil rights movement, the movements for women's rights, environment and issues of racial equality provided the context for the raising awareness on the issue of disability. Disability movement emerged in this environment and belongs to this genre of social movements. However, while other movements such as gender, race, Dalit and environment and their literature were starting to grow from the 1960s onwards, disability movement took much longer to consolidate its presence. It should be noted here that it was only in the late 1980s and early 1990s that disability issues started gaining in importance in different parts of the world including India, although there were exceptions like Aoi Shiba group in Japan which was established in the 1970s. Aoi Shiba started a modern political movement of PWDs including those with cerebral palsy and became an inspiration for others.

BARRIERS IN THE DEVELOPMENT OF DISABILITY MOVEMENT

It is important at this juncture to state the reasons due to which the disability issues remained dormant for a long time, whereas those related to women, farmers, race and so on were in the forefront. A very important reason is the dominance of medical model as a guide to perceive disability in the early years. Related to this is the issue of slow development of alliances and solidarities of persons with different types of disabilities across the spectrum of disability. Then there are demographic, geographical, social and cultural factors. A detailed account of these is given in the following sections.

PERCEIVING DISABILITY THROUGH THE MEDICAL MODEL

Until a few decades back, PWDs as a group largely remained neglected, stigmatized and invisible in cultures around the world. So was disability as a subject of enquiry. The construction of disability then was in biological or medical terms and it was treated as a medical condition which had negative social ramifications. It was this image of disability which was there in the early literature such as in the theories of Darwin, Durkheim and, later on, Talcott Parsons. Darwin's theory of evolution and the concept of survival of the fittest gave impetus to negative views on bodily and intellectual constraints, thus justifying the case for medical intervention (Reddy 2011).

In a similar vein, Durkheim saw disability as a pathological and deviant condition whereas Parsons included it in his concept of sick role[2] and perceived it as a type of disease needing treatment and rehabilitation. For medical professionals, PWDs were like objects with flawed bodies and/or mind, thus, a hazard for society and an impediment to social advancement (Barnes and Mercer 2003). These and other similar views created a culture of discrimination, isolation and pity where focus was on rectification of blemished bodies, forced sterilizations, confinement and even euthanasia. Nazi eugenics programme used medical sciences to build a political strategy of liquidating PWDs. It is this perspective which gave the control of PWDs to rehabilitation experts, social educators, medical doctors, physiotherapists, care givers and psychiatrists. It should be mentioned that those who gave rehabilitation services were themselves responsible for stigmatization as the image they portrayed was that of limitation, helplessness and dependency through which they retained their control. Political engagement in this perspective implied demanding more benefits and resources for prevention, treatment, rehabilitation and research. It was generally the professionals who engaged in this type of political connect (Peters 2000).

Thus, the initial definition of disability was in accordance with the diagnostic categories assigned on the basis of medical condition of the person by doctors. A person who looked different and/or who behaved differently was considered a PWD. Disability implied a physical or psychological inadequacy due to which a person faces explicit drop in bodily functions (functional limitation) and in everyday activities (activity restriction) (Einar Helander 1995, cited in Mehrotra 2013, 26). Based on this perspective, the PWDs were divided into different categories according to their physical or mental impairment such as blindness, low vision, locomotor disability, leprosy cured, hearing impairment, mental retardation and mental illness. It is important to note here that the physical or mental conditions which are included in the category of persons with disability have increased in number and will continue to increase as perceptions towards disability keep evolving.

Clearly then, across cultures and nations, it was this medicalization of impairment which led to objectification of disability in which it was seen as a deviant and pathological condition, burdensome for the family and the society and a misfortune for the person himself/herself.

TRANSITION TO THE SOCIAL MODEL

Slowly, among scholars and activists, this dominant perception of disability started to change. A shift from medical to social factors as disabling cause started taking root. It was in the year 1976 that a group of activists who called themselves as the 'Union of the Physically Impaired Against

---

[2] Sick role concept was originally given by L. J. Henderson and later elaborated by Talcott Parsons. It is defined as a deviant role in which the individual is not expected to maintain normal obligations and is absolved of any responsibility of his or her deviant behaviour. However, it is expected of the person to realize that his or her being ill is undesirable and he or she should try and overcome it with help from professionals and by cooperating with them. The concept throws light on social aspects of illness.

Segregation (UPIAS)' asserted that disability is not about the impaired body but it is about societal attitudes. This came to be known as the social model or social construction model of disability. It started taking root as disability activists in North America and Europe reiterated that it is the society which creates barriers for a person with disability, not his/her impairment. The supporters of the social model distinguished disability from impairment. Although impairment was that of the individual and his/her body, disability was due to societal attitudes and structures. The society disables persons with impairment. It is true that people with different impairments have different experiences (there are some who talk about deaf culture, blind culture and so on); the supporters of the social model focused on the collective experiences of exclusion and stigma. As the social model started to emerge, the perception of disability started changing.

Michael Oliver's voice was among the most prominent voices to advocate the social model. Oliver defined disability as 'all things that impose restrictions on the disabled people ranging from individual prejudice to institutional discrimination' (Oliver 1996, 33). He firmly believed that it is collective action that can address the problems of PWD rather than medical professionals. In the social model, the focus shifted away from the body to the outside environment—social, political, cultural and architectural. 'The problem of disability lies not only in the impairment of function... but also, more importantly, in the areas of our relationship with "normal" people' (cited in Barnes and Mercer 2003, 9).

'The "dis" (in disability) connotes a particular social arrangement that signifies the act of exclusion perpetrated by society on the individual although it is true that this exclusion may have partially come from his or her impairment' (Reddy 2011, 289).

A deeper understanding of disability, disablement and ability was put forward by Erving Goffman who, in his famous work *Stigma*, explains the role of society in identifying and differentiating PWD from those with ability through his concepts of 'virtual' and 'actual' social identity. Social identity for him is based on expectations by other actors. These expectations over time become demands. The demands made on a person account for his or her virtual social identity. The actual social identity refers to his or her genuine characteristics. Benchmarks are set through virtual social identities which become the basis for determining the actual social identity of an outsider. Thus, a person could be seen as normal if he or she is close to the virtual social identity and peculiar, strange and spoilt if s/he deviates widely. The latter is assigned as stigmatized identity. He discussed how a person with impairment manages his identity by struggling to meet the expectations of others (Goffman 1963). There are criticisms of Goffman's view on stigma. A person with hearing impairment is concerned about meeting his/her everyday needs rather than about managing his/her identity (Higgins 1981).

The social construct, thus treated the PWD as an oppressed minority group which likened disability to gender, caste and race. For many, disability was a far greater cause of oppression as it cuts across other types of oppressed identities. For instance, a lower caste woman with disability suffers multiple oppression. It is the social model which has highlighted the multiple marginalities faced by PWDs.

The supporters of the social model reject the very act of counting the persons who have disability and of measuring their extent of disability. They focus on the social barriers and on fighting the forces that deny them dignity and rights for their equal status in society. It is this model which facilitated the development of a distinct identity for PWDs as an oppressed minority having political and social rights like any other citizen. They advocate affirmative action, comprehensive laws, barrier-free environment, non-discrimination and equal opportunities in all spheres of life. It is the social model which gave an impetus to disability movement.

LIMITATIONS OF THE SOCIAL MODEL

Although the social model has pulled the PWDs from a nearly hopeless and pitiable situation to a state of hope and brought the issue of disability to the negotiating table to demand for equality and dignity, it has its limitations. While the social model highlights the courage of PWDs, care has to be taken to address the issues of medical needs and assistance. To achieve one, you need to address the other as well (Galvin 2003).

It may be more useful to look at impairment and disability together rather than in isolation of each other. It is amply clear that by separating disability from impairment, they have even shifted the focus of the policy makers and service givers away from severe impairment which is of disservice to those suffering from it. The need to get medical aid which is so essential for a person with severe impairment is itself seen as a stigmatized activity. For a person with severe mental illness, rights and dignity cannot be emphasized at the expense of medicines and care. Moreover, the central focus of the social model is on those with manageable physical or orthopaedic challenges. They have not taken into consideration those with severe conditions whether physical, mental or developmental which certainly require sustained personal medical care. Hence, impairment cannot be ignored as it is an essential aspect of life for a PWD. The rights approach as part of the social model should find fresh ways to tackle impairment (Shakespeare 2000).

Going past the medical and the social model, a thought which has been persistently put forward by a number of people is that a pluralistic space which recognizes and accepts plurality in abilities should be created in society instead of a single homogeneous expanse.

IDENTITY FORMATION AMONG PWD: THE OBSTACLES THEREIN

In the backdrop of the debate between the medical and social model is the issue of disability identity. As mentioned earlier, while identity politics and identity movements such as race, gender and ethnicity were in the forefront, disability identity was slow to develop. This was due to multi-stranded complex factors related to disability including the predominance of the medical model.

'Disability identity like most identity formations necessitates the presence of three components: role models, history and community' (Garland-Thomson and Bailey 2010, 407).

Getting role models for PWDs has been difficult. Society tends to group people together on the basis of certain particularities. PWDs are put in the diverse category of 'sick, deformed, ugly, old, maimed, afflicted, retarded, insane...' who do not conform to the cultural standard of normal and are thus, stigmatized. This is in contrast to the other category of intelligent, beautiful, healthy and so on. The damaged identity of the former, privileges the latter (Garland-Thomson and Bailey 2010, 405).

It is difficult for people to accept stigma, to form an identity around stigmatized characteristics is clearly problematic and challenging. To find persons who are disabled and who look at their disability in a positive way, as something which is facilitative rather than regressive is certainly rare. As is often said, to make one's disability a badge of pride is difficult. Further, as most of the persons with disability grow up, move around and live with people who do not have disability, the emphasis is on distancing oneself from one's disability, a tendency called 'role distance'[3] by Goffman. Even interactions between PWDs may at times increase stigma. This may act as a deterrent to communication between them and may instigate some to make distinctions such as good or bad impairment. Disability is mostly a private experience which a person would want to forget. Often one fights stereotypes for the sake of solving personal problems rather than to correct people's attitudes. It is, thus, exceedingly difficult for PWDs to have role models around whom they could develop a sense of dignity so essential for identity formation. Role models like Stephen Hawking are rare to come by.

Disability history, similarly, is a neglected area. It is neither developed nor accessible. In fact, women's and racial history have only been recently introduced as curriculum in schools (Garland-Thomson and Bailey 2010).

Identities like race and gender are known to have been formed around family and community through shared cultures. Institutions built around such identities are forceful and accepted. Such common features may facilitate political action. This is difficult in the case of disability as it is complicated and there are many impediments to the formation of a community around which a disability identity could be formed. Disability includes physical, psychological, sensory, cognitive and/or emotional conditions, and conceptualizing them as a cohesive identity based on similar life experiences is a major challenge. The different types of disabilities are an obstacle in the way of creating a community so essential for forming a common identity. There are diversities even within each type of disability like within locomotor disability which has a variety of conditions. To add to this are variations like the time of onset of disability, whether it is from birth or came later, in childhood or as an adult. People with orthopaedic disabilities may often have a feeling of superiority when they compare themselves with those having developmental or mental disabilities embroiled in their fuzzy ambiguous worlds. To further complicate matters, these

---

[3] Role distance, is a term coined by Erving Goffman which refers to a situation where the performer subjectively disengages himself from the role he is to perform. He neither acts according to the expectations of the role nor is he committed to it. Instead, he detaches himself from it.

different types of disabilities cut across caste, class, race, ethnic groups and gender making it even more difficult to form cohesive communities.

As pointed out earlier, people with disabilities grow up in families where others are non-disabled. They might often have little or no access to institutions which will facilitate a disability identity. However, medical and rehabilitation institutions catering to each disability, although seen as efforts to segregate them, have also, at times, helped in community formation and in solidifying disability identity, although these are limited geographically and conceptually. An interesting example is that of deaf persons who reject the disability tag and call themselves a minority culture which has its own language, the sign language and its own deaf culture. Many may not agree but this has been possible only because of institutional settings and close community formation. There are other examples such as war veterans or miners with disabilities who share occupational ties and can thus develop political action. It is also true that PWDs who are in institutional care could develop a common culture to manage the indignities and stigma they face. However, researchers have found that it is very rare for such a group to keep the collective identity and develop activism once they move out of the institution. An exception could be the 'ex-mental patients' who develop associations and work through them. With present focus on mainstreaming and integrating PWDs and doing away with special institutions, identity formation is taking place with the help of disability activists through political groupings across regions.

There are other factors which come in the way of creating a disability identity. The categories such as ethnic group, gender or race are more or less permanent, where a person is likely to be a member on a constant basis. On the other hand, disability identity is more fluid as is disability as a category. There is the case of temporary disabilities where a person may move in and out of disability category. It is also true that at times a person who is absolutely normal one moment may suddenly and tragically become disabled like Christopher Reeve[4] who at one moment was superman but became a quadriplegic the next moment. The fluid nature of disability category has to do with the fact that our bodies are in a state of flux and change in accordance with our environment.

DISABILITY IDENTITY IN THE MODERN DAY

Despite the many impediments, disability identity in the modern day is getting transformed from a historical and a medical identity to a politicized social identity. This has emerged as a consequence of shift from the medical to social model, certain legislations, and changes in the stance of international agencies, material and ideological factors which have occurred in the last 40–50

---

[4] Christopher D'Olier Reeve (1952–2004) was an American actor, well known for his portrayal of superman in the motion picture *Superman* (1978) for which he won the BAFTA award. Other acclaimed films include *The Bostonians, Street Smart* (1987) and *The Remains of the Day* (1993). In 1995, Reeve was thrown of a horse during an equestrian competition and was left a quadriplegic.

years. The civil rights movement of the 1950s and the 1960s in the USA motivated a number of marginalized groups including PWDs to look into their oppression in the language of identity politics. There was a conceptual reframing of disability which came to be seen as a civil and human rights issue and PWDs as a minority group having sociopolitical agenda of seeking integration, equal rights and privileges. Anspach has called this 'identity politics', 'a sort of phenomenological warfare, a struggle over social meanings attached to attributes' (Anspach 1979, 773). Thus, redefining disability has been an important prerequisite of the disability movement. Looking at them as people who are excluded from the mainstream unfairly and who are capable of effective political action is to bring about change for their betterment.

OTHER IMPEDIMENTS TO DISABILITY MOVEMENT

In addition to impediments such as the medical model or the absence of a cohesive disability identity, there are other factors which delayed the disability movement from developing. These include their marginalized status as they are generally poor, illiterate or with low education and low to very low participation in the workforce. They generally face barriers in getting education and jobs. Figures show that a majority of them live in backward rural areas where there is neither awareness nor services which are overwhelmingly concentrated in urban areas. Further, there are risks involved in lower class lifestyle which itself could aggravate or even lead to disability.

Discrimination against PWDs

Everyday discriminations against PWDs include using offensive language targeting the disability; insisting upon highlighting differences; highlighting the disability in public; asking a customer with disability to provide more information in comparison to others; and patronizing attitude.

DEVELOPMENT OF THE DISABILITY MOVEMENT INTERNATIONALLY

IMPACT OF CIVIL RIGHTS MOVEMENT

While the civil rights movement played a crucial role in the formation of the disability identity, the Civil Rights Act of 1964 became the basis of disability laws such as the Americans with Disabilities Act of 1990 (ADA), Persons with Disabilities Act 1995 and other similar Acts in different countries.

Early protests for disability rights emerged from the civil rights activists. For instance, an early disability activist Ed Roberts sued the University of California school system for disallowing him admission due to his disability. His protest paved the way for four persons with paraplegia to get admission in the university. This gave impetus to other such protests (Longmore and Unmasky 2001; Johnson 2005). Some of the issues raised by early activists varied from deinstitutionalization and accessible buildings to non-discrimination. Many opposed pity and charity and batted for rights and dignity. Harriet McBryde Johnson, a wheelchair user and a lawyer, who often argued cases under the ADA, opposed the annual fund raising activity of Muscular Dystrophy Association which portrayed such persons as being in need of pity and charity in her book *Too Late to Die Young* (Johnson 2005). Johnson opposed euthanasia for PWD, a demand made by Peter Singer (1993), and extensively wrote against it.

ROLE OF INTERNATIONAL AGENCIES

Beginning with the 1980s, there was increased concern with disability issues among international agencies like the United Nations and its ancillary organizations. For any understanding of the disability movement, the role of international agencies and their changing stance needs to be recognized. It was in the year 1980 that WHO made a major contribution to the contemporary perception of disability and impairment by putting forward three interconnected terms and their definitions. These are impairment, disability and handicap.

- 'Only loss or abnormality of psychological, physiological or anatomical structure or function is *impairment*.
- Any restriction or lack of ability (resulting from an impairment) to perform an activity in the manner or within the range considered normal for a human being is *disability*.
- A disadvantage for a given individual resulting from an impairment or disability that limits or prevents the fulfilment of a role that is normal depending on age, sex, social and cultural factors, for that individual is *handicap*. Handicap is, therefore, a function of the relationship between PWD and their environment' (WHO 1980).

This International Classification of Impairment, Disabilities and Handicaps (ICIDH) is a linear representation of transition from disease, impairment, disability to handicap. It understands 'handicap' as a social disadvantage resulting from impairment or disability.

The ICIDH was criticized for its over emphasis on the medical model. It focused on impairment as the cause of disability and handicap rather than the social, cultural, political and economic factors which deprive and disadvantage persons with impairments. Its focus, thus, was on bodily impairment and its treatment and not on their marginalization by the society (Barnes and Mercer 2003, 15).

A major shift towards the social model occurred with the United Nations pronouncement of the International Year of the Disabled Persons in 1981. In the same year, there was development of Disabled Peoples' International (DPI), a cross disability, international non-governmental organization (INGO), headquartered in Ottawa, Canada and with regional offices in Asia-Pacific, the Middle East, Europe, Africa, Latin America, and North America and the Caribbean. DPI perceived disability through the social model. DPI is now a network of national organizations of PWD, established by a Singaporean, Ron Chandran-Dudley, to promote the human rights of PWD through full participation, equalization of opportunity and development. DPI works with organizations in over 152 nations including India to overcome the everyday problems faced by PWD in different sociocultural settings. They also host assemblies and symposiums across the world with their different national branches.

The declaration of 'The United Nations Decade of Disabled Persons' (1983–1992) ushered in an era of increased awareness and activities related to the rights of PWDs. Guidelines to promote training and employment of PWD were put forward. The decade enthused individuals and organizations working for PWD with a new confidence.

In the year 1991, the United Nations General Assembly adopted the Principles for Protection of Persons with Mental Illness and for the Improvement of Mental Health Care ensuring their basic rights and freedoms. The United Nations Standard Rules on Equalization of Opportunities for Persons with Disabilities was adopted in 1993. In the same year, there was declaration of the Asian and Pacific Decade of Disabled Persons which gave a push to movements in the Asia-Pacific region.

A recent, new and reformed perspective on disability was put forward by WHO in 2001 called International Classification of Functioning, Disability and Health (ICF). Combining both the medical and social models, ICF includes the biological and social with the psychological to come up with a more logical perspective (Reddy 2011). While impairment, like in ICIDH means bodily deficiencies, the term 'disability' is replaced here with 'activity' implying achieving tasks by the individual and 'handicap' with participation meaning living through the life experiences of the individual. In some societies, social disadvantages for PWD are much more than others. It has, thus, been recently suggested that the term handicap should be replaced by 'level of participation in life situations' which varies according to the cultural norms and values, stage of development of a society and the like (Mitra 2006). ICF focuses on medical interventions for impairment and building capabilities of the individual to augment activities and participation. At times, it is termed as 'biopsychosocial' model of disability which takes into consideration the intricate interaction of biological, social and psychological factors related to disability. There have, however, been criticisms.

> ...the ICF model attempts to put the cart before the horse. The shift of focus from social causes of disability to the body functionality and capability not only brings body into the centre of discourse on disability, but also reflects the sedimented, deep-rooted modes of thinking on human abilities that consider deprivations as loss or lack. (Reddy 2011, 295, 297–98)

In 2007, The Convention on the Rights of Persons with Disabilities as an international human rights treaty was formulated by the United Nations and ratified by more than 160 countries including India. It intended to protect the rights and dignity of PWDs as equal citizens.

It will be correct to say that the United Nations and its ancillaries have facilitated and impacted the disability movement through its journey from initial medical model with its focus on individual impairment and charity to its social model reinventing PWDs as minorities having political rights. The transition from ICIDH to ICF and further speaks for the important role played by them. It is also true that international agencies along with globalization and the development of networks through mass media have helped in bringing disability movements from different countries closer to each other in the recent past. This closeness was visible during the Tsunami of December 2004, when joint relief and rehabilitation was organized in the affected areas.

TECHNOLOGY ENHANCING CAPABILITY AS A FACILITATING FACTOR

In this struggle for dignity and equality, a very important role has been played by technology and science which have helped in enhancing the capability of PWDs, at times leading to a complete overhaul of society's perception. Amartya Sen's capability model (1980s) defines capability as opportunities a person gets in society and disability as lack of opportunities. Following these leads, a number of disability activists and academics have, in recent years, focused on how opportunities and technology are being used to enhance 'functionality and capability'. Whether it is artificial limbs, wheelchair, sensory signals or prosthetics, they have increased functionality at many levels. In recent years, the advancement in technology has been such that it has at times led to reconstituting the impaired body with machines. Often referred to as *cyborg*, meaning part human part machine, technology has helped to enhance capabilities immensely. A case in point is that of the South African, Oscar Leonard Carl Pistorious, a Paralympic sprinter often called 'the fastest man on no legs' who confronted the able bodied in athletics using prosthesis. The challenge he posed was so real that 'The International Association of Athletics Federation' disallowed Pistorious from participating in 2008 Olympics by introducing a ban on use of technology (Reddy 2011, 296).

> *You are not disabled by the disabilities you have, you are able by the abilities you have.* —Oscar
> *Leonard Carl Pistorious (cited in Reddy 2011, 296)*

There is not an iota of doubt that in contemporary times, modern technology, whether it is machines, software devices, signage and artificial limbs, enhances and empowers PWDs like never before. However, the use of these devices once again lays emphasis on the individual and his/her disability. It once again makes the medical model take precedence over the social model and revives the old deep-rooted prejudices.

Abilympics

Abilympics (Olympics of abilities) is a competition of vocational skills of PWDs, show-casing their abilities. Although it started much earlier, the first international Abilympics was organized in 1981 in Tokyo to commemorate the United Nations International Year of PWD. It is organized every four years. It was held in New Delhi, India in 2003.

ISSUES RAISED BY THE DISABILITY MOVEMENT

The world over, PWDs have fought for a life of dignity and respect with equal rights and oppor-tunities in every sphere be it education, employment, training or accessibility. Thus, their demands have varied from inclusive education, reservations in jobs, getting vocational training, barrier-free environment, banishing stigma to allocation of more resources. Tom Shakespeare has especially mentioned how the disability movement in Britain has been fighting for allocation of more resources for PWDs. They have 'challenged the distributive logic of capitalism' (Shakespeare 2000) based on the market forces of demand and supply.

The many issues raised by the movement have resulted in accumulation of a storehouse of information and blueprints on inclusive education of persons with different types of disabilities; barrier-free buildings and the concept of universal access; ways to combat everyday discriminations and cross-cultural campaigns for equal opportunities are available and widely shared across countries.

Universal Access

The concept of universal access offers an exclusive alternative to the concept of acces-sibility. It entails making such designs of buildings and products so that everyone who has some mobility can use them. It recognizes that people without disability can fit through a wider doorway, drink from a lower water fountain, or walk up a ramp instead of a staircase. So can persons with limited mobility. Thus, the design should try and cater to the needs of the widest cross-section of society. Any idea of 'special' accommodation will lead to their isolation. Similar changes in transport system will remove barriers for PWDs.

Creating Accessible Spaces

A fundamental issue for PWDs is freedom of physical access. Whether in the hunt for housing or employment, going for a trip or to the market or a cinema hall, they face many physical barriers. These barriers depend on the type and extent of the disability, as well as on the environment in which they live.

For instance, to find their way around a large building complex, blind people must have a mental map of the area so that they can keep track of their route. A blind person can easily lose his/her way in large open spaces as they offer few tactile or auditory clues. Further, it is very difficult for a blind person to make a mental map of a complex building because it has many levels, curves and angles.

There is also the issue of lack of access to information. Most public information is given in print such as street signs; bus and train schedules; product labels and directions. These are inaccessible to blind people who need audible information. However, audible information would be useless for persons who are deaf. On the other hand, for people with mental disabilities, any complex information whether auditory or visual is difficult to handle.

While access which takes into consideration various persons with different type of disabilities and their need for getting education, employment and having a social life is to a great extent possible in developed countries, it is still a mirage for the majority in India. This has been an important issue of the disability movement in India.

Access Audit at the Taj, 2001

Photograph Courtesy: National Centre for Promotion of Employment for Disabled People. Reproduced with permission.

Drg Dharna of Residence of Finance Minister

Photograph Courtesy: National Centre for Promotion of Employment for Disabled People. Reproduced with permission.

Meeting with the President of India, 2002

Photograph Courtesy: National Centre for Promotion of Employment for Disabled People. Reproduced with permission.

Seminar on Employment Opportunities for People with Disability (27 March 1999) (1)

Photograph Courtesy: National Centre for Promotion of Employment for Disabled People. Reproduced with permission.

The Disability Act, 1995 (New Delhi 5–6 October 1998)

Photograph Courtesy: National Centre for Promotion of Employment for Disabled People. Reproduced with permission.

Workshop on Access to Historical Monuments for Disabled People in India

Photograph Courtesy: National Centre for Promotion of Employment for Disabled People. Reproduced with permission.

World Disability Day, 2001 (2)

Photograph Courtesy: National Centre for Promotion of Employment for Disabled People. Reproduced with permission.

World Disability Day, 2005

Photograph Courtesy: National Centre for Promotion of Employment for Disabled People. Reproduced with permission.

DISABILITY MOVEMENT IN INDIA: PRE 1995

EARLY YEARS

Disability movement in India has had a chequered history. During the colonial times, the approach to disability was that of welfare and charity, a top-down approach just like it was for the other marginalized groups. With patronage from the government, missionaries dotted the Indian sub-continent in large numbers (Miles 2001). While some benefits reached the poor, there was no visible impact on the PWDs who were never given special emphasis being treated as one of the crowd.

In line with this approach, after Independence, the Government of India set up the National Council for Handicapped Welfare, an agency having representatives from central and state governments as well as rehabilitation experts to outline policy initiatives for the government and the non-governmental sector. The basis of policy formulation was the medical model, looking at disability in narrow medical terms. The emphasis was on corrective means to make them as normal as possible. Rehabilitation was to be done through vocational training and education. The whole policy was based on the views of the experts such as doctors, special educators, occupational therapists and social workers. There was no space for the opinion of PWDs. They were only beneficiaries, not active members. There was no realization of the role of society in marginalizing the PWDs. The approach was purely apolitical.

There are conflicting views on the origins of disability movement in India. Although there are some who think that disability groups were apolitical and marginal till the early 1990s (Bhambani 2005), there are others who believe that disability was already becoming a political issue in the government-run institutes for visually impaired much earlier (Chander 2013).

1980s TO EARLY 1990s

There was a policy change of the Government of India from welfare to development from the 1980s onwards. With a shift to the social model, a more responsible State policy was emerging which helped to give a push to the disability movement. This period also witnessed the increased involvement of a number of local NGOs in disability rights issues, at times in collaboration with the State agencies. The strong presence of women's movement had a positive impact on the demand for disability rights (Mehrotra 2013). Persons with disability were no longer passive indebted receivers of services that agencies chose to give them. They slowly found their voices and became participants in transforming their own lives.

It is important to emphasize here that the NGOs have been among the main stakeholders in the disability movement in India as in many other countries. According to a rough estimate, there are more than 4,500 organizations and thousands of individuals, professionals and carers working on disability issues, with and for PWDs in India. Many organizations which work in the disability sector have been set up by PWDs themselves or their family members. Others have them in key positions. The voluntary sector has been involved in multifarious activities including advocacy, awareness generation, giving services including rehabilitation, research, skill development, prevention and so on. India has seen a mushrooming of such organizations since the 1990s.

It was in the early 1990s that several individuals and non-governmental groups of persons with different types of disabilities congregated under a disability cluster that intersected through all disabilities. Together they came to be known as the Disability Rights Group (DRG), later Disability Rights Movement (DRM). Three important factors, which cut across disabilities, have aided mobilization for the disability movement in India. These include demands (such as jobs and services); issues (related to their rights for equal opportunities and inclusion) and resources (such as money and human resources) (Bhambani 2005).

Initiatives under PWD Act, 1995

Some initiatives taken under the Act of 1995 for creating friendly access for PWDs include setting up of central access audit team; training of access auditors in all states; promotion of barrier-free environment in airports and railway stations, educational institutions, commercial and cultural complexes, museums and cinema halls, resettlement colonies and modes of transport.

Once formed, DRG was mobilizing, protesting and lobbying for equal status for PWDs. Their activities received a major push with the declaration of the Asian and Pacific Decade of Disabled Persons in the year 1993 along with globalization, development of modern media, greater networking and better flow of information as well as increased opportunities for getting funds (Mehrotra 2013). In the same year, a national seminar on disability was organized by the Government of India. The seminar highlighted the need for an all-inclusive legislation to ameliorate the status of persons with disability. Stickers in yellow and blue (yellow being the colour of disability and blue for their rights) demanding the 'rights for the disabled now' were printed in large numbers and were distributed. These were used to spread the movement about a Bill being prepared for introduction in the Parliament. As a result of collective efforts made by a number of distinguished activists, eminent persons drawn from all walks of life and all political parties, the Bill was passed as the Persons with Disabilities (Equal Opportunities, Protection of Rights and Full Participation) Act, 1995. Despite these efforts, 'the passing of the Persons of Disabilities (Equal Opportunities Protection of Rights and Full Participation) Act in 1995 owes much more to international pressure than to lobbying and protests by disability rights groups' (Mehrotra 2013, 99).

POST 1995

The Disability Act of 1995 was in a sense a turning point in the struggle for disability rights. It, along with the influence of an international movement for the rights of the PWDs, increasing activism by, with and for PWDs. In addition, new opportunities offered by technology, science, medicine, architecture and engineering further gave a push to disability movement. If the year 1995 was considered as a landmark year, the subsequent decades have shown that it triggered a more massive, more intense struggle for the implementation of the existing Act, for addressing its limitations and for formulation of a new Act.

In the early phase, mainly persons with physical disabilities joined the movement. Those with mental and developmental disabilities were almost unrepresented. They were seen as persons with impairments whose problems were medical in nature. Soon, however, their families started forming NGOs such as Spastic Society of India, now Able Disabled All People Together (ADAPT) and Action for Autism and became politically active. It is these and other similar groups who were greatly responsible for pressurizing the government to pass National Trust for Welfare of Persons with Autism, Cerebral Palsy, Mental Retardation and Multiple Disabilities Act, 1999.

Since 1995, the task of many NGOs has been to work for the implementation of the Act through mobilization, advocacy and spread of awareness. Such efforts have been endorsed over the years by all sections of society including the political class, film stars, media persons, school teachers, vice chancellors, professors, judges, lawyers and ordinary people.

Following the Acts of 1995 and 1999, a pivotal role was played by Javed Abidi and his organization National Centre for Promotion of Employment for Disabled People (NCPEDP) to carry the movement forward. They started a national campaign 'Disability 2000'. In 32 states and union territories, advocacy organizations, disability rights groups and local government bodies were mobilized to join in a nation-wide National Disability Network. In each of these locations, a partner was identified to actively take up rights-based issues in their own area and making contributions at the national level (Hosamane 2007). In the context of these developments, the disability movement started redefining disability issues and reinventing PWDs—capable and ready to go that extra mile to fight for their dignity and rights. Their fight was for a new position in a structurally different world (Baldwin 2006).

CONTEMPORARY STRATEGIES IN THE DISABILITY MOVEMENT

Broadly, there are three trends in the disability movement which are running parallel to each other (Malhotra 2001). One is that of advocacy organizations who are using the rights-based approach to ameliorate the lives of PWDs. Then there are community-based rehabilitation organizations and self-help groups (SHGs) trying to uplift PWD through their rehabilitation programmes and financial security. Finally, there are disability intellectuals, within the academia who are into research and analysis, collating and disseminating information through their writings. Each of these trends are discussed in the following sections.

THROUGH ADVOCACY GROUPS

These groups are mostly urban based, often run by educated PWD or their sympathizers who fight for their rights by influencing government policies and programmes. They demand equal participation in every sphere of life. Their issues could vary from barrier-free environment to inclusive education, to reservations in jobs, to implementation of disability legislations, to sensitizing society on disability issues through dissemination of information and all-important, a new, more inclusive and effective law. Their specific issues could be making a demand for ramps and lifts in public places such as museums, markets and cinema halls; for disabled-friendly buses, for signage and so on. Quite often, these are individual-based cross disability NGOs. It is these groups which played a crucial role in forming the DRG and National Disability Network. In recent years, a number of lawyers have joined these groups to litigate on the behalf of PWDs.

Ribbon Campaign for the dignity of PWDs

Concerned Action Now (CAN), a Delhi-based NGO, has been advocating for the rights of PWD through its use of yellow and blue ribbon campaign, a major event organized on 3 December each year to observe the International Day of Disabled Persons. Over the years, many NGOs, media personnel, college and school students and teachers and society at large have participated in the campaign by wearing yellow and blue ribbons and have helped to spread awareness on disability issues not only in Delhi but across India and abroad.

Although such groups have and continue to play an important advocacy role, they have at times been accused of having urban and upper class bias. For instance, demands for comfortable air travel or specially marked parking does show this bias in a highly unequal socio economic context. It has also been observed that there is very little or even negligible representation of women and other genders with disability in these groups, thus leading to a neglect of their issues. Rightfully, a number of female, transgender and queer disability activists have raised this point of male dominance and a male-centric approach of the disability movement. On the other hand, they have also highlighted the neglect of the issues of women with disabilities by the feminist movement (Hans and Patri 2002; Ghai 2003). No wonder then that a number of women from across disabilities have joined into the fray to raise their voice in recent years (see Chapter 3).

Although these groups bring up issues on behalf of all type of persons with disability, there is certainly a dominance of persons with locomotor disability. Often, in public places, disability is symbolized by a wheel chair. Other groups which are of some prominence are the visually challenged and people who are deaf.

The methods used by such groups to make their voices heard include gherao, lobbying, campaigns, strikes, workshops, seminars and so on. Most of the urban advocates of disability issues use modern technology to achieve their objectives. Whether it is through websites, newspapers, television programmes (*Ek Ghar Aas Paas*[5]) or magazines, they often successfully highlight their issues. There is *Disability News and Information Service* (*DNIS*), a fortnightly news service for India which provides authentic data, guidelines and news related to disability. It is produced and managed by NCPEDP, a Delhi-based NGO.

Inclusive Education of Disabled Children (IED)

IED means educating the children in a conducive and enabling environment along with other students in the regular school setting. Some of the challenges to inclusive education are lack of flexibility in courses, evaluation process and classroom rules; highly competitive environment; lack of trained teachers and staff; lack of sensitivity towards these children; non-availability of barrier-free environment in school premises and negative attitudes.

THROUGH COMMUNITY-BASED REHABILITATION SERVICES AND SHGs

Government and non-governmental agencies have played an important role in rehabilitation of PWDs. A number of centres, often called as community-based rehabilitation centres, have been opened all over, often with the help of PWDs or their families. Although many such centres play an important role and bring a ray of hope for them, they are mostly found in urban areas and function like urban formal organizations with no or negligible presence in rural areas. It is need-less to say that they are incompatible with informal structures in rural areas.

Simple Steps to Create Access

Simple common sense changes to create access include installing handrails and ramps; widening doors; using lever taps as those with less strength can also use them; painting edges of stairs with white for maximum contrast; have good lighting and have sign boards with large print.

---

[5] *Ek Ghar Aas Paas* was a television serial produced by Doordarshan in two parts of 13 episodes each in the 1980s and 1990s, which focused on the advantages of community-based rehabilitation for persons (both male and female) with mental disability.

On the other hand, a number of studies have highlighted the role of SHGs[6] in empowering PWDs in rural areas. These have been at times a source of income generation for PWDs; have benefitted them to access government schemes and provisions; have helped them to get assistive devices and have given them the strength to fight discrimination. Although there is merit in fighting for their rights through SHGs, there is a counterview according to which exclusive SHGs of PWDs further isolate them from the larger society. Despite this counterview, SHGs have on the whole played a positive role for them in building their identity as a cohesive group, in garnering dignity and freedom for them and in giving a fillip to the participation of PWDs in rural areas in the disability movement (Reddy 2011).

THROUGH DISABILITY LITERATURE

In tandem with the medical model, early disability studies remained confined to areas of prevention, rehabilitation, occupational therapies, assistive devices, institutional care and the like. The concept of their rights came in later as the social model started to take precedence. Along with it, there emerged a new genre of studies on disability taken up by social scientists. Although limited, these studies have highlighted the need to analyse disability from the perspective of marginalization and the economic and cultural ramifications in India.

THE DEMOGRAPHIC SCENE: NUMBER JUMBLES

A number of academics have highlighted the anomalies in enumeration of PWDs in India as different agencies have defined disability differently and have used varied procedures (Mitra and Sambamoorthi 2006; Bakshi 2010). The two main listing agencies in India are the Census of India and the National Sample Survey Organization (NSSO). Although both have identified disability in a similar way as locomotor, mental, hearing, speech and visual, their figures have varied significantly (Mitra and Sambamoorthi 2006). This has been because they have often defined particular disabilities differently. For example, while census defines visual impairment mainly on the basis of hazy vision, NSSO judges a person as visually impaired through a special test which assesses a persons' ability to see light and count fingers using spectacles, 3 m apart (Mitra and Sambamoorthi 2006). Given these anomalies, when the census places the number of visually challenged at 10.6 million, almost 50 per cent of the total PWD, NSSO's count is only 2.8 million, just 15 per cent of the total number of PWDs. A similar situation exists in locomotor disability. Census includes 'absence of toes, all fingers, deformity, the inability to move without aid, and the inability to lift and carry any small article' in locomotor disability (Reddy 2011, 299). The definition used by NSSO, on the other hand, is very broad. It includes conditions such as

---

[6] SHGs are generally village-based voluntarily formed groups of local women or men who make small savings on a regular basis often in a local bank. SHGs may or may not be registered. Once the saving is sizeable, it can lend money to the members, if required. Often, SHGs can get micro credit from the bank. SHGs are not only a means of saving money and of mutual help but they facilitate women empowerment and developing leadership skills among them.

TABLE 5.1 PWDs Profile in India	
Total number of PWDs in India	2.68 crore
Number of PWDs in movement	54.3 lakh
Number of PWDs in hearing	50.7 lakh
Number of PWDs in seeing	50.3 lakh
Total number of literates among PWDs	1.46 crore or 54.5 per cent[a]
Literacy among disabled females	44.6 per cent[b]
Literacy among disabled males	62.4 per cent[c]

Source: Census 2011
Notes:
[a] Of these, only 8.5 per cent were graduates and above.
[b] Of these, 7.7 per cent were graduates and above.
[c] Of these, 9 per cent are graduates and above.

paralysis, dwarfism, malfunction of joints and amputation among others as conditions of locomotor disability. Hence, their figures are very different. According to the census, it is 6.1 million (28% of the total disabled), whereas NSSO assesses it at 10.6 million, as much as 58 per cent of the total (Reddy 2011, 299).

A similar discrepancy exists between Indian figures and World Bank figures on total number of PWDs in the country. As published in a report of 2010 by Kamal Bakshi, while the census figure stood at 2.13 per cent or 21 million, the World Bank figure (O'Keefe 2007) was 4 per cent to 8 per cent, that is, 40 to 90 million.

Numbers do tell a part of the story, the real status of PWD should, however, be understood through their deprivation (see Table 5.1). In 2006, A. K. Mishra and R. Gupta (2006) formulated a new instrument to measure deprivations which they called 'Disability Index' (DI). Based on Human Development Report and data sources such as NSSO and census, they developed a DI for different states in India. According to them, there are three criteria through which deprivation can be measured. These include opportunities for education, skill development and employment. The DI score indicated that deprivation levels are higher in rural as compared to urban areas, in states like Odisha as compared to Himachal Pradesh and among persons with mental retardation as compared to those with physical disabilities.

Other studies have corroborated that PWDs face acute deprivation and stigma as compared to those in the Western countries (Klasing 2007). In India, as mentioned earlier, there is no clarity of the number of persons having disability and the percentage in each disability. Further, as is well known, impairment, illiteracy and poverty tend to coexist and complement each other.

To add to this, a majority of those with disabilities are found in rural areas (around 80%), and the various services whether it is health, rehabilitation or skill development are concentrated in the urban areas. The condition of PWDs in rural areas of India is particularly bad. The facilities provided by the government are severely lacking in prevention, detection and rehabilitation. For instance, there is no provision for psychiatric care which is essential to tackle mental illness. Thus, while rural folk are more prone to getting disabilities of different types, they are also less likely to get education, receive vocational training, get barrier-free environment, find suitable jobs and become independent. They are most dependent on their families and are most confined to their homes. Further, impairment, poverty and stigmatized attitudes tend to force them to live a life which is full of physical hardships and mental trauma (Klasing 2007).

High illiteracy among PWDs is not just due to poverty, there are more pressing reasons for it (see Table 5.1). These include negative sociocultural environment. Due to acute stigma, a PWD often faces humiliation in the community and the school. PWDs are the butt of jokes and mockery. Other factors include inaccessible schools, classrooms and toilets; untrained teachers who have no knowledge of dealing with special children; lack of flexibility in school rules to accommodate PWDs and unwillingness of the teachers to take on extra work for these children (Klasing 2007). These hardships become manifold in the case of women with disabilities. 'Ek to ladki, oopar se apahij' (one, a girl and that too disabled) is a well-known Hindi phrase which explains it all (Ghai 2002, 53).

Marriage is a difficult, often impossible proposition for both men and women with disabilities. Strangely however, more women with disabilities get married in comparison to men (Klasing 2007). In a traditional society, a daughter's marriage is the only remaining responsibility of parents which must be fulfilled. They may at times do it by hiding facts, by giving huge dowry, if they can afford it, or by other means such as marrying their young girl to an old man, divorcee or a widower. It is needless to say that in most of these situations, they are exploited and demeaned. Men with disabilities also have difficulties in getting married as they do not fit into the image of a typical husband and a breadwinner.

Although in India, there is more literature in the form of NGO reports, contextual, subjective information or medical books, serious research examining disability in a critical way is beginning to develop. Academic works are seeing disability more in terms of different cultures and identities such as gender, caste, class and religion rather than as a homogeneous experience.

A VICTORY OF THE MOVEMENT: THE RIGHTS OF PWDs BILL, 2016

The long struggle after the 1995 Act to address its anomalies and to formulate a new Act ended in December 2016 when a new bill was passed in the Indian Parliament. There was enough data to prove that the 1995 Act had many discrepancies. Moreover, it recognized only seven disabilities (blindness, low vision, locomotor disability, leprosy cured, hearing impairment, mental retardation and mental illness), while many other conditions needed to be included. On top of it, it was poorly implemented. According to the annual report of 2015–2016 of the Department of Empowerment of Persons with Disabilities, of the total PWDs listed in the 2011 census, only 49.5 per cent had disability certificate as on 31 August 2015. Moreover, the certificate was given on the basis of the medical condition of the person as judged by medical professionals. If a person, according to their judgement had 40 per cent disability, such a person would be given the disability certificate and he/she would then be entitled to the various provisions of the Act. The PWD was at the mercy of the State and the State-deputed doctors.

Disability activists while working towards the implementation of the 1995 Act had also been raising demands for amendments to the Act which, according to them, had serious limitations. It was only in December 2016 that The Rights of Persons with Disabilities Bill, 2016 was passed in the Lok Sabha replacing the 1995 Act. The journey from 1995 to 2016 was a long and arduous one. The 2016 Bill was in the making from 2011 onwards. A diluted form of the proposed bill was approved by the Union Cabinet on 30 December 2013. However, the disability rights activists led by Javed Abidi opposed it. Through intensive negotiations the government incorporated the issues raised by the activists and included 16 odd amendments. This led to the 'The Rights of the Persons with Disabilities Bill, 2014'. The 2014 Bill strengthened the definition of disability, included 19 physical and mental conditions as disabilities and provided 5 per cent reservation for PWDs in government jobs and in higher educational institutions.

The 2014 Bill has been further amended and finally, a more acceptable 'The Rights of Persons with Disabilities Bill, 2016' has come into existence. To the seven categories of Disability Act of 1995, 14 more conditions have been added such as speech and language disability, specific learning disability, acid attack victims, dwarfism and muscular dystrophy. The new categories also include three blood disorders, namely thalassemia, haemophilia and sickle cell disease.

Induction of PWDs in the highest echelon of the government like the IAS was until now delayed or at times denied. There was no punishment for those who did not comply with the provisions of the Act. The new Act has installed punishment in the form of fines. Further, the quota (4%) for employment of PWDs will not be from identified posts as in the previous Act but from the total number of vacancies in that cadre strength. Private agencies are included in the definition of 'establishment'. There is provision for free and inclusive education in the age group of 6–18 for those with benchmark disabilities. Special provisions are there in the new Act for women and children with disabilities. There is provision for making public places accessible within a time frame. Another welcome provision under the new Act, however, is that a disability certificate issued in any part of India will be valid all over the country which was not so in the earlier Act.

CHALLENGES FACING THE NEW DISABILITY ACT

Although this new Act is a great advancement over the earlier Act and has many welcome provisions (Murlitharan 2016), it also poses new challenges. It is important to note that under the 1995 Act, less than half the population got disability certificates up to 2015 when it included only seven disabilities. The present Act includes a much larger population and 17 more conditions. To issue certificates to such a big group would be a daunting task. Moreover, the certificates will still be issued by medical professionals on the basis of the extent of impairment (40%) and not on the basis of disabling social environment, making it similar to the 1995 Act. Many countries have disability laws based on the social model—judging disability as any physical, mental, sensory or intellectual condition which works together with social barriers which impede participation on an equal basis. The 2016 Bill assumes this definition when it comes to issues like non-discrimination but ignores it when selection for more quantifiable benefits have to be made like reservations in jobs or in educational institutions. Then, the medical assessment of 40 per cent for defining benchmark disability is the basis like in the earlier Act. It should also be noted that it is not always easy to judge the extent of disability in case of psychosocial or intellectual disabilities. In a broad sense, the 2016 Bill is to a great extent based on the medical model.

CONCLUSION

In conclusion, one can say that the disability movement has taken root in the Indian society and has achieved a momentum in urban areas with some success in terms of legislations and concessions. The two most important legislations of 1995 and 2016 have been possible, though partly due to international pressures but most importantly due to an indigenous and ever widening network of disability activists and organizations who have played a crucial role in it. PWDs have come out of the confines of anonymity with a capability to influence decisions and act as pressure groups. While those with orthopaedic disability, hearing or visual impairment have been in the forefront of the movement, the ones with developmental disabilities and mental illness have largely remained out of it. However, in recent years, some representation is there through their kin. It is also true that a large majority of PWDs live in rural areas and are as yet untouched by the movement.

The movement thus faces many challenges. The next immediate test is the implementation of the 2016 Act, though the larger aim is to push for creating structurally pluralistic spaces where there is place for everyone. The 'wall of exclusion' will only go if society takes big and bold steps in this direction. The battle seems to have just begun.

POINTS FOR DISCUSSION

- Discuss the nature of structural changes the disability movement should take up in order to bring discernible changes in the lives of PWDs in India.
- How should the International Day of PWDs be celebrated to give momentum to the disability movement?
- Two invisible sections are women and other genders with disabilities and the PWDs living in rural areas in India. Discuss some ways of addressing the issues that concern them.

REFERENCES AND READINGS

Addlakha, Renu. 2008a. 'Disability, Gender and Society'. *Indian Journal of Gender Studies* (Special Issue), 15 (2): 191–207.

———. 2008b. *Deconstructing Mental Illness: An Ethnography of Psychiatry, Women and Family*. New Delhi: Zubaan.

———, eds. 2013. *Disability Studies in India*. New Delhi: Routledge.

Addlakha, Renu, Stuart Blume, Patrick Devlieger, Osamu Nagase, and Myriam Winance, eds. 2009. *Disability and Society: A Reader*. Hyderabad: Orient BlackSwan.

Anspach, R. R. 1979. 'From Stigma to Identity Politics: Political Activism among the Physically Disabled and Former Mental Patients'. *Social Science and Medicine*, 13A: 765–73.

Bakshi, Kamal. 2010. 'Disability and Census of 2011: Counting the Invisible Children of Mother India'. *The Hindu* (Hyderabad), June 23, 9.

Baldwin, J. L. 2006. 'Designing Disability Services in South Asia: Understanding the Role that Disability Organizations Play in Transforming A Rights-based Approach to Disability'. MA thesis, University of Pittsburgh.

Baquer, Ali, and Anjali Sharma. 1997. *Disability: Challenges vs. Responses*. New Delhi: Concerned Action Now.

Barnes, Colin, and Geof Mercer. 2003. *Disability*. Cambridge: Polity Press.

Bhambani, Meenu. 2005. 'The Politics of Disability Rights Movement in India'. *International Journal of Disability Studies*, 1 (1): 3–28.

Chander, Jagdish. 2013. 'Disability Rights and the Emergence of Disability Studies'. In *Disability Studies in India: Global Discourses and Local Realities*, edited by Renu Addlakha. New Delhi: Routledge, Taylor and Francis group.Coleman, Lerita M. 1986. 'Stigma: An Enigma Demystified'. In *A Multidisciplinary View of Stigma*, edited by S. Ainlay, G. Becker, and L. M. Coleman, 211–34. New York, NY: Plenum.

Davar, Bhargavi V. 1999. *Mental Health of Indian Women: A Feminist Agenda*. New Delhi: SAGE Publications.

———, ed. 2001. *Mental Health from a Gender Perspective*. New Delhi: SAGE Publications.

Dhanda, Amita. 2000. *Legal Order and Mental Disorder*. New Delhi: SAGE Publications.

Foucault, Michel. (1965) 1973. *Madness and Civilization: A History of Insanity in the Age of Reason*. New York, NY: Vintage Books.

Galvin, Rose. 2003. 'The Paradox of Disability Culture: The Need to Combine versus the Imperative to Let Go'. *Disability and Society*, 18 (5): 675–90.

Garland-Thomson, Rosemarie, and Moya Bailey. 'Never Fixed: Modernity and Disability Identities'. In *The SAGE Handbook of Identities*, edited by Margaret Wetherell, and Chandra Talpade Mohanty, 403–416. Los Angeles, CA: SAGE Publications.

Ghai, Anita. 2002. 'Disabled Women: An Excluded Agenda of Indian Feminism'. *Hypatia*, 17 (3): 49–66.

————. 2003. *(Dis) Embodied Form: Issues of Disabled Women*. New Delhi: HarAnand Publications.

————. 2015. *Rethinking Disability in India*. New Delhi: Routledge, Taylor and Francis Group.

Goffman, Erving. 1961. *Asylums*. Garden City: Anchor Books.

————. 1963. *Stigma: Some Notes on the Management of Spoilt Identity*. Englewood Cliffs, NJ: PrenticeHall.

Hans, Asha, and Annie Patri, eds. 2002. *Women, Disability and Identity*. New Delhi: SAGE Publications.

Higgins, P. C. 1981. *Outsiders in a Hearing World*. Los Angeles, CA: SAGE Publications.

Hosamane, S. B. 2007. 'Developing the Gender Dimension in India's Disability Rights Movement'. Available at: http://www.isiswomen.org/index.php?option=com_content&view=article&id=659&Itemid=346 (Accessed 15 February 2019).

Johnson, H. M. 2005. *Too Late to Die Young*. New York, NY: Henry Holt and Co.

Kapur, Malavika. 1995. *Mental Health of Indian Children*. New Delhi/Thousand Oaks, CA/London: SAGE Publications.

Klasing, Insa. 2007. '*Disability and Social Exclusion in Rural India*. Jaipur: Rawat Publications.

Longmore, P. K., and L. Umansky. 2001. *The New Disability History: American Perspectives*. New York, NY: New York University Press.

Malhotra, R. 2001. 'The Politics of Disability Rights Movements'. *New Politics*, 31: 65–75.

Mehrotra, Nilika. 2013. *Disability, Gender and State Policy: Exploring Margins*. Jaipur: Rawat Publications.

Miles, M. 2001. 'Studying Responses to Disability in South Asian Histories: Approaches Personal, Prakrital and Pragmatical'. *Disability and Society*, 16 (1): 143–60.

Mishra, A. K., and R. Gupta. 2006. 'Disability Index: A Measure of Deprivation among Disabled'. *Economic and Political Weekly*, 41 (38): 4026–29.

Mitra, Sophie. 2006. 'The Capability Approach and Disability'. *Journal of Disability Policy Studies*, 16 (4): 236–47.

Mitra, Sophie, and Usha Sambamoorthi. 2006. 'Disability Estimates in India'. *Economic and Political Weekly*, 41 (38): 4022–26.

Murlitharan. 2016. 'Bill of Rights'. *Indian Express*, 20 December, 14.

O'Keefe, Philip. 2007. *People with Disabilities in India: From Commitment to Outcomes*. Washington, DC: World Bank.

Oliver, M. 1990. *The Politics of Disablement: A Sociological Approach*. London: Macmillan.

————. 1996. *Understanding Disability: From Theory to Practice*. Basingstoke: Macmillan.

Peters, Susan. 2000. 'Is There a Disability Culture? A Syncretisation of Three Possible World Views'. *Disability and Society*, 15 (4): 583–601.

Reddy, Raghava C. 2011, May–August. 'From Impairment to Disability and Beyond: Critical Explorations in Disability Studies'. *Sociological Bulletin*, 60 (2): 287–306.

Scotch, R. K. 1984. *From Goodwill to Civil Rights*. Philadelphia: Temple University Press.

Shakespeare, Tom. 2000. 'Disability Sexuality: Towards Rights and Recognition'. *Sexuality and Disability*, 18 (3): 159–66.

Siebers, Tobin. 2008. *Disability Theory*. Ann Arbor: University of Michigan Press.

Wendell, S. 1997. 'Toward a Feminist Theory of Disability'. In *The Disability Studies Reader*, edited by L. J. David, 243–56 (Second edition). New York, NY: Routledge.

WHO (World Health Organization). 1976. *Document A29/INF.DOC/1*. Geneva: WHO.

————. 1980. *International Classification of Impairments, Disabilities and Handicaps*. Geneva: WHO.

————. 2001. *International Classification of Functioning, Disability and Health*. Geneva: WHO.

————. 2001–2002. *International Classification of Functioning, Disability and Health (ICF)*. Geneva: WHO.

6

Nature and People: Environmental Movement

I became very realistically aware of the terrible floods which pour down from the Ganga catchment area, and I had taken care to have all the buildings constructed above the flood high mark. Within a year or two I witnessed a shocking flood: as the swirling waters increased, there came first bushes and...great logs of wood, then in the turmoil of more and more water came whole trees, cattle of all sizes and from time to time a human being clinging to the remnants of his hut.... Merciless deforestation as well as cultivation of profitable pines in place of broad-leaf trees was clearly the cause....

—Mira Behn[1]

Few will deny that humanity is standing at the door step of ecological ruin. Its debris is threatening to destroy the balance of nature and mankind. It is no wonder then that some of the most powerful social movements have arisen around environmental issues. 'It is entirely possible that when the history of the twentieth century is finally written, the single most important social movement of the period will be judged to be environmentalism' (Nisbet 1982, 101). Labelled as new social movements, they have acquired a place of significance the world over. In the West, the environmental movement organizations are often formal bureaucratic organizations which either have their own political parties like the Green Party of the USA or they have a substantial presence in mainstream parties. In Germany, France and Italy, they have held positions in the government of the day. In countries like India, environmental movements are in the forefront of people's uprisings which are known to have influenced policies and programmes perceived as negative for the environment and for the people themselves.

It all started in the 1970s when the world witnessed a number of mobilizations 'searching for a new kind of peace—peace with nature. Despite the differences in the stage and in the actors,

---

[1] Mira Behn was the European disciple of Mahatma Gandhi who had made Garhwal hills her home.

these movements shared the common objective of a search for an alternative development that is more in harmony with nature's rhythms, patterns and processes' (Shiva 2010, 275). These mobilizations were symptomatic of the environmental degradation that the world was facing through its many variants such as greenhouse effect, global warming, air and water pollution, deforestation, diminution of fauna and flora, loss of biodiversity and depletion of Ozone layer. A consciousness was dawning on the world that the degradation was due to factors such as indiscriminate use of modern technology, reckless-industrialization and urbanization, modern developmental models and the excessive misuse of natural resources. Protests around environmental issues started with the realization that sustainable development was the key to safeguarding nature and the future of humankind.

In India, the search was not only for peace with nature but was also accompanied by a search for justice. Indian environmental movements have been identified as movements of the 'dispossessed' for 'just peace', as movements in search for nature-friendly development along with justice (Shiva 2010, 275). Expressing a similar sentiment, Ramchandra Guha said, 'Indian environmental movement is an umbrella term that covers a multitude of local conflicts, initiatives, and struggles where the poor confront the rich in order to protect the scarce diminishing natural resources that are needed for survival' (Guha and Martinez 1998, 4). Whether it is the hill dwellers against the rich and powerful, indulging in commercial felling of trees as in Chipko, or poor tribals and small landholders against the builders of big dams as in Narmada Bachao Andolan (NBA), or the poor fish workers pitted against trawling companies as in Kerala Fishworkers' movement; in all these cases, the struggle has been between those who have used natural resources in a sustainable manner for ages against those who exploit them and in the process destroy them for personal gain.

> *The 'iron triangle' of politicians and bureaucrats use public resources to extend patronage to, and receive support from industry, large landowners and urban middle class populations. These resource omnivores live on islands of prosperity at the cost of India's vast numbers of ecosystem people who are submerged in a sea of poverty.*

Indian environmentalism has thus often been referred to as the 'environmentalism of the poor'[2] (Gadgil and Guha 1995, 34–45) or even as 'utilitarian conservationism' (Kumar 2015, 313).

India has had a long history of sensitivity with nature and human being's responsibility towards it. However, with the establishment of colonial rule, natural resources turned into profit generating commodities to be exploited in order to generate revenue for the British. In modern times, it has been highlighted by Mahatma Gandhi who had said, 'Earth provides for every man's need but

---

[2] It should however be noted that at times even the rich and landed participate in such protests when their livelihood is threatened like in the movement against Sardar Sarovar dam and Maheshwar dam where a sizeable number of them are also facing displacement (Baviskar 167–68).

not for every man's greed'. He insisted that containing the use of natural resources such as forest, water and land facilitates environmental stability and creates a society based on fairness and justice. Predatory tendencies to satisfy the greed of few humans are destructive of nature and the life-sustaining systems of the rest of humanity (Rootes 1990, 5–17).

TYPES OF ENVIRONMENTAL MOVEMENTS

It should be noted that environmental movements are not homogeneous or of one type but are highly varied raising different issues. It is also true that these movements did not arise because of a single event or due to a spontaneous reaction to certain changes.

Gadgil and Guha have classified environmental movements as political, material and ideological (Kumar 2015). Those movements which question the policies and programmes of the state, especially its developmental model which is known to have led to environmental degradation, are termed as political. The ones which fight for the rights of the deprived and marginalized over natural resources are identified as material. Further, those environmental movements with a distinct dominant ideology such as the Gandhian and Marxist are labelled as ideological.

In a more specific classification, Harsh Sethi has talked of five main types of environmental movements. These include those opposing construction of big dams and the consequent displacement; those fighting for the use of forest resources and against the policy of protected areas; then there are movements fighting for prudent use of marine resources; further, there are those against the use of pollutants and harmful chemicals in agriculture; and finally are the ones fighting against pollution and wasteful use of resources in industries.

A more elaborate classification into eight categories based on different issues has been given by Andharia and Sengupta. These include 'forest and land based' such as the Chipko[3] and Appiko, 'marine resources and fisheries aquiculture' like the fishworkers' movement in Kerala and 'industrial pollution' like 'Zahirili Gas Morcha' in Bhopal. There are others based on development projects such as dams and irrigation (Silent Valley, NBA), power projects (Koel Karo Jan Sangthan in Bihar), mining (anti-mining project in Doon valley), industrial plants, railway and airport projects, military projects (Amravati Bachao Abhiyan against a large chemical complex, anti-missile test range in Baliapal and at Netrahat, Bihar) (Kumar 2015). Then there are movements around wildlife sanctuaries like Ekjoot in Bhimashankar in Maharashtra. In addition, there are tourism-related movements like Himachal Bachao Andolan. There are those related to advocacy groups like the Centre for Science and Technology and others who have promoted the use of appropriate technology like the well-known architect Laurie Baker.

---

[3] The recent campaign by citizens of Delhi against the large-scale felling of trees has a resonance of Chipko movement.

ROLE OF IDEOLOGY

Like other movements, environmental movements have often been classified and understood on the basis of their differing ideologies such as Gandhian, Marxist and appropriate technology use. A number of movements use multiple ideologies to substantiate their crusade.

The Gandhian ideology has played an important role in guiding a number of environmental movements in India. This approach fuses concerns for the environment with a commitment to social justice. They reject aggressive industrialization and indiscriminate spread of modern lifestyle which have led to materialism and consumerism triggering environmental degradation and an imbalance between human beings and nature. In a typical Gandhian way, they propagate a pattern of life which is in harmony with nature. Their methods are also Gandhian such as holding fasts, sit-ins, *padyatras* (journeys on foot), non-cooperation and *jal samadhi*.

The Marxist ideology, on the other hand, looks at environmental crisis through the economic and the political prism. Profiteering, which is the central principle of capitalism, results in environmental degradation. Ecological Marxists, as they are at times referred to, talk about the need for structural changes. Redistribution of economic resources and political power, they argue, would facilitate ecological balance.

Advocates of appropriate technology are often seen as taking a 'middle path'. According to this view, technology which is suitable for the social and economic conditions of a particular geographical area should be applied. Not only is it sustainable but it also promotes self-reliance among those using it. It advocates a fine balance between industry and agriculture, traditional methods and modern ones, and big and small entities (Kumar 2015, 313–17).

ARCHETYPAL ENVIRONMENTAL MOVEMENTS IN INDIA

MOVEMENTS AROUND FORESTS AND PROTECTED AREAS

Movements related to forests began with the inception of state control over forests and their commercial exploitation. The colonial government understood the value of forests for getting resources like timber for building railway tracks, ships and so on. In order to strengthen its hold over forests, the colonial government set up Indian Forest Department (then called the Imperial Forest Department) in 1864. Deforestation and commercial exploitation of forests increased, while access of the local people to forests was curtailed. The government introduced the Indian Forest Act of 1927 under which certain forests were granted protection which led to denial of access to the local people. This affected their livelihood and added to their woes and their resentment against the government. Nomads, artisans, shifting cultivators, food gatherers, hunters, pastoral people, peasants and many others went against the government's forest policies. Skirmishes and conflicts started occurring in different areas.

Ironically, similar forest policies were adopted by the state after Independence. The National Forest Policy of 1952 was very similar to the forest Policy adopted by the British in 1894. It enforced the exclusive rights of the state over forests, its control, protection, growth and use. This policy was in tandem with the developmental model adopted by the government of a modern industrial, urbanized nation based on modern technology and science. This model required mobilization of resources in large and ever increasing quantities, thus putting immense pressure on natural resources like the forests. The unimpeded exploitation of the forests by the corrupt, powerful and rich led to their devastation and ecological crisis (Bandopadhyay 1985).

Although protests around forests occurred in pre-Independence times, in contemporary India, there is some difference between the two types of uprisings. While the earlier protests were against the claims of the state over forests as against that of the people, now they should also be seen in the context of fast diminishing forest resources.

The following sections contain an account of few of the classical movements around forests including Chipko, Appiko and Silent valley along with an account of the various issues related to protected areas and uprisings around them.

CHIPKO MOVEMENT

Chipko movement is often known as the first organized environmental movement in India which brought the environmental issues to the forefront of policy making. Before Chipko, there was little collective awareness of the ecological issues confronting the country. Although India signed the Stockholm Declaration of 1972 on environment under the aegis of United Nations, it was far behind many developed nations who had already passed legislations in this regard. It is only with a grassroots level mobilization like Chipko that environment became an issue of prominence in India (Chakraborty 1999).

Chipko was a prototype of a protest against commercial felling of trees. While for the people, the forests represented in their words, 'What do forests bear? Soil, water and pure air'. On the other hand, the contractors who fell the trees saw the forests as, 'What do forests bear? Profit, resin and timber' (Shiva 2010, 284).

This movement inspired similar uprisings in India and abroad. An important 'new social movement', at times, also referred to as a peasant, women's or even a movement for a separate state, it is indicative of the various features which either intertwine with it or have developed in different stages of the movement leading to serious debates among academicians.

The movement developed in the 1970s in the Tehri Garhwal hills of the then Uttar Pradesh, although it is widely believed that its origins lie in 1968 celebration (30 May) of the Tilari martyrs day, when many were killed or injured by the British forces for protesting against their control and exploitation of the Himalayan forests at Tilari in Tehri Garhwal region in 1930 (Chakraborty 1999). It was on this day in 1968 that people of western Himalayas took a pledge to protect their forests from commercial exploitation and deforestation.

Chipko, which means 'hugging the tree', is known for its unique method of preventing the felling of trees. The first record of this type of resistance (of hugging the tree with one's body to stop their lopping) is that of Bishnois of Jodhpur, Rajasthan who prevented tree felling by the princely state in 1730. The state had to give up its programme following the protest. 'The image of a woman embracing a tree as a divine spirit or as she would her child is one that men cannot violate with impunity'. It is difficult to say whether this form of protest actually travelled from Rajasthan to the Garhwal hills or whether it was a natural form of protest among people from a similar sociocultural milieu (Brara 2004, 110).

While studying the history of Garhwal region, Ramchandra Guha highlighted how the colonial state indulged in commercial use of the forests leading to environmental degradation. This triggered off peasant revolts. While the peasants wanted subsistence use of the forests such as fuel, fodder, timber and other minor forest products, the state exploited its resources leading to ecological disasters. The coming of Independence did not change the situation. If at all the exploitation of the forests and the hills increased putting immense pressure on the ecological system and the people. By the 1960s, felling of trees, replacing mixed deciduous forests with profitable pine plantations, road building, houses and so on increased immensely making the area vulnerable to disasters.

It was the floods of Alaknanda river in 1970 (of the kind mentioned by Mira Behn, quoted in the beginning of this chapter) and the massive devastation that occurred which made people realize the grim situation that they were faced with. The trigger for the movement came from these floods which made people realize the importance of maintaining ecological balance in their livelihood and lives. A realization started dawning that while deforestation has to be controlled and minimized, rejuvenation of forests should happen simultaneously. A number of progressive individuals came forward to increase people's awareness and mobilize them for collective action. One such person was Ghanashyam Silani, who highlighted the plight of the hills and the people through his folk poetry. His songs helped in creating a positive atmosphere for a grassroots level movement (Chakraborty 1999).

During this time, there was a dominance of Gandhian influence in this region which led to the setting up of a number of Gram Swarajya Sanghs (village self-rule leagues) which aimed to build 'alternative technology to use forest products' and promote employment and small industries at the local level (Omvedt 1993, 132). In the early phase of the movement, it was one of these groups by the name of Dasholi Gram Swarajya Sangh led by Chandi Prasad Bhatt which played a central role. The immediate event which started the people's protest happened in early 1973 when the government officials refused to give permission to the villagers to fell some ash trees for making tools for use in agriculture, while it allowed a sports goods manufacturing company to do so. This led to meetings and massive protests against the contract system. People from the Sarvodaya movement and the youth supporting left-wing ideology also joined in the agitations. It was in a meeting held in Gopeshwar in 1973, which was attended by the local people, village heads, journalists and political workers, that a strategy was formulated to prevent contractors from felling the trees. This was done at times by chasing them away and at other times by hugging the trees with their bodies to prevent felling.

The protests spread to other areas with women participating in large numbers as they have always been more closely connected to nature and forests, while majority of the men were migrant labourers who worked on the plains. This became amply visible in the case of Reni incident of 1974.[4] Under the leadership of Gaura Devi, a large number of women, mainly agricultural labourers, prevented the felling of trees in this region by embracing the trees. There were no male leaders or activists. This initiative of women to protect their traditional right on forests gave a new direction to the movement (Chakraborty 1999; Joshi 1982).

While women played an important role in the movement, there were students from different parts of the hill region, mostly inspired by Marxist ideology, who came to support the movement. Initially, their fight was for the rights of the forest labourers which was later modified to include their opposition to the forest policies and the commercial felling of trees. These groups supported Gandhians and their agenda in the movement. There were points of confluence between the two streams of thinking—to work for the upliftment of the local people, to help them set up small scale, forest-based industries and to prevent commercial forestry. Under the leadership of Uttarakhand Sangharsh Vahini (USV), many pro-left students joined hands to prevent a paper industry in the Chanchridhar forest of Almora district to cut trees in 1978.

A Gandhian, Sunderlal Bahuguna, working in the Bhagirathi valley, took the movement forward from here. Bahuguna is often referred to as an 'ecological radical' as he at one time rejected agriculture itself since 'it took more land to feed people with grain than with tree products'. A saintly figure, he tirelessly undertook padyatras through the length and breadth of the region to spread awareness and mobilize people around the movement. Fasts in Gandhian style, lectures and through writings, Bahuguna gave a momentum to the movement.

...Chipko movement has developed into a powerful mass based ecological movement for permanent economy against the traditional short-sighted and destructive economy. The main contention of this movement is that the main gift of the Himalayas to the nation is water and its function is to produce,

---

[4] In 1974, large area of the forest was auctioned to a private contractor by the forest department near Reni village in Joshimath block, an area which was devastated in the Alaknanda floods of 1970.

maintain and improve soil structure. Hence felling of green trees for commercial purposes should be stopped forthwith for at least ten to fifteen years, until green coverage of at least 60 percent area is restored as professed in the National Forest Policy of 1952. (Bahuguna 1981, 7–8)

Bahuguna undertook a padyatra from Kashmir to Kohima, a distance of 4,870 kilometres from 1981 to 1983 to create awareness on the need to preserve natural resources. The movement under Bahuguna achieved a major success in 1981 when the government suspended all commercial forestry for a period of 15 years.

Debates around Chipko Movement

As has been pointed earlier, Chipko movement has been identified in different ways by different people. At times, it is designated as a peasant movement, at other times as ecofeminist, and often as an environmental movement according to different ideological persuasions and understanding of the movement. Guha sees Chipko movement as one movement in a series of peasant uprisings which occurred over the years due to commercial forestry imposed on the Garhwal hills, initially by the British and later by the government of independent India. Although early protests were not identified as ecological in nature at that time, they were voices against commercial forestry and for subsistence use of natural resources. Thus, Chipko for Guha is essentially a peasant and an ecological movement (Guha 1989).

On the other hand, activists like Vandana Shiva are of the view that Chipko is a movement of ecofeminism,[5] thus giving a feminist identity to it.

…underlying the Chipko movement is an appreciation of the fact that women's interests in the environment arise from a gendered division of labour wherein they are largely responsible for the daily provisioning of fodder, water, and fuel, and Chipko as an archetype draws on this reserve. (Brara 2004, 110)

It has been said that women and their *mahila mandals* have been concerned with food, fodder and other minor forest products and thus have been inclined towards subsistence economy and protection of the forest from commercial use. On the other hand, men, many of whom work as migrant labour on the plains and control the gram panchayats are more inclined towards commercial activities in the forest areas. It is believed that men would often sell commercially grown produce to buy liquor and tobacco (for further details see Chapter 3).

Gabriele Dietrich has pointed out two important limitations of Vandana Shiva's framework of ecofeminism. The first is that Shiva unproblematically uses the term 'feminine principle' derived

---

[5] The term ecofeminism draws attention to the view that development of science and technology leads to subordination of nature and simultaneously to the subordination of women. The term was first given by French writer Francoise d'Eaubonne.

largely from upper caste Hindu sensibilities which in a way excludes the sensibilities of lower caste Hindus as well as non-Hindus. This, she fears, in the context of growing majoritarianism, could very well be appropriated by what is sometimes described as the Hindu Right. Dietrich also points out that Shiva's framework does not question the role of caste-based hierarchy in the kind of relationship between humans and nature that she advocates. In other words, a caste-based patriarchal society could well be living an ecologically sustainable system.

Bina Agarwal (1992) is the other scholar who has a comprehensive critique of Shiva's positions. She is uncomfortable with the latter's attempts to essentialize women as nature which in the process bypasses the question of the material rooting of the relationship of men and women to nature. Shiva characterizes pre-colonial India as having democratic and community based systems to manage the environment. This too is a lens that is not acceptable to Agarwal, since history and sociology do not substantiate these assumptions. She argues that the pre-colonial arrangements were also based on power and property relations which were unequal and certainly unjust. Hence, she advances an alternative to ecofeminism and terms it as environmental feminism—an approach that would be mindful of the social and economic relations that went into the making of varying ecological management approaches.

Underlying Philosophies of Chipko

Chipko has often been perceived as a 'fractured movement' as it was influenced by different ideologies and viewpoints in its different phases. On the one hand, there was the Gandhian ideology and its influence on two of the most important leaders of the movement, Chandi Prasad Bhatt and Sunderlal Bahuguna, although they differed in important respects. On the other hand, there was Marxist influence through USV (Chakraborty 1999, 39).

Chandi Prasad Bhatt, a Gandhian, was an important leader in the initial stages of the movement, from 1968 to 1976. While condemning exploitation of forests by outsiders, he advocated that forest resources should be available to the local people for their use and for small forest-based labour intensive industries. This could be achieved through 'people's cooperatives'. He did not reject all exploitation of forest resources but instead believed that such resources should be available to the local people who could set up local industries and who would also look after the forests. 'Preservation of forests was considered necessary not for water, air or soil alone but more than that to ensure supply of raw materials to local industries'. He advocated appropriate technology as a way forward (Chakraborty 1999, 35).

Sunderlal Bahuguna gave a broader, ecological explanation of the crisis in this region and an ecological solution. Economic development is based on 'new distribution of goods produced by the existing resource intensive and resource wasteful technologies' (Bahuguna 1994). 'At the resource level, it consumes more resources to produce less useful goods.... At the human level, it displaces labour in labour-surplus context and thus destroys livelihoods instead of creating them'

(Bandyopadhyay and Shiva 1988). It was Bahuguna who, in true Gandhian style, gave an ecological solution to the problems of hill people through a call for 're-establishment of a harmonious relationship between man and nature' (Bahuguna 1994, 21).

USV was entrenched in Marxist ideology, and thus, they perceived the relationship of man and nature through class concept. They talked about structural economic changes which would facilitate ecological balance.

Despite these ideological differences and perceived objectives, each of these strands greatly influenced the movement, helped in mobilizing the masses and participated collectively in different phases of the movement. It should also be noted that none of these ideological streams had at any stage a total control of the movement.

By 1980s, the movement started to decline, although Sunderlal Bahuguna, with support from a small section, continued by opposing the construction of Tehri dam.

> *However, part of the Chipko critique, that government policy in Uttar Pradesh hills was insensitive to the region's ecological and social specificity and was driven by the concern to maximize revenues which were appropriated by a bureaucracy based in the plains, formed the core of a movement for regional autonomy. (Rangan 2000, 167–70, 180–84)*

For the next two decades, a movement for a separate hill state ravaged this region. It was in the year 2000 that a new state comprising the hill districts called Uttarakhand was finally formed.

Analysts have raised many questions regarding Chipko and its identity as an environmental movement. While it was popularized in India and globally as a 'subaltern environmental movement' which signified the 'environmentalism of the poor', questions are being raised regarding these credentials of the movement (Baviskar 2005, 167).

APPIKO MOVEMENT

Inspired by Chipko, a movement developed in the Uttara Kannada district of Karnataka, which came to be known as Appiko movement. This area is an ecologically sensitive area of the Western Ghats. Led by Panduranga Hegde, the movement developed as a reaction against commercial forestry which was destroying the forests, leading to deforestation, soil erosion and drying up of water resources. These factors were negatively impacting the lives and livelihoods of the local people. In the year 1983, many people including women and children of Salkani village success-fully prevented felling of trees by hugging them. The youth took an oath to prevent felling of trees. Not only did the Appiko activists demand a complete ban on felling of trees, they also aggressively pursued afforestation in the denuded areas. In addition to this, they played an important role in creating awareness about the importance of Western Ghats and their valuable natural reserves. They also advocated discovering alternative sources of energy to protect forests. Their approach was non-violent just as in Chipko movement. Sit-ins, rallies, street plays and folk dances became their standard way of putting pressure on those in power. An organization by the name Parisar Sanrakshan Kendra (Environment Conservation Centre) played a crucial role in this movement.

'The movement succeeded in protecting the existing forest cover, afforestation, rational use of natural resources and saving the livelihood resources for the people' (Kumar 2015, 322).

SILENT VALLEY MOVEMENT

Silent Valley is the southernmost part of the Western Ghats, nestled in the Malabar region at a height of about 100 metres in the Palakkad district of the state of Kerala. It has Nilambar and Nilgiri forests to the north and Attapadi forests to the east. Silent Valley comprises 8,950 hectares of unspoiled forest rich in fauna and flora. It boasts of some rare and endangered species like the lion-tailed macaque, the second most threatened primate species in the world. The valley has some rare species of herbal plants. It has at least 20 genes for pest and disease control of rice (Chakraborty 1998).

The movement began when the Kerala State Electricity Board (KSEB) decided to construct a 240 MW hydroelectric dam (medium sized) over the Kunthipuzha[6] River. The British first thought of making a dam here in 1929. It was many decades later in the late 1970s that the proposal materialized. There were multiple reasons cited in favour of the dam. It was in line with the country's objectives to bring about industrial development. For this, production of power is essential, hence the dam. Another justification for the dam was the low economic status of the people of Kerala, especially that of the Northern part. The project got a lot of support from the local people because they thought it would help to ameliorate their status and facilitate development of the whole region. It was also supported by the political class of all hues as it was seen as a populist project. 'The Silent Valley issue in Kerala demonstrated the aggressive All-Party ignorance of ecological balance' (Iyer 1992, 130). Other reasons given in favour of the dam are that hydel power uses renewable natural resources, is less polluting and cheaper.

The proposal for the construction of the dam sent shock waves in the state. A network called Kerala Sasthra Sahithya Parishad[7] (KSSP), which included teachers from rural schools along with

---

[6] There is a belief in this region that the name of the river Kunthipuzha was given by the Pandavas after the name of their mother Kunti, when they stayed for some time in this valley during their exile.
[7] Kerala Sasthra Sahithya Parishad (meaning Kerala Science Literature Movement) was founded in 1962 in Kozhikode, Kerala. It has over 60,000 members and more than 2,000 centres all over the state. Its main goal has been to popularize and spread science and scientific outlook among the masses. Protection of environment is one of its defined goals.

middle class professionals and the local people and had been active in the state since 1962, realized the destructive potential of such a dam in this rare storehouse of nature's bounty. Although closely aligned to the Communist Party of India (Marxist) (CPI [M]) which was supporting the dam project, KSSP aggressively opposed it. Many well-known persons of different hues gave their support to the movement. These include Dr M. S. Swaminathan, Dr Salim Ali and the poet Sugatha Kumari. In fact, Sugatha Kumari's poem, 'Marathinu Stuti: Poetry to a Tree' symbolized the movement (Kumar 2015).

Along with KSSP and its supporters, the Silent Valley movement got its inspiration from environment activists and organizations, some of whom approached the government at the centre highlighting the importance of Silent Valley as a valuable natural resource and urged it to stop the dam project. Following this, the central government set up a task force to look into the matter with Zafar Futehally (then the vice-president of World Wildlife Fund [WWF]) as the chairman (D'Monte 1985). The task force powerfully recommended the scrapping of the dam project and highlighted the unique biodiversity of the Silent Valley region in 1977. In the same year, more support for this stand came from WWF and International Union for Conservation of Nature and Natural Resources (IUCN) comprising a group of primatologists from America who passed a resolution favouring preservation of Silent Valley. Others like 'Friends of Trees' in Bombay filed a public interest litigation (PIL) in 1978 in Kerala High Court and got a stay on dam construction for two weeks. In 1979, a 'Save Silent Valley Committee' was formed which comprised individuals including academicians, scientists, some industrialists as well as organizations such as the Natural Histories Societies of Bombay and Kerala and the Botanical Survey of India (Madras). Along with this, state-run Kerala Forest Research Institute also recommended closing of the project and declaring the area as biosphere reserve. By the late 1970s, a realization was dawning on a large number of people that a dam in this area would destroy a sizeable part of the rainforest and flood a unique natural forest.

Simultaneously, there were voices in favour of the dam such as those of the local people and politicians, mainly under the guidance of KSEB who questioned the ecological value of Silent Valley.

After years of protests, the state government was forced to appoint a high-level committee to go into the ecological, social and economic repercussions of the proposed project. Based on the committee's recommendations, the government through a notification in 1982 decided to give up the project and declared Silent Valley as a national park. Silent Valley movement is one of the successful environmental movements.

PROTESTS AROUND PROTECTED AREAS

A number of uprisings, big and small, have arisen in India around protected areas, particularly in relation to wildlife sanctuaries and national parks. There has been a regular increase in such areas since the early 1970s. For people living inside and around the protected areas, there are a lot of restrictions on entry and use which in turn affect their entitlement portfolio. There is also the issue of displacement without adequate and appropriate compensation. All this is justified by the authorities in the name of conservation, protection, national duty and the like. For them, the local people are responsible for damage to the forests. Many struggles have thus risen around forest resources (Dwivedi 2010, 297–98).

Some measures have been developed to address these issues of the local people. These include creating 'buffer zones' as 'areas between the strictly preserved area and the human settlements'. This has been done under the 'Man and Biosphere Programme' of UNESCO. The aim is to allow some activities to the local people in the buffer zone. However, 'attempts to promote agricultural and rural development programmes alongside conservation measures have yielded poor results because of their largely experimental character, designed principally to reduce conflicts at the local level, rather than to generate sustainable livelihood opportunities and alternatives' (Dwivedi 2010, 297–98).

Protected Areas in India

Protected areas comprise wildlife sanctuaries, national parks and conservation and community reserves. Their numbers and area have continuously increased since 1971. According to a recent estimate, there are (as of July 2016) a total of 733 protected areas in India. They cover 4.89 per cent of its geographical area. Protected areas include 103 national parks, 537 wildlife sanctuaries, 67 conservation reserves and 26 community reserves.

Maximum number of national parks are there in Madhya Pradesh (10), followed by Andaman and Nicobar islands (9), Kerala, West Bengal, Maharashtra and Uttarakhand (6 each). There are as many as 96 wildlife sanctuaries in Andaman and Nicobar, followed by Maharashtra (42) and Tamil Nadu (29). (Edake 2016)

The attitude of the authorities towards the local people as being a threat to both wildlife and the forests is to a great extent corroborated by the urban-based environmentalists. They believe that if these areas are not protected, it will lead to their depletion. The arguments in favour of conservation and protection of forests are that they help to control poaching, enhance awareness and sensitivity towards environment including fauna and flora, decrease the dependence of the local people on forests and create opportunities for alternative occupations. A number of laws have been made due to demands from these environmentalists. These include Wildlife Protection Act (1972 and 1991), the Forest Conservation Act (1980) and the Environment Protection Act (1986).

A NEW DISCOURSE

With increase in protests, a new way of thinking started emerging which questioned the state's policies on protected areas as well as of those environmentalists who supported them. While the state has been accused of having a 'top-down approach' with no involvement or participation of the people, the urban-based environmentalists have been called 'elitist' who have no idea of the ground reality. This new discourse represents the grassroots level protests around forest resources and has been made possible by many NGOs which have helped to articulate their concerns and mobilize public opinion in their favour. Their main demand is to protect rights of the people as well as those of animals. The Forest Rights Act of 2006 was enacted due to their efforts. It gives credence to the rights of the people living in and around the forests on the forest resources. It also gives accountability to conservation.

Tiger Reserves

There are 50 tiger reserves in India. These are those national parks and wildlife sanctuaries which have a sizeable population of tigers and have thus been labelled as tiger reserves. They have a special status and have utmost protection. (Edake 2016)

It was in the year 1994 that a group of NGOs and activists got together in New Delhi to look into the issues confronting the people who live in and around protected areas. It was unanimously agreed that they need a forum to become their voice, a forum that will help to create a dialogue between the officials of forest and wildlife departments and the people, majority of whom are marginalized tribals. The forum would also find alternative approaches to conservation. Following this meeting, in early 1995, a yatra (peaceful march) was organized to visit 18 national parks and sanctuaries, including some of the most famous ones, spread over the states of Gujarat, Madhya Pradesh, Maharashtra, Rajasthan, Uttar Pradesh and Delhi. They covered a distance of 14,000 kilometres in 50 days. The participants were representatives of the local people, NGOs and environment activists. The aim of the yatra (Jungle Jivan Bachao Yatra) was manifold. It varied from understanding the status of the forests and the wildlife, the issues of contention with the local people and creating awareness on environment issues in the process (Dwivedi 2010).

Mukul Sharma in his book *Green and Saffron* argues that environmentalism and politics cannot be seen as disconnected from one another. Ultra-nationalist ideologies often espouse the cause of environment divorced from questions of equity and justice. (Sharma 2012)

Wildlife Sanctuaries and National Parks

Wildlife sanctuaries and national parks are ecologically rich and comprise a vast variety of fauna and flora including some rare and endangered species. As a protected area, a national park is meant for conservation of animals where human beings are not allowed any activities which would harm them in any way. Any minor or major activities whether it is timber harvesting, collecting forest products for subsistence or private ownership rights are disallowed. The wildlife sanctuaries which also aim at conservation of animals allow such human activities as mentioned earlier, provided they do not harm or interfere in the lives of the animals and their interests. While conservation of animals is paramount in both, there are certain important differences. The boundaries of a national park are well defined, whereas that of a sanctuary are more porous; grazing of livestock is strictly prohibited in national parks, whereas it is allowed in a controlled manner in sanctuaries; certain rights of people are allowed in a sanctuary but they have to be settled in national parks and finally, a national park cannot be downgraded to a sanctuary, whereas a sanctuary can be upgraded to a national park.

ISSUES OF CONTENTION AND THE PROTESTS AROUND THEM

Several contentious issues around which protests and movements have occurred which came to the lime light during the yatra are given in the following.

Grazing Rights

Grazing rights were traditionally enjoyed by the local communities but were now visibly restricted in the protected areas such as Rajaji National Park in Uttarakhand and Ranthambore and Bharatpur in Rajasthan. In Rajaji National Park, the local Gujjar community has been agitating for these traditional rights to be restored. In the meanwhile, bribing the forest officials or letting the cattle stray into the protected area in violation of the rules are common. In Melghat in Maharashtra, the forest officials allowed the locals to carry head loads of grass from the buffer zone to feed their cattle. This was resented by them as they felt that it is extra work to carry grass when the cattle could just enter the area and graze.

Fuel Wood

Another issue that has led to confrontation between the locals and the forest officials is that of fuel wood. The locals use it for cooking, keeping their homes warm during winter months and for special occasions such as marriages and funerals when they would require large quantities.

Earlier, they had free access to fuel wood but now this access is restricted or denied. As a result, they routinely bribe forest officials to get fuel wood, often, more than what they actually require. There are fixed rates for a head load. The extra wood is sold by the locals, mainly women and children, to nearby rural areas where there is more scarcity. While the activists say that free access will mean judicious usage and no bribes, the officials believe that it will lead to wasteful usage and deforestation.

Joint Forest Management (JFM) Scheme: To address this issue of fuel wood, some state governments have launched a JFM scheme which is based on managing the forest jointly by the forest officials and the locals. Under this scheme, the forest department, in partnership with the locals 'takes on protection, regeneration and plantation of forests'. It addresses the problem of fuel wood and fodder for the locals. There are other benefits for the locals. Dense forest patches are cleared intermittently by JFM committee. Of the timber which is sold in the market, 25 per cent of it goes to the local community. 'After twenty five years, when the forest matures for harvesting, 50% of the sales proceeds would accrue to the local community'. It has been considered as a successful scheme. While the fodder, fuel and other requirements like logs for house repairs and so on are taken care of under the supervision of JFM committees, it also protects the forest area from depletion. There are, however, disadvantages of the scheme as well. As the JFM committee controls the village pasture land, access to it is controlled by the JFM committee and is meant only for the members, whereas earlier it was free access for all. Moreover, it is the rural landowner male population who often control the JFM committee, whereas poor tribals, the landless and women do not have a say. It is ironical that these are the very people who control agricultural land and they also control forest areas. Further, the scheme 'promotes monoculture of the species which have high market value, thereby reducing biodiversity. The proposed harvest of the forest in 20 years implies that nothing of the "forest" would remain after the harvest' (Dwivedi 2010, 302–03).

It is also true that the whole scheme was to be based on participation of all but it has been observed that there is dominance of forest officials in decision-making. Then there are usual delays and inadequacy in implementation of various provisions of the scheme.

Issue of Minor Forest Products (MFPs)

The issue of MFPs is the other major issue of confrontation. These products include gum, honey, bidi/*kendu* leaves, berries, roots, fruits, saag seeds, vegetables, lac, *mahua* and so on. The MFPs are essential for survival of the local tribals and other marginalized groups till agriculture season starts after the rains. While this is so, it is also true that state forest departments control those MFPs which give big profits such as the bidi/*kendu* leaves and gum in Madhya Pradesh and Gujarat where profits run in crores.

The locals in Vasava villages in Shoolpaneshwar, Gujarat, under the leadership of Gujarat Vanavasi Sangathan have been demanding free access to MFPs. Similar agitations have been taking place in some other protected areas as well.

Commercial Use of Forests

The use of forest lands by the local communities has also been hampered by commercial and industrial considerations which at times weigh upon forest officials to take decisions in favour of the rich and the influential. It has been seen that commercial and industrial activities have been allowed in a number of protected areas which has resulted in their degradation. Then powerful groups put pressure on the officials to denotify these areas so that industries can be set up in these areas, purely for commercial considerations.

Biosphere Reserves

UNESCO started 'Man and the Biosphere Programme (MAB)' in 1971 with the aim of conserving all forms of life in their natural ecosystem and develop a referral system for monitoring changes. There are 18 such biospheres in India. Among them are Sunderbans in West Bengal, Khangchendzonga mountains in Sikkim, Rann of Kutch in Gujarat, Gulf of Mannar in Tamil Nadu, Nanda Devi mountains in Uttarakhand and so on.

It was found that many commercial activities such as 'bamboo extraction' from Shoolpaneshwar Sanctuary by Central Pulp Mills and 'open-cast marble mining' in Jamva Ramgarh Sanctuary in Rajasthan are being carried out, whereas the local people are troubled for usufruct. It should also be noted that a number of national parks and wildlife sanctuaries have been or are on the verge of being denotified. 'The Narayan Sarovar Sanctuary in Kutch, for example, has recently been denotified to make way for a cement factory, while the Gulf of Kutch marine national park faces denotification because of a proposed oil refinery by the Reliance industries' (Dwivedi 2010, 304).

It is clear that those who are meant to protect allow such activities to take place, all in the name of conservation, protection of wildlife and the like. While the justification given for mining was employment opportunities for the local people, bamboo extraction was said to be good for herbivorous animals that need sunshine.

Destroying of Crops by Stray Animals

Another issue of contention is that of crop damage by stray animals. Wild boars often damage crops of local farmers leading to confrontation between the conservationists and the local population living in and around the protected area. This has led to a huge loss to the local economy as well. Organizations like Maharashtra Arogya Mandal have been involved in quantifying and highlighting these losses which are often phenomenal. The different state governments do not give compensation for crop damage as, according to them, it is difficult to assess the extent of damage and to work out on compensation. They, however, give compensation for any harm to persons or cattle by the wild animals like elephants.

It is clear that instances of damage to crops occur more often because of the increase in the population of herbivores. While the forest officials are quick to claim that it is because of success of conservation, there is a flip side to it. It also indicates that the population of carnivores is decreasing. It has been found that wherever cases of poaching of carnivores occur, there the population of herbivores is high.

Claims on Forest Lands

Occupying forest lands, cultivating them and making demands for regularization is a common practice. While for the forest officials and conservationists, it is illegal and an infringement of public property, for the local tribals and other marginalized persons, they have always used forest areas and it is a matter of survival for them.

Sunderban Islands: A Theatre of Strife

Sunderbans is an ecologically sensitive zone, the largest remaining natural habitat of the Royal Bengal tiger and the largest Mangrove forest area. It has been designated as a National Park and the World Heritage site. A recent study based on public hearings (conducted in 2016) revealed the extent of hardships faced by the local people (who are mainly Dalits, Adivasis and backward Muslim castes) despite the Forest Rights Act of 2006 which recognizes the rights of those living in and around forests to forest resources.

The study questions the role of the forest department in severely curtailing the use of the forests by the locals which has led to large-scale migrations in the area.

The fact that when people risk their lives and go for honey collection, they are more afraid of the Forest Department officials seeing them and harassing them (no matter whether they have the licences and papers), than a Tiger attack, is a matter that must enter the debate around 'man and animal conflict'. (The Research Collective [TRC], unit of Programme For Social Action 2017, 73)

Sunderbans Public Hearing on FRA Implementation in 2016

Source: Media Collective
Photograph Courtesy: The Media Collective. Reproduced with Permission.

MOVEMENTS AROUND DAMS: INTERROGATING THE ROUTE TO DEVELOPMENT

Construction of big multipurpose dams in different parts of the country have brought environmentalists together to highlight their negative impact on the environment and on the people in the line of fire, by displacing them and depriving them of their livelihood and culture. Almost always, these negative fallouts have affected the poor and the marginalized tribes more than others. Hence, a number of movements have developed around dam projects like Tungabhadra and Ghataprabha in the south, Tehri and Pong dams in the north, Bedthi and Bhopalpatnam in the west, Kosi and Gandak in the east and the Narmada valley project in central India.

NARMADA BACHAO ANDOLAN

Few movements in India have achieved the kind of worldwide publicity which NBA has received. Among the most talked about and documented movements till date, NBA has a history of more than three decades. It was in 1985 that the movement started its crusade against the building of several dams across the Narmada river such as the Sardar Sarovar Project, Maheshwar dam and the Narmada Sagar Project (NSP) under the Narmada River Project of the government in central India.

In different areas where the dams are being built, people from different backgrounds and classes are participating in the movement. The protests against Sardar Sarovar Dam (SSD) have brought together upper caste landowners from the plains and poor tribals from the hills. In the case of Maheshwar Dam, those protesting are 'poor lower caste boatmen' and 'caste Hindu farmers'. The factors that link these diverse groups are their concern of displacement, of losing their livelihood and land. For the tribals, the concern is also of losing their rich culture and their ecologically sustainable lifestyle. It is well known that the use of natural resources by the tribals or other marginalized groups is never destructive but it is judicious and environment friendly in comparison to the aggressive and highly destructive use for industries or commerce (Baviskar 2005, 167).

NBA Agitation

Source: Media Collective and Narmada Archives
Photograph Courtesy: The Media Collective. Reproduced with Permission.

NBA Satyagraha in 1996

Source: Media Collective and Narmada Archives
Photograph Courtesy: The Media Collective. Reproduced with Permission.

NBA AGAINST SSD

Among the various movements around Narmada dams, the most prominent has been the one against the SSD. Although the movement was already brewing since 1985, it emerged as a consolidated uprising in 1989 under the leadership of Medha Patkar. As pointed earlier, barring some upper caste Hindu landowners, a majority of the local people who joined the movement were poor marginalized tribals. The massive size and height of SSD, although on the one hand promised power and water to thousands, it brought untold miseries to very large populations, mainly in Madhya Pradesh tribal belt whose very existence was threatened by it. Their 'distinctive life in the forested hills of the river valley and dependence on forests and a close-knit village community' came under a cloud with no possibility of ever replacing it (Baviskar 2005, 167).

Two conflicting groups

It should be noted that there are two distinct groups associated with the SSD who have opposing goals. There are those activists, academics and intellectuals who are associated with the movement and oppose the dam as anti-people, against cultures and environment. Then there are others including those who are benefitting from the dam and the technocrats, politicians, bureaucrats associated with it who consider the dam as a symbol of development which will bring prosperity. They consider those opposing it as anti-national.

Sardar Sarovar Dam

SSD is a gravity dam built on Narmada river near Navagam, Gujarat. The project was inaugurated by Jawaharlal Nehru on 15 April 1961. It took shape in 1979. It is among the biggest dams in India for producing hydroelectricity and increasing irrigation. The dam was declared complete and was dedicated to the nation by the Prime Minister of India on 17 September 2017.

The resettlement and rehabilitation (R&R) of the Sardar Sarovar affected families is governed by the Narmada Water Dispute Tribunal Award (NWDTA), each of the states' policy, the two main judgments of the Supreme Court of India (2000 and 2005) and the latest order of the Supreme Court on R&R which came on 8 February 2017.

Three Levels of Protest

Oommen has identified three levels of protest against SSD. One is at the grassroots level where demands vary from compensation, resettlement to rehabilitation. The issues here are the quality and quantity of compensation, livelihood opportunities, shelter and other such material concerns. The mobilizations at this level are micro level; they are not against the dam per se but reflect concerns for material benefits. 'These mobilizations do not make a movement in that there is no articulated ideological content to them. They are elementary collective behaviour caused by insecurity due to the feared loss of shelter and means of livelihood' (Oommen 2010, 323).

The second level is regarding displacement. The questions they raise are on whether displacement is necessary and advocate that it should be reduced to the very minimum. These mobilizations are ideological as they question the very logic of dams which compromises the interests of thousands. The mobilization at this level is 'norm-oriented' and 'meso in orientation'. It involves activists and academics (Oommen 2010).

The third level of mobilizations question the development model itself, with its focus on big technology-driven projects like SSD. These are macro level mobilizations by intellectuals at the level of the nation or internationally. They are 'value oriented' movements which question the issue of ecological imbalance and damaging of people's lives. While the grassroots level mobilizations may not be aware of these issues or may not be able to articulate them, the academics and activists at the meso level are aware but are not endowed to raise them. Such issues are raised by the intellectuals who are better equipped to look at the larger picture. It is believed that macro level mobilizations are few and far between (Oommen 2010, 324).

'The NBA-initiated mobilizations have all these three components coalesced into one'. Starting with material benefits of first level, through displacement issue of the second to contesting the basic idea of development at the third level, the NBA movement has them all. This transition occurred gradually due to the interaction of the NBA activists with the state. Initial mobilizations began at the grassroots level to expedite the generous compensation announced by the state like giving land in lieu of land and even to the landless, in the 'command area of the project'. After a while, people found the government dithering on its promises. All it was doing was to divert their attention in order to avoid any confrontation. It was in these circumstances that the movement revisited the core issues. They took a major ideological stand rejecting the development model applied by the government as anti-people and anti-environment. In defiance of the government, the movement labelled SSD type of projects as destructive (Oommen 2010, 324).

For a movement to survive, the macro ideological goals stated by its leaders should be in tandem with the material needs of the people. According to Oommen, this union is present in the case of the NBA movement making it a congenial and effective movement that has continued for so long.

SUPPORT FOR THE NBA

As the movement progressed over the decades, a number of organizations and eminent personalities from both within and outside India joined hands at different points of time to give it the necessary push and to make it one of the most famous environmental movements in India as well as internationally. NGOs such as 'Narmada Ghati Nav Nirman Samiti' in Madhya Pradesh, 'Vahini and Narmada Asargrastha Samiti' in Gujarat and 'Narmada Dharangrastha Samiti' in Maharashtra backed the movement. International organizations such as 'European Greens groups', 'International Rivers Network', 'Friends of Earth', 'Environmental Defence Fund' and 'Sierra Club' strongly supported the movement.

It was under pressure from organizations like these that World Bank withdrew its funding for SSD in 1992. When despite the withdrawal of the World Bank, the dam work continued, the movement approached the Supreme Court which temporarily halted work on the dam. However, the Supreme Court allowed the raising of the height of the dam in 1999. Many intellectuals like Arundhati Roy and others joined the movement. Roy along with the film maker Jharna Javeri went on a lecture cum film showing tour called 'Rally for the Valley' in September 1999 to North America and Europe which was a thumping success. The movement gained in publicity both in and outside the country. Many personalities from the world of cinema/literature etc. voiced their support. It was around this time that the foreign partners for Maheshwar dam withdrew due to pressure from various quarters.

PRESENT STATUS

A press release by NBA on 25 July 2017 is indicative of the present state of affairs. In a desperate appeal it said,

> *without completing just rehabilitation of thousands of families in Madhya Pradesh, the government of Madhya Pradesh with the centre's blessings is all ready to forcibly evict and throw the families with the children and aged, out in the tin sheds of 180 sq. feet which can't even accommodate their belongings, why talk of persons and their cattle. Yesterday the police force brought in for this operation carried out a mock drill in Badwani and continued with its intimidation tactics towards vacating the villages.*

Government of Madhya Pradesh seemed to be ready to sacrifice the lives and rights of lakhs of people with police force and water floods.

Ignoring such appeals and the serious social and environmental issues related to the dam height of 138.68 m, the government at the centre and the states, have gone ahead with the project, even declaring the R&R (rehabilitation and resettlement) process as more or less complete.

30 Year Celebration of NBA in Delhi in 2014

Source: Media Collective and Narmada Archives
Photograph Courtesy: The Media Collective. Reproduced with Permission.

With much fanfare, the Prime Minister of India inaugurated the SSD on 17 September 2017, claiming that it will give power and water to millions in Gujarat, Maharashtra and Madhya Pradesh. While this was going on, many led by Medha Patkar stood in waist deep water, demanding just and fair rehabilitation for thousands uprooted by the project. The movement continues its long uphill task for getting thousands their due.

MOVEMENTS AROUND MARINE RESOURCES: FISHWORKERS' MOVEMENT

As India treaded towards the path of modernization, commercialization and mechanization of fisheries started which led to many negative consequences including a threat to the livelihood of traditional fish workers and an imbalance in the whole 'coastal ecosystem'. These changes brought 'new economic agents in the sea. They were in search of quick profits and favoured large scale capital intensive development of fisheries under corporate control' (Kurien 1996, 33). Thus fishing equipment was modernized. Large number of trawlers and mechanized boats entered into the seas as state subsidies became available at cheaper rates. Investments increased substantially. Over time, the demand for shrimps and prawns really increased in the foreign markets. Indiscriminate fishing, quick harvesting became the trend. Fishing period shortened. A mad rush to catch more and more fish, especially shrimps led them to fish closer to the shore. This resulted in destruction of several fish species. An imbalance developed in the ecosystem drastically reducing the total stock of fish available for fishing by traditional fish workers. This led to a crisis in the fisheries sector.

The fish workers initially thought that the stock has depleted only due to monsoon trawling. They later realized that there are a multiple causes of the depletion including mechanization, capitalist pattern of investment and the like. They understood that the only way to save their livelihood is to form strong trade unions. The trade unions have been in the forefront of their movements—whether in Goa, Karnataka or Kerala. The interests of the various unions are today represented by an all India organization, the National Fishworkers Forum (NFF), which has successfully brought the many state level unions together. NFF is an active body which has given a push to the issues confronting fish workers at the national level.

Given further is an illustration of fishworkers' movement in Kerala.

THE FISHWORKERS' MOVEMENT IN KERALA

Located in the coastal districts of Kerala among traditional fishing communities, the movement brought 'the "liberation theology" Christians and Marxists in confrontation and dialogue as it developed almost beyond the visions of both into a popular ecology struggle' (Omvedt 1993, 134).

With the aim of bringing prosperity to the people, the Government of India tied up with the Norwegian government to launch Indo-Norwegian Project (INP) for mechanization of fisheries in three villages of Kerala in 1953. Under this project, technology of trawling (sweeping of the sea floor with mechanized boats) was acquired. The objective was to improve the infrastructure, make the fishing practices better and transform it into a modern industry.

By the 1960s, there started an increased demand for prawns and shrimps. This gave a push to prawn fishery for the purposes of export. In this scenario, the INP diverted its attention to harvesting prawns. They organized training for fishermen to use trawl nets and developed mechanized boats for this purpose. These changes meant high investment, and thus, clamouring towards more exports and more profits. Fishery was no longer an activity of the local people for their sustenance. It got transformed in every sense of the term. New technology as against old simple techniques, trained persons from outside to operate the equipment and not the local fishermen, new players such as traders and exporters making it into a business enterprise as against sale in the local market or for one's own consumption and finally, profit motive as the driving force rather than subsistence. These changes led to many negative impacts. The 'coastal ecosystem' came under threat of destruction. People's livelihood was compromised with in a drastic way. Use of bottom trawlers was destroying the sea base as well as fish eggs and juvenile fish, thus leading to destruction of future fish resource. Further, 'purse seining' involving heavy equipment was depleting fish stock affecting traditional fishermen. These changes threatened the balance in the coastal ecosystem, the immediate catch and the potential resources of the traditional fishermen.

As a result of this situation, conflicts started occurring between the local fishermen and those associated with mechanized fisheries. The conflicts would become more acute during monsoon season as that is also the breeding season of the fish. If trawlers are used, especially near the shore at this time, the catch which is the lifeline of the local fishermen gets severely affected. In the year 1977, a state-level organization called the Latin Catholic Fishermen's Federation (LCFF) sent a memorandum to the chief minister of Kerala with a demand that mechanized boats should operate 5 kilometres away from the coast, that there should be a ban on use of trawlers during monsoon season and that the government should stop pollution on inland water resources.

To press for their demand, LCFF organized a relay hunger strike in November 1978 which lasted for 59 days. However, the mechanized boats continued to operate, so did the clashes. A month later, a fisherman, Babu, died in a clash between his boat and a mechanized boat. This incident sent shock waves among fish workers who organized massive protests. LCFF organized a jeep rally following which its president went on an indefinite hunger strike demanding compensation for Babu's family, police protection for local fishermen and a marine regulation law. The government agreed to all the demands and the strike was called off.

LCFF reinvented itself in 1980, changed its name to make it a secular body representing people from all religions and independent of all political parties. It called itself Kerala 'Swathantra' (independent) 'Matsyathozhilali' (fishworker) Federation (KSMTF). Father Albert Parasivala, a Catholic priest became its president. In May 1981, an order was passed by the state government to ban all trawling during monsoon season. However, within days the government made an exception of Neenadakara, an area with highest number of mechanized boats. Understandably, KSMTF opposed this action and on 25 June, its leaders Father Kocherry and Joychen Antony went on an indefinite hunger strike getting support of thousands of fish workers. Many, who gheraoed the collector's office, were arrested. The government gave in under pressure and decided to set up an expert committee to look into the matter. The committee was called Babu Paul Commission. Although the commission recommended that the interests of the local fishermen should be protected, it did not ban monsoon trawling (Aerthayil 2000).

Meanwhile following a split, with one faction taking on religious identity, KSMTF emerged as a powerful trade union of fish workers with secular credentials inviting members from all religions.

The Babu Paul Commission's recommendations though limited were not implemented which led KSMTF to start another round of agitations in April 1984. A memorandum of demands was presented to the chief minister. With no response forthcoming, rallies, sit-ins, torch light processions and indefinite fasts were organized in different districts of the state. Some 7,000 courted arrest. Around a thousand women protested on the national highways. The agitation attracted huge media coverage. Eventually the government invited the agitators for talks and announced a ban on night trawling and a welfare package of 180 million rupees (Aerthayil 2000).

The struggle continued. It got a major push when two MLAs joined the hunger strike and subsequently, in support of the movement, the whole opposition walked out of the legislative assembly. Thousands marched to the assembly. To appease the protesters, the chief minister met them and announced a package for their pension and education of their children. Although KSMTF called off the agitation, they were not satisfied and vowed to come back. True to their word, they restarted the agitation with rallies, 'fill in the jails' hunger strikes and so on and presented a number of demands to the government. On the government's assurance, the 183 days agitation was finally called off. In the process, the agitation, its objectives and its main leaders got a massive publicity, although there was still no ban on monsoon trawling.

Some years later in 1988, protests were organized in seven districts of the state against monsoon trawling. With no response coming from the government, Father Thomas Kocherry went on an indefinite fast. '1000 fish workers in about 125 big country crafts surrounded the fishing harbour from morning till afternoon'. Following this, at long last, the government announced a ban on monsoon trawling except in Neendakara. However, the announcement did not become an official statute (Aerthayil 2000, 86).

A year later on 26 June 1989, an expert committee on 'marine fisheries resource management' approved a ban on monsoon trawling. This gave a new momentum to the movement and the agitations intensified. Finally, the government gave in and announced a ban on monsoon trawling between 20 July and 31 August all over the coastal line of Kerala. This order was endorsed and ratified by the Kerala High Court followed by the Supreme Court. This was a very big victory for KSMTF, in particular, and the fish workers and their many organizations, in general.

RECENT PROTESTS

In more recent years, fish workers of Kerala have registered their protest against free trade under the Indo ASEAN free trade agreement, as they fear that their interests will be compromised with if free and cheap imports are allowed from these countries. The agitation started in 2009 with KSMTF at the helm of it with a number of other unions. In 2009 itself, the various unions of fish workers in Kerala formed a larger organization called the Kerala Fishworkers Coordination Committee. Under its banner, large numbers converged outside the Parliament house to press for their demands.

WOMEN FISH WORKERS

A special group called the Coastal Women's Forum has been fighting for the cause of women fish workers in Kerala since the 1980s. One example of their acumen is their fight for the right to use public transport to take their ware for selling in the market. They were not allowed to do so due to stigma, hence they were forced to walk long distances. This led to them losing out as those who reached early sold their products easily. After a protracted agitation, these women vendors not only got their right to travel by public transport but they were also given special bus in some areas.

From the aforementioned account, it can be said that the main objectives of the fishworkers' movement in Kerala have been twofold. One, to protect the marine life against indiscriminate exploitation and second to shield their livelihoods from the resource omnivores, in this case, those indulging in mechanized fisheries. The success of the movement is due to a number of factors including formation of a strong trade union, the nature of its objectives, the ability of its leaders to redefine objectives in accordance with changes; the commitment of its leaders and the fish workers; its ability to mobilize fish workers from all over Kerala and other parts of the country; its acumen to gather large-scale support from the mainstream media and the public at large; to be able to sustain the movement over long periods and to be able to regroup with the same enthusiasm when required. These are the reasons for its identity as a successful environmental movement.

CONCLUSION

Beginning with a general overview, this chapter has mainly concentrated on the environmental movements in India, their various causes and locations as well as the commonalities between them. Although limited in its scope, an effort has been made to present in detail Chipko, NBA and Kerala fishworkers' movement which are often identified as three most significant movements which not only impacted the environmental discourse but also inspired other uprisings. It should be noted that there are a vast number of environmental movements spread across India which could not be included here.

At a broad level, it can be said that many of the environmental uprisings are around issues related to forests, their commercial exploitation and their control by authorities in the name of protection; the model of development aggressively pursued by the government whether it is dams and irrigation, mining and industries; commercial use and mechanization of marine resources and their exploitation as well as pollution and wasteful use of resources. Despite these manifold issues and their different locations, there is a common thread which connects them to each other—the demand for an ecologically receptive society pursuing an alternative model of development which is sensitive to human beings and to nature. Implied in this are livelihood issues but at a broader level there is the demand for fixing responsibility, insisting on participation, information sharing, transparency and accountability of the agencies or governments who are entrusted by people to take decisions on their behalf.

POINTS FOR DISCUSSION

- Environmental movements are among the most diverse movements with a wide variety of sites and issues. What are the broad commonalities between them?
- Compare the environmental movements in India with those in the developed world?
- Does the tag of 'environmentalism of the poor' correctly explain environmental movements in India?

REFERENCES AND READINGS

Aerthayil, M. 2000. *Fishworkers' Movement in Kerala (1977–1994)*. New Delhi: Indian Social Institute.

Bandopadhyay, J., and Vandana Shiva. 1988, 11 June 11. 'Political Economy of Ecological Movements'. *Economic and Political Weekly*, 23: 1223–1232.

Bandopadhyay, J., ed. 1985. *India's Environment: Crisis and Responses*. Dehradun: Natraj Publishers.

Bahuguna, Sunderlal. 1981. *Chipko: A Novel Movement for the Establishment of Cordial Relationship between Man and Nature*. 2 vols. Silyara: Chipko Information Centre.

————. 1994. 'Chipko Message: Whither Development'. Silgara, Tehri Garhwal. Chipko Information Centre, Parvatiya Navjivan Mandal.

Baviskar, Amita. 2005. 'Red in Tooth and Claw? Looking for Class in Struggles over Nature'. In *Social Movements in India*, edited by Raka Ray and Mary Fainsod Katzenstein, 161–174. Lanham, MD: Rowman & Littlefield Publishers, INC.

Brara, Rita. 2004. 'Ecology and Environment'. In *Handbook of Indian Sociology*, edited by Veena Das, 88–113. New Delhi: Oxford University Press.

Chakraborty, Somen. 1998. 'The Silent Valley Movement'. In *Contemporary Social Movements in India: Achievements and Hurdles*, edited by Sebasti L. Raj, and Arundhuti Roy Choudhury, 188–200. New Delhi: Indian Social Institute.

————. 1999. *A Critique of Social Movements in India: Experiences of Chipko, Uttarakhand and Fishworkers' Movement*. New Delhi: Indian Social Institute.

D'Monte, Darryl. 1985. *Temples or Tombs? Industry versus Environment, Three Controversies*. New Delhi: Centre for Science and Environment.

Dwivedi, Ranjit. 2010. 'Parks, People and Protest: The Mediating Role of Environmental Action Groups'. In *Social Movements II: Concerns of Equity and Security*, edited by T. K. Oommen, 297–314. New Delhi: Oxford University Press.

Edake, Siddharth S. 17 December 2016. 'The Protected Area Network of India'. TERI (The Energy and Resources Institute). Available at: http://www.teriin.org/opinion/protected-area-network-india (Accessed 11 February 2019).

Gadgil, Madhav, and Ramachandra Guha. 1995. *Ecology and Equity: The Use and Abuse of Nature in Contemporary India*. New Delhi: Penguin.

Guha, Ramachandra. 1989. *The Unquiet Woods: Ecological Change and Peasant Resistance in the Himalaya*. New Delhi: Oxford University Press.

————. 2000. *Environmentalism: A Global History*. New Delhi: Oxford University Press.

Guha, Ramachandra, and Juan Martinez-Alier. 1998. *Varieties of Environmentalism: Essays North and South*. New Delhi: Oxford University Press.

Iyer, V. R. Krishna. 1992. *Environment Protection and Legal Defence*. New Delhi: Sterling Publishers.

Joshi, Gopa. 1982. 'Afforestation of Deforested Himalaya'. In *Hugging the Himalayas: The Chipko Experience*, edited by Shishupal Singh Kunwar, 36–43. Chamoli: Dasholi Gram Swarajya Mandal (DGSM).

Kumar, Dinesh. 2015. 'Environmental Movements in India'. In *Development Process and Social Movements in Contemporary India*, edited by Abhay Prasad Singh, 312–334. New Delhi: Pinnacle Learning.

Kurien, John. 1996. *Towards a New Agenda for Sustainable Small Scale Fisheries Development*. Thiruvananthapuram: South Indian Federation of Fishery Sector.

Menon, Nivedita, ed. 2001. *Gender and Politics in India*. New Delhi: Oxford University Press.

Nisbet, Robert N. 1982. *Prejudices: A Philosophical Dictionary*. Cambridge, MA: Harvard University Press.

Omvedt, Gail. 1993. *Reinventing Revolution: New Social Movements and the Socialist Tradition in India*. Armonk, NY: An East Gate Book, M. E. Sharpe.

Oommen, T. K. 2010. 'Protest against Displacement by Development Projects'. In *Social Movements II: Concerns of Equity and Security*, edited by T. K. Oommen, 317–332. New Delhi: Oxford University Press.

Rangan, Haripriya. 2000. *Of Myths and Movements: Rewriting Chipko into Himalayan History*. New Delhi: Oxford University Press.

Rootes, C. A. 1990. 'Theory of Social Movements: Theory for Social Movements?' *Philosophy and Action*, 16 (4): 5–17.

Rootes, Christopher. 2004. 'Environmental Movements'. In *The Blackwell Companion to Social Movements*, edited by David A. Snow, Sarah A. Soule, and Hanspeter Kriesi, 608–640. Malden, MA: Blackwell Publishing.

Scott, J. C. 1986. *Weapons of the Weak: Everyday Forms of Peasant Resistance*. New Haven, CT: Yale University Press.

Sharma, Mukul. 2012. *Green and Saffron*.

Shiva, Vandana. 1988. *Staying Alive: Women, Ecology and Survival in India*. New Delhi: Kali for Women Press.

———. 2010. 'Ecology Movements in India'. In *Social Movements II: Concerns of Equity and Security*, edited by T. K. Oommen, 275–295. New Delhi: Oxford University Press.

The Research Collective (TRC). 2017. *Visible Tiger; Invisible People: Study and Report Based on the Public Hearing Held at Sunderban Islands, India*. New Delhi: PSA.

Touraine, Alain, Zsuzsa Hegedus, Francois Dubet, and Michel Wieviorka. 1983. *Anti-Nuclear Protest: The Opposition to Nuclear Energy in France*. Cambridge: Cambridge University Press.

7

Difference and Democracy: Queer Movement

Some men like Jack
And some like Jill
I'm glad that I like
Them both, but still

I wonder if
This freewheeling
Really is an
Enlightened thing

Or is its greater
Scope a sign
Of deviance from
Some party line?

In the strict ranks of
Gay and Straight
What is my status:
Stray? or Great?

—Vikram Seth

The word queer is new to Indian politics, and a queer movement is only at a nascent stage as yet. Understanding the queer movement is very significant for a society such as ours that seeks to be inclusive and democratic. Would there be physical safety, social sanction and economic and political opportunities for citizens who do not fit into the current definition of the 'majority'; how would equality, dignity and freedom be understood—these are some of the important issues that the queer movement raises.

The answers to these questions are rather telling—they would determine the character and nature of Indian democracy. Would Indian democracy be a place where the 'majority' tramples over the voices and concerns of the minorities, in other words, would it degenerate into crass majoritarianism or would it be sensitive to the voices and aspirations of those on the margins and perhaps not powerful enough to get their voices heard? Hence, the response of the Indian State and society to the challenges raised by the queer movement would tell us a great deal not just about the future of queer people in India but about the future of Indian democracy itself.

Agitation in Delhi, 2017

Source: Media Collective
Photograph Courtesy: The Media Collective. Reproduced with Permission.

Gay Pride at Display in Delhi, 2017

Source: Media Collective
Photograph Courtesy: The Media Collective. Reproduced with Permission.

New Delhi, 2017

Source: Media Collective
Photograph Courtesy: The Media Collective. Reproduced with Permission.

Protest at Delhi, 2017

Source: Media Collective
Photograph Courtesy: The Media Collective. Reproduced with Permission.

UNDERSTANDING THE TERM QUEER

We shall begin by trying to understand the term queer. As argued by Narrain and Bhan (2005), the term evokes not only personal choice but also political defiance. It suggests a questioning of what has often been referred to as compulsory heteronormativity. Queer politics argues that identities including gender identities are socially constructed and have concrete material consequences. It is based on this premise that the movement seeks to challenge the imposition of strict binary divisions based on sex. Rather, the queer movement argues that sexuality and identities based on sexual orientation occupy a continuum and are far more flexible than are generally understood (Menon 2012).

It is important to point out that these identities are not just a matter of personal lifestyle choice but have very real economic and sociocultural consequences. Men who 'do not seem enough like men' or women who 'appear to be more like men' (many such permutations and variations are possible) live in our society a life that is tenuous and rather risky. Education, job and indeed social acceptance become difficult. Routine activities such as getting a house on rent or getting a bank loan become challenges.

Instances of violent hate crimes and intolerance towards those who refuse to be pinned down by the twofold division of sex/gender and the social and sexual behaviour that is predicated upon it are innumerable.[1] Desire, love, sexual relations, marriage and family, property and descent are based on the principle that the only legitimate form of desire and conjugality is that which is based on relationship between the opposite sexes. Any deviation from this is seen as a threat to morality, family structures, property ties, legal system and finally to the State itself and the 'natural order of things'. Queer movements refer to a varied group of people who make choices and lead lives that are not in strict conformity with the ideals of heterosexuality.

Michel Foucault has argued that industrializing societies depend on highly organized and efficient techniques of social control and regulation as compared with pre-modern societies. This resulted in the creation of the Panoptican.[2] The Panoptican refers to a centralized principle and arrangement of surveillance that is so all pervasive that the subjects of this relentless survey begin to internalize the system and accept it unquestioningly leading to a situation where they begin to keep themselves under scrutiny and surveillance. Foucault argues that it is this that becomes the glue of modern societies wherein all institutions are organized on this principle. This includes diverse institutions such as the school, factory and family and of course norms of sexuality. The 'normal' is determined by the Panoptican, and any deviation from this would be disciplined through various means to go back to the position of normalcy. Foucault, in his accounts of the history of sexuality, describes the normalization of heterosexuality and the efforts to punish the deviant homosexual behaviour as yet another instance of modern societies using power to normalize any deviant or different attribute or behaviour (Adams and Dyson 2007, 220).

Interestingly, the term queer was not employed in a flattering way; the meaning suggests someone strange or peculiar. However, over the years, many homosexual groups asserted their right to describe and encompass a variety of choices that people make outside of the heterosexual matrix. The queer movements are engaged in going beyond identity or minority rights politics. It positions itself as a movement that seeks to liberate all human beings who are compulsorily placed within rigid binaries and the ensuing surveillance mechanisms. As argued by Foucault, this binary division is seen as normal and elaborate social, cultural, economic and other codes and institutional arrangements are set in place to ensure the continuation of such binaries. Any departure is seen as abnormality and measures are in place to prevent or penalize such departures.

---

[1] http://www.democracynow.org/2009/6/26/stonewall_riots_40th_anniversary_a_look (Accessed 10 October 2015).
[2] https://www.ucl.ac.uk/Bentham-Project/who/panopticon (Accessed 10 October 2015).

VIEW FROM INDIA

It is a fact that in India the term queer is yet to find common currency; however, the number of groups and experiences that would be addressed by this term are many and varied. Gautam Bhan and Arvind Narrain list hijras, kothis,[3] lesbian, gay, bisexual and transgender (LGBT) communities and traditional identities based on sexual non-conformity, for example, jogappas, ganacharis and so on (Narrain and Bhan 2005).

The feminist movement in contemporary India has made it possible to raise issues of sexuality as political issues, not limited to mere lifestyle or personal choices. Feminist politics has repeatedly established the political nature of sexual arrangements in society. Who has sex with whom and how; these are clearly more than private matters. The answers to these questions seem to have far-reaching social, economic and political consequences. The elaborate surveillance mechanisms to regulate women's sexuality are a proof of this fact. Feminist politics has established the close connection between sexuality and pleasure and of course the denial of it. Unequal power relations in society make the enjoyment of sexual pleasures difficult.

Such conversations have opened up the possibilities for questioning heteronormativity. One of the sharpest challenges to power in Indian society has come from people trying to forge friendships, marriages and sexual relationships cutting across caste, religious and linguistic boundaries. The 'violation' of sexual norms that forbid same-sex love, hence, has to be understood as an attempt to question the 'natural' arrangement of power in society. For family, property, marriage, financial arrangements and much else is based on the assumption of the heterosexual family.

There is often a suggestion that non-conformist sexuality is a Western import; however, evidence from literature, sculpture and painting, and of course, history demonstrates that this is not necessarily the case. Property, marriage and domestic arrangements based on non-heterosexual arrangements were in existence in pre-modern societies, even in India. Of course, this is not to suggest that there was some mythical past that was perfect and modernity ruined it all, rather to suggest that history has not always been progressive in its linear march (Menon 2007).

Pre-modern traditions might throw up instances of tolerance and even acceptance of same-sex relationships. India encountered modernity mediated by the colonial administration that was keen on disciplining the deviant societies that it then proceeded to reform and punish. These deviations reinforced the notion that the 'natives' were degenerate, and hence unfit for self-governance. Mrinalini Sinha has argued that this message was enthusiastically internalized by the newly emergent English educated Indian middle classes who sought to banish 'deviant' sexual behaviour as emasculating. They internalized the idea that this justified the denial of self-governance

---

[3] Kothi is a term used by the hijra community to describe non-hijra feminine males and now is used to describe feminine males, transvestites, cross-dressers and others.

(Sinha 1995). Thus, an inextricable link is established between sex and political power and in post-Independence India with culture, traditions and national identity.

This was the context in which the now infamous Section 377 of the Indian Penal Code got introduced. This law prohibits all carnal intercourse 'against the order of nature'. Convictions under this Section had been considerably rare. However, from the 1990s, Indian society has witnessed many kinds of changes. On the one hand has been the opening up of the economy, which has inevitably brought in many social and cultural changes as well. There is a general anxiety among the Indian elite about the openness that permits the questioning of existing power structures of family, marriage and the State. While the bounties of the modern market economy are welcome, there seem to be great trepidation vis-à-vis the social and cultural changes that accompany it. These anxieties helped reinforce the conservative positions on issues such as homosexuality, steeped in a nationalist discourse that constructed these 'deviations' as threats to national integrity and honour, and as symbols of the depraved West.

SOME IMPORTANT MILESTONES

Skirmishes around the issues of sexuality and queerness were highlighted in the controversy around the film *Fire* that depicted a lesbian relationship in a Hindu upper caste family.

The film was attacked for bringing in Western morals that were corrupt and depraved (Ghosh 2010). Naisargi N. Dave (2012) has argued that the invisibility of lesbian oppression is the unique feature of much of queer activism in India. Lesbians are excluded from all social and cultural recognition, so that even the comfort of collective anger, the possibility of resistance and the knowledge of what to resist is unavailable (see Fernandez and Gomathy 2005). For lesbians groups in India, unlike for the hijras or the kothis, the issues are not so much about access to public spaces and freedom of movement and so on. Lesbian women have had to wage a battle even to be acknowledged as a distinct group. Their being born women, creates a set of disadvantages that the women's movement has so effectively mapped. Hence, a very obvious alliance with the women's movement does exist. Although, many of the left-oriented women's groups did take a long time to accept the importance and significance of these issues.

The other trend that needs to be mentioned here is the causal connection that is sought to be drawn between the liberalization of the Indian economy and the assertion of rights by sexual minorities, almost implying an exclusive urban, upper middle class character to these assertions, thereby completely ignoring the experience of communities such as the hijras or the kothis.

The fact is that there is no single unified queer movement in India. Caste, class, location, urban/rural, gay/lesbian and many more attributes determine the nature of the specific issues raised. For instance, gay men are, of course, stigmatized in urban India, but the already disempowered position of women in a patriarchal context further marginalizes, indeed invisibilizes lesbian women. Thus, diversity is written into the queer movement in India. Nevertheless, it is possible to identify some broad groups (Chakravarti and Dutta 2011).

Broadly, the aim of this movement is to create an acknowledgement of the concerns and challenges faced by queer people in India. It seeks to establish the diversity of sexual experiences and rejects the violence and coercion that queer people are subjected to. It is primarily a movement that seeks to assert the citizenship claims of queer people, and thus strengthen Indian democracy. These aims are sought to be translated into reality through many modes of resistance and challenge ranging from legal campaigns to cultural productions and of course marches and demonstrations.

The gay/lesbian groups that are characterized largely by their urban location and articulate and deft handling of the media and who engage in sophisticated campaigns would be the most visible part of the movement. The second large group consists of MSM (men who have sex with men) groups along with kothi groups largely engaged with HIV-AIDS prevention and other similar campaigns. The third distinct component would be the traditional community of hijras who seek recognition by the State and electoral opportunities.[4] Of course, these distinctions are not watertight and there is a great deal of fluidity and indeed solidarity.

The 1990s saw a great deal of mobilization by self-described gay and lesbian groups and activists in urban centres, especially Delhi and Mumbai. Apart from establishing groups, many of them published magazines and newsletters. Some of the iconic names in the context of gay mobilization would be Counsel Club in Kolkata, AIDS Bhedbhav Virodhi Andolan (ABVA) in Delhi, Good As You in Bangalore[5] and the magazine *Bombay Dost* among many others (Singh et al. 2013).[6]

These initiatives have struggled for space and acceptance, and it is not surprising that lesbian women have found it even more difficult to undertake such initiatives (Narrain and Bhan 2005). It is pertinent to point out that many of the lesbian groups have close links with both the feminist movement and gay rights campaigns. A diverse range of such groups exists in India, Deepa V. N.'s interesting account of one such group—Sahayatrika in Kerala—is a case in point.

THE AIDS BHEDBHAV VIRODHI ANDOLAN

The ABVA, established in 1991, was among the first groups to integrate issues of gay rights, with concerns for health and well-being of gay persons as well as place the discussion in a larger

---

[4] http://www.bangaloremirror.com/bangalore/others/Transgenders-shun-religion-tag/articleshow/52424908.cms (Accessed 26 May 2016).
[5] http://goodasyoublr.blogspot.in/
[6] http://www.bombaydost.co.in/Bombay_Dost_-_About.html

context of human rights (Balasubrahmanyam 1996, 257–58). On 11 August 1992, ABVA staged the first known protest against police harassment of LGBT people in India; the protest was against police raids that targeted men cruising for men in Central Park, Connaught Place in Delhi. The protest was held at the police headquarters in the ITO area of Delhi (Dave 2012). ABVA was, in 1991, the first organization to challenge Section 377 of the Indian Penal Code.[7] Its historic publication *Less than Gay: A Citizen's Report* is certainly a milestone in the queer politics in India.[8]

This became important because in the frenzy of anti-AIDS campaign, men having sex with men became the hapless targets of law enforcement agencies, which in the backdrop of the draconian Section 377 led to unwarranted harassment of gay men by police and the legal machinery.

However, these groups focused largely on men in urban locations. A large group of men outside this category consisting of lower class men who have sex with men, transvestites and cross-dressers were drawn into the queer movement through the efforts of groups such as the NAZ foundation, Humsafar Trust and Sahodaran (Chakravarti and Dutta 2011). Such groups have emerged all over the country. Most of these groups though exclude female-born persons because of the focus on MSM and AIDS prevention activities.

The NAZ Foundation

For long, casual and unprotected sex was considered to be one of the most common routes for contracting the HIV-AIDS infection. This automatically diverted the focus of the movement towards gay men and commercial sex workers who were identified as 'high risk groups'. This resulted in many international NGOs and donor agencies joining the efforts, which in turn led to the increasing misapprehension about homosexuality and the supposed corollary of HIV-AIDS being Western imports. Homosexuality came to be denounced as a Western scourge that was corrupting Indian culture and the NGOs that sought to defend the rights of homosexuals and MSM were branded anti-national.

---

[7] Section 377 of Indian Penal Code—which came into force in 1862—defines unnatural offences. It says, 'Whoever voluntarily has carnal intercourse against the order of nature with any man, woman or animal shall be punished with imprisonment for life, or with imprisonment of either description for a term which may extend to 10 years, and shall also be liable to fine'.
[8] http://orinam.net/indias-lgbt-activism-history-early-1990s/#sthash.UImPaSiH.dpuf (Accessed 26 May 2016).

There is no denying that a certain amount of internationalization of the queer movement has happened and this is almost inevitable given the nature of the world that we live in today. The fact is that although non-English languages in India might not have precise translations for words such as gay and lesbian, the experiences of being cast out because of differing sexual orientations are very similar across cultures and languages. Besides in a furiously globalizing world, there is a great deal of exchange of ideas and experiences.

The terms gay and lesbian have acquired a specific Indian inflection, and traditional groups like the hijras have gained a great deal by exchanging notes with gay and lesbian activists from India and abroad.

SAME-SEX RELATIONSHIPS IN INDIA

The category of MSM is a case in point. Same-sex relationships are not alien to the Indian context, and many men do engage in it while carrying on with heterosexual marriages. Often these homosexual encounters are accorded the status of 'treats' and described as *masti* or a little bit of fun. Thus, it was not just homosexual men who had to be addressed in India in the context of the HIV-AIDS prevention activism. These interactions and introspections have created new tensions as well as new identities. Kothi, the term used by hijras in Tamil Nadu to describe effeminate men who are not necessarily a part of the community but do engage in sex with men has found favour all over India, along with the term panthi that the kothis use to refer to the 'real' men that they like to have sex with. These terms and identities have been questioned and debated within the queer movement.

'INDIAN CULTURE' AND THE QUESTION OF HOMOSEXUALITY

The question of Indian culture and the place that it has for homosexuality is yet another contentious one. In response to the allegations of same-sex relations being a Western import, some groups and scholars such as Ruth Vanita and Saleem Kidwai have tried to establish the antiquity of same-sex love in India (Vanita and Kidwai 2000). Unless handled with great care, this position could lay itself open to the criticism of privileging Hindu high culture, while attributing homophobia to Muslim 'invasions'.

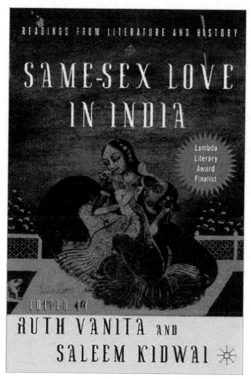

Cover Page of *Same-Sex Love in India* **(Vanita and Kidwai 2000)**

Source: https://link.springer.com/book/10.1007/978-1-137-05480-7

Although references to same-sex love might be found in non-English language books and resources in India, the fact is that the conception of modern India and the history that it would like to be built upon as argued by Mrinalini Sinha has no or very little space for gay and lesbian, hijra and other histories within it (Sinha 2006).

Although such a tradition might have existed, the fact is that modernity in India has sought to construct itself with a carefully selected list of ingredients from the past, and homosexuality most certainly does not feature in it. Lesbianism and other forms of 'deviant sexual behaviour' are clearly unacceptable to the neoliberal Indian elite as much as it was to the newly emergent English educated Indian elite that spearheaded the nationalist struggle. In fact, such behaviour, it was argued, was responsible for emasculation and consequently colonial rule.

To argue that homosexuality has ancient roots in Indian history is fraught with trouble, for it is historically a cumbersome argument. It hinges upon the issue of how India is defined and indeed how history is perceived apart from what it seeks to establish. More often than not it is to glorify a supposedly liberal open past cruelly snapped by 'invaders'. Who exactly are the invaders would depend once again on the specific notion of India and its boundaries. At other times, history is invoked to establish the complete absence of same-sex relationships. Both accounts are limited in their understanding. The fact is that although the past has always been varied and complex with more than numerous illustrations of same-sex relationships, but it does not necessarily imply that hence the past was a liberal and open society. What is fairly obvious is that the project of modern national construction that we are familiar with has been contingent on selective picks from the historical basket. Evidence of same-sex relationships has most certainly not been picked up in this construction, and hence any group in contemporary India that seeks to promote the rights of homosexual people can possibly be branded as anti-national or Westernized.

Apart from this challenge of establishing an indigenous tradition of homosexuality, the queer movement, much like the feminist movement in India, has had to face up to the fact that queer people are also divided along the lines of class, caste, location and other fault lines. One of the most severe cracks in the queer movement is the one that separates gay men from middle class backgrounds, on the one hand, and MSM/kothis on the other hand. To complicate matters further, many hijras might actually prefer to identify themselves as women and not necessarily as men who have sex with men.

HIJRAS

Hijras have often been referred to as the third gender of India. This is an internally varied group of male born and some intersexed persons. As early as 1994, some hijra groups in Delhi made a plea for government initiatives to address the issues and absence of rights of sexually under-privileged groups. This was an interesting and important turn, for these groups were making use of the Constitutional language and framework. These groups have been keen on joining the political mainstream by contesting elections and participating in representative politics with gusto, an initiative that is not seen in other gay rights groups. A new collective called Prism (People for the Rights of Indian Sexual Minorities) was set up in 2001 (Dave 2012).

Many hijras have contested elections successfully and won positions in local representative bodies, for instance, Shobha Nehru was elected as a city council member in Hisar in 1989 and Shabnam Mausi Bano became the first hijra to be elected to the Madhya Pradesh Assembly in 2000. Laxmi Narayan Tripathi and many other hijra activists have initiated prominent activist networks in various parts of the country.[9]

Some state governments, like in Tamil Nadu, have been more responsive than others to the demands raised by hijra groups like the Thamilnadu Aravanigal Association established in 1989.

---

[9] Tripathi's Astitva in Mumbai is a very well-known organization.

The government set up a 'Transgender Welfare Board' in 2008, an initiative which emulated by the government of Karnataka as well. Bangalore-based groups Vividha and Sangama organized a large-scale gathering of hijra groups in 2002—the Hijra Habba. Soon, despite large scale mobilizations of hijras and other traditional communities by the NGOs, the internal divisions and limitations of such mobilizational efforts were beginning to get exposed. In the year 2010, an effort was made to create distinct groups of hijras and transgender persons to the exclusion of MSM groups. Meanwhile, these initiatives resulted in the Government of India and some universities and educational institutions initiating the category of 'third gender'.[10] The 2011 Census has already included the enumeration of the third gender, which is of course a significant step in this context.[11] Any enumeration by the government, of course, immediately raises concerns about greater possibilities of surveillance and control albeit garbed in the discourse of welfare and rights, invoking all the dimensions of the concept of governmentality as proposed by Michel Foucault.[12]

Initiatives towards Inclusion

Kerala introduced the Transgender Policy in 2015, and Kochi Metro became the first government project in India to provide equal opportunities of employment and initiating a change in public perception towards transgender people. However, this has not been a smooth process, there are many challenges such as:

- The biggest challenge is to educate colleagues and commuters on the metro about the question of gender identity of the transgender workers.
- Complete lack of awareness of the existence of transgender people as well as the belief that trans people double up as sex workers, create unhealthy suspicions in the minds of the community.
- The police in Kerala, too, had been accused of hounding the transgender people and calling them sex workers for several years.
- Kochi Metro's transgender employees face a host of unprecedented problems. Lack of gender-specific washrooms, accommodation problems and commuting costs are among the most common. As a temporary measure, transgender employees at the Metro have begun using washrooms meant for people with disabilities. However, this is a bold initiative.

---

[10] http://www.thehindu.com/news/national/other-states/du-jamia-include-third-gender-category-in-application-forms/article7160426.ece"ttp://www.newstatesman.com/world-affairs/2014/04/india-s-supreme-court-recognises-third-gender

[11] http://www.gaystarnews.com/article/indian-census-counts-transgender-people-first-time-finds-half-million020614/

[12] http://www.michel-foucault.com/concepts/Foucault originally used the term 'governmentality' to describe a particular way of administering populations in modern European history within the context of the rise of the idea of the State. He later expanded his definition to encompass the techniques and procedures which are designed to govern the conduct of both individuals and populations at every level not just the administrative or political level.

These governmental recognitions and electoral opportunities do create a world of possibilities. India now has many people from the trans community playing very public and important roles in society. However, these new openings also bring the movement to a crossroad and the question of what next. (Dave 2012). Despite the electoral avenues and some changes in the bureaucratic formalities of the State, the fact is that the queer movement in India is a movement that is far from having exhausted its potential; in fact, it is best characterized as a movement that is engaged in creating a radical world (Povinelli 2001). Radical worlds are always in process, linked through their shared existence in a field of possibility.

ENGAGING WITH THE LAW: SECTION 377

Feminist movement in India has had a difficult relationship with the terrain of law and yet has engaged repeatedly with it. Similar have been the experiences of the queer movement in India, especially with regard to the infamous Section 377. Critics like Tellis have interrogated this engagement with the domain of law by pointing out the inevitable normalizing tendencies and surveillance mechanisms that follow in the wake of legal interventions. This, some critics fear, would inevitably lead to the domestication of the queer movement that has started out as a radical questioning of normative standards of regulating human life (Tellis 2012). Be that as it may, the fact is that no discussion of queer politics in India can afford to ignore the struggle against Section 377.

Section 377 of the Indian Penal Code criminalizes same-sex relations on the grounds that it is against nature. The law as it existed, privileged heterosexual activity, preferably for procreative purposes within the institution of marriage. Sections 375 and 376 along with Section 377 are the most important parts of the law dealing with sexual conduct of Indians.

The argument is not that legalizing same-sex relations would transform our society into a democratic and progressive one, rather that it would be a vital ingredient in the march towards an egalitarian and non-hierarchical society. Sexual rights cannot be understood in isolation from other kinds of rights. As Ponni Arasu has pointed out, Israel accepts same-sex relations, but we cannot ignore the fact that this recognition is being extended by a State that violated the human rights of vast numbers of Arabs in the region (Arasu 2011).

One of the earliest instances of a law against same-sex relations was the Buggery Act, 1533 in vogue in England. It was finally removed from the statutes in 1957, when it was accepted that homosexual behaviour between consenting adults in private could no longer constitute a criminal offence. This colonial legacy has stayed on in many of the former colonies of the British. In the South Asian region, Nepal has taken the boldest initiatives towards legalizing same-sex relations. This has perhaps been possible in some measure due to the overall atmosphere of change and the presence of radical groups in politics.

Of course, legal initiatives in this regard are not uniform and display a great deal of diversity across nations. In some countries, consensual sexual relations between persons of the same sex is allowed, whereas civil partnerships and right to beget children through artificial insemination and joint ownership of property and other similar rights are allowed in other countries. Still other countries allow asylum seekers on the basis of their sexual orientation. Decriminalization is only one end of the spectrum, the other end would be the wide network of non-discriminatory and enabling rights and policies.

In most British colonies, an attempt at civilizing and Christianizing the 'natives' resulted in a slew of legislations on various aspects of the sociocultural organization of life. The ban on Devadasi performances in the temples of southern India or the criminalization of homosexual activity are examples of such attempts by the British. Prior to this, no such codification existed, this is, of course, not to suggest that same-sex relations were celebrated in pre-colonial India.

It was only in the closing years of the 20th century that Section 377 was challenged by the ABVA in 1994. The immediate provocation for this was the refusal by prison authorities to distribute condoms among prisoners in the Tihar jail on the grounds that this would encourage homosexual activity. Petitioners challenged this by invoking the right to health and also cited the traditional acceptance of homosexuality. In the international context of the campaigns to arrest the spread of HIV-AIDS virus, special focus was on homosexual behaviour as this was understood to be one of the most important routes for the spread of the virus.

VOICES AGAINST 377

By 2001, the NAZ foundation which too worked on similar campaigns joined the legal struggle and filed a PIL petition questioning Section 377. They were joined by various other groups that came to be finally described as the 'Voices against 377'. Using the pretext of this law, homosexual people have often been intimidated and attacked, harassed and blackmailed by law enforcing agencies as well as by hooligans and miscreants. Of course, this is not to suggest that such homophobia is the result of the law alone, but rather to suggest that the existence of such a law makes such harassment easier. Because of all these experiences, a plea was made to the Delhi High Court to read down the law, since repeal was not feasible as this Section was routinely invoked to deal with instances of child sexual abuse in the absence of any specific law. The initial response from the High Court was not very encouraging,[13] but the case came back to the court and the petitioners made effective use of international case law, including the Wolfenden Report and Lawrence versus Texas.[14]

---

[13] In 2004, the High Court turned the petition down, but it came back to the Court in 2006 on the basis of a special leave petition filed in the Supreme Court. The Supreme Court directed the Delhi High Court to consider the petition in public interest.

[14] It is precisely the use of international case law that Ashley Tellis has cited as example of the Westernized ethos and sensibility of queer politics.

The Delhi High Court finally read down Section 377 to suggest consensual sex between adults in private cannot be criminalized on grounds that such criminalization violated Articles 21, 14 and 15—Fundamental Rights to Life and Liberty, and Equality. This moment was celebrated by queer activists, while also acknowledging the fact that the law addressed itself basically to male persons. Queer women, it has to be pointed, do face a great deal of harassment not just in the public sphere, but within the domestic sphere as well. This campaign against the law did not take into account instances of such harassment at all. Many queer persons face threats and harassment on the basis of their caste status or regional identities and so on. This too was overlooked.

The Delhi High Court decision was challenged by Suresh Kumar Koushal, an astrologer, along with other religious outfits in the Supreme Court. The Supreme Court said in its decision that the Parliament can look at this matter. The Parliament on its part could not discuss the matter because it was sub judice.

The Supreme Court in response to this PIL turned down the High Court judgment. This dramatic turn of events draws our attention to the rather slippery nature of the legal terrain. The decision was overturned by the Supreme Court in 2013, resulting in despair, disbelief and protests.

Writer and Poet Vikram Seth Reflects the Anguish of the LGBT Community on the Supreme Court's Refusal to Reconsider Its Order on Gay Rights

Source: India Today, https://www.indiatoday.in/india/north/story/vikram-seth-on-sec-377-poem-to-sneer-at-love-is-unnatural-crime-178889-2014-01-29

Curative petitions against the Supreme Court order were filed in end March/early April, 2014. On 22 April 2014, the Supreme Court directed that the curative petitions would be heard in an open court. Chief Justice Thakur, early in 2016, said the petitions posed several questions with 'constitutional dimensions of importance' while dictating the order of reference to a Constitution Bench he would be setting up shortly. This Bench neither admitted the petitions nor issued notice to the government, leaving it to the future Constitution Bench to do so, if found necessary. Rebelling against its own procedural conventions in dealing with curative pleas, the Supreme Court indicated its openness to reconsider the constitutionality of Section 377 with new eyes.[15]

Section 377 of the Indian Penal Code is Now Decriminalized

The Supreme Court in September 2018 read down the archaic Section 377 of the Indian Penal Code, in a relief to millions of people across India.

The top court said, 'Homosexuality is not an offence'.

'Sexual orientation is one of many biological phenomena. It is natural and no discrimination can exist. Any violation is against freedom of speech and expression', the court said.

The court said, 'Section 377 so far as it criminalizes same sex or heterosexual relationships is volatile of the Constitution'.

Articles 14, 15, 19 and 21 of the Indian Constitution were invoked by the judgment, thus making this an issue of constitutional rights and freedoms with larger reference to the nature of democracy in Indian society than being an issue limited to 'homosexual' people alone.

CONCLUSION

The status of Indian democracy would be determined by the kind of life minorities can lead. A democracy is not characterized by brute strength and might of the majority. The idea that there can be a fixed majority is anathema to the understanding of a democracy. Rather, a democracy would be that where those who are numerically small or even insignificant and vulnerable would feel secure and confident. After all, there is no guarantee that one group of people would remain a majority always. Thus, the kind of life sexual minorities would have access to in India, would

---

[15] http://www.thehindu.com/news/national/supreme-court-refers-plea-against-section-377-to-5judge-bench/article8183860.ece

determine the kind of democracy India wants to construct. Hence, like all other social movements that have been discussed, the queer movement is imagining an India that would push the frontiers of democracy even further.

But such struggles cannot be isolated from other forms of violent suppression of rights—be it centred around caste, class, religion, disability or the ability to express dissent.

Hence, the queer movement, despite some criticism to the contrary, has increasingly tried to forge solidarity with numerous infringements on personal and social liberties of various communities, speaking up alongside a rising tide of writers, scientists and historians protesting against shrinking spaces for dissent.

Important queer activists have asserted that it is time to end all fears and barriers in society, and that queer freedom is inseparable from a broader culture of respect and space for diversity.

The claims that queer activism in India makes of being a movement have been contested on the grounds that it is hardly a movement and more a manufactured product to cater to the needs of international governance regimes of the United Nations and other similar bodies (Tellis 2012). Tellis argues that the leadership of such groups that advocate the rights of sexual minorities in India is rather limited in its vision as well as in its political engagements. He has suggested that such movements are led by urban, upper caste men from privileged backgrounds that are happy to act as conduits of international governance mechanisms. Tellis bemoans what he feels is the exclusive nature of the movement, since in his opinion no linkages have been made with the struggles of the workers, farmers, sex workers and others on the margins of the Indian society (Tellis 2012).

Tellis argues that these groups are largely bourgeois in their orientation and happy to negotiate with the State for piecemeal legal reforms like the struggle against Section 377. The High Court judgment that decriminalized homosexuality has been cited by queer activist as a landmark victory. Tellis has argued that the judgment illustrates his anxieties about international governance finding its way into India as is demonstrated by the fact that in the text of the High Court judgment, all the precedents on sexuality quoted in it are international, all the language is global and in perfect consonance with global governance (Tellis 2012).

Tellis further interrogates the source of funding that these queer activist groups in India have been linked with while also suggesting that the very terminology and the discourse employed by the groups is of non-indigenous origins—only to suit the understanding and sensibilities of the Western donors.

Queer politics is most certainly attempting to move beyond identity politics based on what has become an ever increasing alphabet soup of LGBTQKH.... It seeks to posit a new image of Indian society, one that is based on room for difference and is characterized by absence of hegemonic hierarchies. It sees the link between what might seem like personal choices regulating sexual matters with deeper questions of freedom and dignity. Queer politics has successfully questioned entrenched norms on matters such as marriage and sex. In destabilizing these, it has also destabilized many adjunct assumptions about caste and religion and, of course, class.

The queer movement while establishing its firm links with the Indian social and cultural fabric is also keen to avoid a chauvinistic slant. It also seeks to forge ties across identities, seeing most identities as conjectural. Many of the criticisms levelled against the queer movement are rather similar to the ones levelled against the women's movement, especially the criticism levelled in the context of its engagement with law.

Although some of the criticisms levelled against the queer movement are certainly valid, the fact is that there is no escaping the importance of the nation-state and its central regulatory mechanism—law. Seen like this, it is very clear that the law has to be engaged with, albeit not from a starry-eyed perspective that would give to law a position of pre-eminence in society. Legal systems have always reflected the power structures of society. Although law is notorious for its tendency to categorize and create new norms, yet it has on occasion provided a fillip to the process of social change and transformation.

Change cannot come overnight, and law can merely nudge change or suggest a desirable path of action. It is not surprising that Lok Sabha voted twice against the introduction of a private member's Bill, sought to be introduced by Congress MP Shashi Tharoor for decriminalizing homosexuality. The Indian Penal Code (Amendment) Bill, 2016, sought to amend Section 377 of the Indian Penal Code that criminalizes homosexuality.[16] In such a scenario, the responsibility of a broad spectrum movement like the queer movement helps focus attention not only on the immediate issues on hand but on deeper philosophical and ethical questions about the very nature of Indian democracy.

POINTS FOR DISCUSSION

- Do you think the legal structure on its own can bring about a change in Indian society with regard to issues of sexuality and gender?
- Would it be right to say that homosexuality as a taboo subject was a colonial construct, as far as India is concerned?
- How has the mainstream media reported/discussed/portrayed the struggles discussed in this chapter? Do you think the media has succeeded in portraying it as a democratic movement?

[16] http://indianexpress.com/article/india/india-news-india/decriminalising-homosexuality-lok-sabha-votes-against-shashi-tharoors-bill-again/#sthash.LBdmuPcE.dpuf

REFERENCES AND READINGS

Adams, Ian, and R. W. Dyson. 2007. *Fifty Major Political Thinkers*. London: Routledge.

Arasu, Ponni. 2011. 'Queer Theory'. In *Theories of Women's and Gender Studies*. New Delhi: IGNOU.

Balasubrahmanyan, Vimal. 1996. 'Gay Rights in India'. *Economic and Political Weekly*, 31 (5).

Chakravarti, Paromita, and Aniruddha Dutta. 2011. 'Queer Liberation'. In *Theories of Women's and Gender Studies*. New Delhi: IGNOU.

Dave, Naisargi N. 2012. *Queer Activism in India: A Story in Anthropology of Ethics*. Durham: Duke University Press.

Fernandez, B., and N. B. Gomathy. 2005. 'Voicing the Invisible: Violence Faced by Lesbian Women in India'. In *Because I Have a Voice: Queer Politics in India*, edited by Arvind Narrain and Gautam Bhan, 197–216. New Delhi: Yoda Press.

Ghosh, Shohini. 2010. *Fire: A Queer Film Classic*. ReadHowYouWant, 20.

Menon, Nivedita. 2007. *Sexualities*. London/New York, NY: Zed.

———. 2012. *Seeing Like a Feminist*. Delhi: Zubaan-Penguin Books.

Narrain, Arvind, and Gautam Bhan, eds. 2005. *Because I have a Voice: Queer Politics in India*. New Delhi: Yoda Press.

Povinelli, Elizabeth. 2001. 'Radical Worlds: The Anthropology of Incommensurability and Inconceivability'. *Annual Review of Anthropology*, 30: 319–34.

Singh, Suneeta, Sangita Dasgupta, Pallav Patankar, and Minati Sinha. 2013. *A People Stronger: The Collectivization of MSM and TG Groups in India*. New Delhi: SAGE Publications.

Sinha, Mrinalini. 1995. *Colonial Masculinity: The 'Mainly Englishman' and the 'Effeminate Bengali' in the Late Nineteenth Century*. New York, NY: Manchester University Press.

———. 2006. *Spectres of Mother India: The Global Restructuring of an Empire*. Delhi: Zubaan.

Tellis, Ashley. 2012. 'Disrupting the Dinner Table: Re-thinking the "Queer Movement" in Contemporary India'. *Jindal Global Law Review*, 4 (1): 142–57.

Tellis, Ashley, and Sruti Bala, eds. 2015. *The Global Trajectories of Queerness (Thamyris/Intersecting: Place, Sex and Race)*. Amsterdam: Brill | Rodopi.

Vanita, R. 2000. 'Vikram Seth: Poems (English)'. In *Same-Sex Love in India*, edited by R. Vanita and S. Kidwai, 376–77. New York, NY: Palgrave Macmillan.

Vanita, Ruth, and Saleem Kidwai, eds. 2000. *Same-Sex Love in India*. New York, NY: Palgrave Macmillan.

8

Autonomy and Association: Civil Society Mobilizations

Hum Jaanenge, Hum Jeeyenge (We will know, we will live)

—A slogan of Right to Information Movement
(given by Hindi journalist Prabhash Joshi in 1996)

A dominant narrative which sees civil society as the modern crusader for change is leading the social movement discourse everywhere. Although the concept has had its origins in the Western liberal thought from the late 17th century onwards and has been conceptualized in many different ways over the years, its contemporary usage has acquired a kind of storybook fantastical character, 'an ideological construct for a good society' (Comaroff and Comaroff 1999, cited in Elliot 2003, 3). Often identified as the third front, the other two being the state and the market (or for some, the family), civil society is invariably perceived as a vibrant feature of the modern democratic world which mostly works against the state in order to carve out a liberal, equitable, tolerant, secular and just society. This image not only evokes awe and hope for the masses, it also gives the impression that civil society is a cohesive and clearly defined sphere, its role in society is positive, it is aligned to democracy and it is a major force representing people's interests against a dominant state and market. A deeper analysis, however, reveals that this view is a much debated view. As an old concept which has travelled over the centuries, civil society has been perceived in many highly different, at times, opposing ways.

There are debates on what is civil society, whether it is really the third front; is it really a positive and a modern force; does it always oppose the state; is it a feature of democratic societies; what is its relationship with the market and so on. The following sections reflect on its diverse issues in the light of the Western classical theories and the contemporary views regarding its definition and its many sided nature with special focus on India. Subsequently, some important civil society mobilizations in India have been delineated.

THE WESTERN PERSPECTIVES ON CIVIL SOCIETY

Any understanding of the concept of civil society and its role in the contemporary world requires first an insight into the earlier theories popular in the Western context spread over the centuries. At the peak of political and social hegemony of the Roman Catholic Church in the 13th century, the concept of *societas civilis* came into existence to refer to that sphere of life which was governed by laws rather than religious dictates. Free from religious institutions, civil society was seen as an autonomous, secular and democratic space where people could choose their own king.

Beginning with the 17th century, civil society came to be identified as '...a distinct form of political society—one in which the rights of individuals received primacy over all else' (Gurpreet Mahajan, in Elliot 2003, 168). This early Western liberal thought on civil society has often been differentiated into two broad streams, one associated with John Locke and the other with Montesquieu (Taylor 1990). Yet another approach to the concept of civil society is based on the 19th and 20th century thinkers including G. W. F. Hegel, Karl Marx, Antonio Gramsci and Jurgen Habermas.

THE 'PRE-POLITICAL SOCIETY', 'SELF-REGULATION' AND 'LIMITED STATE': JOHN LOCKE

In John Locke's imagery, civil society is distinct from both the 'state of nature' and 'political society'. In his view, human beings live in pre-political societies in the state of nature under the natural law where natural rights are equal for everyone. These societies, however, lack in a legal authority which can protect and secure the rights of the individual granted by nature, thus representing an uncivil condition (Mahajan, in Elliot 2003). Civil society is formed when individuals, feeling the need to secure their rights from those who endanger them, come together and make a contract to set up a political authority which will protect their rights through definite laws and instruments of punishment for the offenders. Although this is seen as the minimum condition of civility, it is not enough for the formation of civil society. 'Civil society emerges only when the citizen's right to life, liberty and property is guaranteed by law'. A political society which does not guarantee individual rights, thus would not qualify as civil society. It is clear that in Locke's view, civil society does not exist outside the realm of the state or works against it. As it celebrates the rights and liberty of the individual citizen, it creates the circumstances for a democratic state to develop. Although Locke did not talk about universal franchise or equal rights, there is centrality of rights of the individual in his view, thus a basis of social equality. These rights not only dispute the existing social inequalities but also prevent the misuse of power by the state. In a situation where the state does not adhere to people's expectations, the individuals have a right to interrogate it. Thus, the metaphors of 'self-directing society' and 'limited state' came up in this context (Elliot 2003, 5).

INDEPENDENT RIGHTS-BASED GROUPS AND GOVERNMENT ACCOUNTABILITY: MONTESQUIEU AND ALEXIS DE TOCQUEVILLE

French scholar Montesquieu and his pupil Alexis de Tocqueville argued that the way to counter 'an absolutist state is to have a constitution defined in law and protected by a counterbalancing force of independent bodies' (Elliot 2003, 5). While the independent bodies, according to Montesquieu, were the 'towns and estates' in medieval Europe which were the centres of autonomous rights-based living, for de Tocqueville they were groups of citizens coming together to act on common issues and capable of countering an aggressive state. For both Montesquieu and de Tocqueville thus, such mediating entities, although technically outside the political state, are its components acting in political ways, making the voices of different social segments be heard and helping to disseminate power.

Thus, while John Locke's view lays a thrust on 'pre-political society', 'self-regulation' and 'limited state', Montesquieu emphasizes on civil society groups as voluntary and independent rights-based groups making governments more accountable and effective. As is clear, the two faces of civil society—self-regulation and providing a counterweight to the state—are present in both the traditions discussed above (Elliot 2003).

STATE, MARKET AND THE CIVIL SOCIETY: HEGEL, MARX, GRAMSCI AND HABERMAS

Largely critical of the liberal tradition, alternative views on civil society, sometimes referred to as the third stream emerged in the milieu of the predicament of the capitalist society in the 19th and 20th centuries. G. W. F. Hegel saw civil society as distinctive area of social interaction, distinct from the market where individuals pursue their own interests. 'Hegel's civil society is egoist, selfish and fragmented' (Elliot 2003, 6). In modern society, people are interdependent on each other and this facilitates community life. But according to Hegel, it cannot prevent individuals from being self-centred pursuing their own interests. In order to overcome this, society requires organizations, laws and a forceful state to keep individuals together, to create a sphere of community life where they could also follow their own specific interests like those of protection of property or life in a free environment. 'Lest social life disintegrate into a mere accumulation of private actions, he emphasized the need for organizations, law, and an overarching state to integrate individuals into the needs of the community and provide a sphere of freedom within which they could pursue particular interests' (Elliot 2003, 6–7). For Hegel, state is a rational agency which defends the freedom and rights of the individual. The civil society is subservient to the state.

Distinct from Hegel's pro-establishment stand, Marx and Engels criticized the state and defined it as an agency, which in association with the dominant sections in the civil society, tends to defend the interests of the propertied class. In *The German Ideology*,[1] they identified civil society as '...the social organization evolving directly out of production and commerce'. It developed with the coming of bourgeoisie class and the erosion of feudal ties. Civil society for them was the whole gamut of social relationships emerging from productive forces of capitalist society. It is the very foundation of the state and the rest of the superstructure. The civil society works to protect the rights of the dominant classes rather than of people at large, in the same way as the capitalist state. The idea of freedom within the civil society is a myth. Many consider Marx's notion of reducing civil society to the economic structure of capitalism as a basic flaw.

While agreeing with Marx, Gramsci went further to associate 'the state with instruments of direct coercion and civil society with the creation of hegemony' (Gurpreet Mahajan, in Elliot 2003, 178). He identified civil society as that sphere of social relationships, organizations and institutions which exists in between the state and the society. In capitalist societies, while the state rules through its coercive power, the civil society manages 'spontaneous consent given by the great masses of the population to the general direction imposed on social life by the dominant fundamental group'. A predominance of the civil society helps to gather consent for the hegemony of the ruling class, thus reducing the need to indulge in much coercion. The state and the civil society tend to work in tandem with each other.

Among the more recent theorists, Jurgen Habermas has viewed civil society as a space where individuals, through discussion and dialogue, define community goals and keep a watch on the working of the state. The basis of this solidarity is neither innate identities nor self-seeking activities but 'reasoned out deliberations'. 'For this discourse to produce freedom, it must be a deliberative exchange of reasoned arguments, not assertion of inherited ideas or identities, nor assertion of selfish interests' (Elliot 2003, 7).

CONTEMPORARY VIEWS

The concept of civil society which originally emerged in the works of liberals from the 17th century onwards was developed by others in subsequent centuries. The concept was resurrected strongly in the academic circles in Europe in the 1980s with the growth of movements for democracy like the Solidarity movement in Poland (Pelczynski 1988) and the rise of political democracy in the aftermath of decline of communism in Eastern European countries (Elliott 2003; Jayaram 2015). Civil society became a potent force in mobilizing people against the authoritarian state in the quest for affirming their rights to free speech, freedom of association and regaining their space in the society. 'Civil society, thus, can be viewed as a rebound or recovery concept' (Jayaram 2005, 15).

---

[1] *The German Ideology* is a set of manuscripts written by Karl Marx and Fredrick Engels in 1846. In this, they referred to civil society as 'the true focus and theatre of all history'.

The civil society discourse soon spread to other countries which did not necessarily have repressive regimes like in the USA. The concept became a saviour for dispersed groups raising varied issues such as 'socialists opposed to globalizing corporate networks, global society theorists disenchanted with the nation-state, critics of the developmental state, protagonists of free market economy, communitarians articulating concerns about community life, leaders of people's movements of various sorts and even those critical of representative democracy itself' (Jayaram 2005, 15). For people from different parts of the world and of different persuasions, the idea of civil society became a messiah of sorts. Whether it was Tiananmen Square uprising by Chinese students, the Latin American movement for seeking a new participatory political system or the various Indian movements for reform, all portray the promise of civil society. This trend continues in the present times where varied groups across the world see it as 'the new magic bullet for development and democracy' (Elliott 2003, 4).

The Indian intellectuals of different hues have been involved in animated debates on issues related to civil society from the late 1980s onwards. There are, however, distinct perceptions of civil society derived from studies of Indian society and polity among the Indian intellectuals.

The early studies on civil society in India are credited to political scientists mainly due to a widespread disillusionment with the post-Independence developmental state as is evident in the works of Rajni Kothari (Beteille, in Elliot 2003). By and large, the emphasis of political scientists has been on civil society and the dynamics of the democratic state. On the other hand, sociologists have seen civil society more in terms of its relation to social movements and the role of NGOs, although they have engaged with its relationship to the democratic state as well. There is now available an impressive omnibus on civil society with its various dimensions in the Indian context, some of which will be described further (Jayaram 2005).

CIVIL SOCIETY IN ITS CURRENT USAGE

The classical and the contemporary views have thrown up certain crucial issues of contention with regard to civil society. At the outset it should be conceded that despite the surge in civil society scholarship and activities from the 1980s onwards, there is no consensus regarding its nature and its characteristics. This is acknowledged by every scholar studying the concept. It has become a 'holdall concept' (Jayaram 2005, 18). However, there are broad areas of agreement which can be a starting point for understanding the concept.

In its current usage, civil society is commonly defined as the 'space between the family and the state where people associate across ties of kinship, aside from the market and independent of the state' (Elliot 2003, 8). On the one hand, it is described as a distinct personalized sphere of activities, associations, informal networks, social movements and voluntary agencies which are autonomous, are formed with intent and which provide space for individuals and groups to pursue their interests. Such entities often vary widely in their goals or even in the way they influence other people's rights and liberties. However, they restrict the power of the state and are seen in a positive way. By this line of reasoning, different types of voluntarily formed groups whether student's union, clubs, child rights groups or even an artist's forum would qualify as civil society. The growth of such groups is often associated with a democratic state. It is seen as the factor that strengthens democracy.

According to another view, the arena of civil society is all those formal organizations, whether colleges, hospitals or professional associations, which exist outside the state and have a rational legal organization, characterized by an open system of stratification with avenues of mobility and a neutral stance (Gurpreet Mahajan, in Elliot 2003).

Thus, broadly speaking, civil society comprises both an informal arena and a sphere of formal organizations which exist outside the state, restricting its powers and is aligned to a democratic environment. Although this description gives us some understanding of civil society, it raises more questions than answers some of which shall be explored further.

AS DISTINCT FROM THE STATE AND THE MARKET

There is a belief that civil society is the distinct third sphere of the society, the other two being the state and the economy (Cohen and Arato 1992, 18). The third sphere argument implies that neither the logic of the political sphere which is characterized by conflict and power nor that of the economic sphere where there is competition for scarce resources would apply to civil society. Cohen and Arato seem to suggest that these three spheres of human action belong to different sectors and have their own logic and organization, distinct from others. Speaking along these lines, they reiterate that though civil society may at times deal with economic activities, it is different from formal economic systems. Hence, civil society and economic system may not be watertight compartments but they are sufficiently distinct from each other. Underlying principles of the two are certainly different. Cohen and Arato look at the political system and civil society in a similar way. Describing the political system, they talk about its two components— the state and the public sphere—the latter refers to 'non-state sphere of politics'. For them, both the state and the public sphere are fundamentally different from the civil society. From this perspective, civil society as a personalized sphere has its own logic and drive. It works in welfare activities such as education, employment and health through a large number of NGOs. In popular thinking, these organizations work separately from the state and the market. Their funding often comes directly from multilateral funding agencies rather than through the state and their activities are often not guided by market considerations. By this contention, civil society is people's space which is autonomous, is ethical and is a healthy mix of social good and individual interests as it integrates and harmonizes individual differences (Seligman 1992). In this view, civil society is the space which gives succour to people living in highly individualistic, impersonal societies where alienation is widespread. Thus, it is an immensely attractive space.

By this contention, collective life can be conceptualized as consisting of the household, civil society, economy and polity. They are assumed to function as independent spheres, while the reality is far from it (Neera Chandoke, in Elliot 2003).

CIVIL SOCIETY AND THE STATE

This has been the most deliberated issue in civil society discourse. Civil society and state, as pointed earlier, are often seen as binary opposites. While civil society is perceived as a remedy against an authoritarian state, the state is viewed as its opponent. This thinking is entrenched in the general belief that the state is the aggressor; it often indulges in overreach, whereas the civil society as an independent moral entity protects the common citizen from the state and helps to build a social life entrenched in freedom. This view, though dominant, has been questioned by many.

STATE FACILITATES AND RESTRICTS CIVIL SOCIETY

Hegel argued that the state is the prerequisite for the civil society to exist. It will be right to say that the very laws which give civil liberties to people and which civil society strives to implement are formulated by the state and facilitated by its components such as the police, judiciary and the bureaucracy. 'Therefore ironically, the very state that civil society supposedly positions itself against enables the latter in the sense that it provides the legal and the political settings for the sphere to exist and maintain itself' (Neera Chandoke, in Elliot 2003, 243).

This gives enormous power to the state over the civil society organizations. The Indian state decides which civil society organizations will be allowed to function by law. While it is likely to allow a bank employees' union to agitate for better wages, it may not allow an NGO to organize an agitation against the building of a dam which has displaced thousands. The reins of power are with the state after all. It is wary of those groups which challenge its authority. The state, for instance, is very hard towards the so-called Maoists who represent the most marginalized tribals and considers them as anti-national elements. On the other hand, it is soft towards politically important farmers' groups demanding better procurement price, free electricity or loan waivers. Looking at this, can we understand that civil society is distinct from the state? Instead, civil society is constrained by the state, both in its discourse and its actions. It must work within the rules framed by the state. Although civil society has the right to oppose the state, it should be done within the definition of law. It can use the legal means available to do so such as mobilizing public opinion, organizing agitations or going to the court. Any overstepping will invite negative consequences.

While it is true that state lays down agendas and programmes for the civil society, it is equally true that the state uses various means to make the civil society accept and follow it. There is another side to the relationship between the state and the civil society. There are times when civil society requires the support of the state. It needs to join forces with the state to carry on with its work. For instance, groups fighting against sexual exploitation of children need the state to bring in appropriate legislations, to facilitate their implementation, to punish the offenders, rehabilitate those rescued and to provide state protection if required.

SEWA

SEWA, a movement of the most marginalized women seeking self-employment, often seeks and gets support from higher levels of state officials while at the same time is in conflict with lower level of the state machinery with whom it works at the grass root level (Oommen 2004).

The function of the state is to organize and codify the power of the social formations in society. While power of social formations is more informal and loose as it is constantly questioned by those in the margins, state formalizes this power and makes it stable and concrete through codi-fied laws and the judicial system. Hence, power is concentrated in the state. However, it should be reiterated that this power comes from society. State extracts its power from the society. Hence, it cannot be unconnected to the civil society. The two are interrelated through contours of power relations and structures. Hence, the view that civil society, which is a democratic space, protects the citizen from an authoritarian state incorrectly undermines the collusion between the two.

Mark Robinson relates the civil society and the 'political society' complete with political parties, legislative functions and election practices in a more holistic way. Although the tendency to put them as binary opposites seems useful as a tool, it has been recognized that in actual reality they may at times overlap, come in conflict with each other or get merged. This is especially true in the Indian context where seeing the two as separate realms will prevent an understanding of 'how consciously designed ideological projects find strategic and organizational expression in civil and political society' (Mark Robinson, in Elliot 2003, 358).

CIVIL SOCIETY AS SOCIAL CAPITAL AND THE STATE

Robert Putnam[2] talks of civil society 'in the sense of dense networks of associations, as generating what he calls as social capital' (Neera Chandoke, in Elliot 2003, 252). Social capital includes those

---

[2] Based on statistical and historical data, Robert Putnam (1993) did a huge study of Italy, *Making Democracy Work*, in which he asserted that civil society makes democratic government more successful.

aspects of social relations which work together for the achievement of goals. The denser the associations, the more they can get rid of differences and create a democratic space. Further, the greater the engagement, the more will be the common norms, trust on each other and integration which are essential features of a democracy.

The question that needs to be answered is whether it is possible to build trust without interference from other institutions. State policies could at times divide the civil society irreparably. In the Indian context, one such instance was the implementation of Mandal commission report for reservation of government jobs for Other Backward Classes in 1990. Bitter hostility gripped some sections of upper caste people in certain parts of the country and divided the civil society into those for and against the provision. Another example is that of disputes over places of worship that have often led to the breakdown of relationships between Hindus and Muslims in India, for example, the dispute over Babri Masjid and Ram Janam Bhumi in Uttar Pradesh. Events such as these prove that the idea of civil society as a sphere of harmonious personalized relationships is far from true.

IS CIVIL SOCIETY A DEMOCRATIC SPACE?

Many believe that the nature and the working of associational life, the component of civil society, is essentially a democratic one, free from power relations. A closer look shows the shallowness of this belief. It is as much entrenched with power relations and inequalities as any other. Whether it is caste, patriarchy, ethnic or religious identities, these are often reinforced and at times undermined by the civil society. It is, thus, impossible to visualize civil society as devoid of power relations. In this hierarchical arena, the dominant sections of the civil society may work against the rest of it, at times with support from the state (Oommen 2004). Civil society may not thus be a space where equality is the basic feature.

CIVIL SOCIETY IN CONTEMPORARY INDIA

While it will be right to say that civil society should not be 'identified with democracy per se, it is a precondition for democracy in as much as it constitutes both a site for democracy and a cluster of values and institutions that are intrinsic to democracy' (Chandoke, in Elliot 2003, 258). In other words, for a democracy to exist there should be a space for people to interact, to communicate their views, to have discussion in a free environment to decide on the type of society they want, their expectations from those in power and the values they nurture. To develop and exist, democracy needs such a space which civil society offers.

Formal democracy often caters to the powerful and the influential. The powerful within the civil society may join hands with the state. By offering space to contest, civil society offers the possibility of struggle against such forces. For instance, the debates and contests between majoritarian and liberal democratic forces in contemporary India are possible because of the existence of a robust civil society. Thus, it is very clear that a strong civil society is a precondition of democracy. At times, there are some civil society groups that take up adversarial role in relation to the state, and at other times, they could cooperate with the state.

Locke and Hegel related civil society to the process of transition from traditional hierarchical institutions to modern democratic ones. If this is so, then it has been suggested by scholars that associations based on ascriptive and hierarchical identities cannot find a place within civil society (Mahajan, in Elliot 2003, 185–6). Arguing along similar lines, Andre Beteille has positioned civil society within the modern ethos of social equality, individual rights and liberty. According to Beteille, traditional groups like those based on caste and religion do not qualify as civil society groups as they are based on primordial principles and not on secular rational ones. Following Alexis de Tocqueville's views on mediating institutions, Andre Beteille looks at the civil society as having the role of a mediator between the state and the citizen. Civil society augments the status of the citizen and makes the state more responsive to citizens in a democratic society. It strengthens democratic traditions (Mahajan, in Elliot, 2003).

Contrary to this view are those who argue that kinship, religion, region, ethnic and caste based associational life is an essential part of Indian society. To ignore this empirical reality and to treat their agendas as morally inferior would make the study of civil society incomplete (Mark Robinson, in Elliot 2003). It can be said that scholars like Rajni Kothari have given legitimacy to social entities which are ascriptive by including them as part of civil society. Thinkers such as M. N. Srinivas, Sussane Hoeber Rudolph, Oommen and Mark Robinson have supported this argument. According to Rudolph, there is similarity between caste associations and modern version of civil society.

> *The caste associations became vehicles of self-organization for social reform and for political formation. Caste, a vehicle for maintenance of a hierarchical society was converted via caste associations into a means for the more numerous lower castes to mobilize and participate in ways that challenged ritual hierarchy. (Rudolph 2000, 1767)*

These associations helped caste members to achieve social and political goals in contemporary Indian society.

It is clear from the above discussion that there are difficulties in applying the Western notion of civil society to non-Western societies like India. Giving a more holistic view, Mark Robinson believes that 'the concept of civil society can be enriched and extended by applying it creatively to the analysis of contemporary Indian realities' (Mark Robinson, in Elliot 2003, 357). In this context, he reiterates that it is not right to treat civil society as a set of associations and organizations only, 'it extends to the realm of ideology' (Mark Robinson, in Elliot 2003, 357). Civil society in India has a two-way nature. On the one hand, these are associations and social movements representing citizens and fighting for their rights and dignity. On the other hand, there are those pursuing narrower agendas characterized by intense and often conflicting ideologies.

From the 1960s, a visible disenchantment towards the Indian state was in evidence. This was followed by a growing importance in the role of civil society associations. These trends were reflected in the scholarship in the Indian state and the role of civil society in India.[3]

MAIN SITES OF CONTESTATION

Groups based on specific religious and other similar identities constitute an important fault line within Indian society and politics. Casteist forces in combination with patriarchal forces intersect vigorously with such religious groups to produce a dangerous cocktail. This phenomenon is reflected in the sharp debates around the idea, practices and institutions of secularism in contemporary India.[4]

CIVIL SOCIETY CONTESTATIONS AGAINST THE STATE

Contemporary India is witnessing an array of contestations which have pitted the civil society groups often representing the poor and marginalized against the policies of an overarching state and its bureaucracy. These include women's groups, human rights organizations, environmental groups, tribal groups and the like. Such groups match the typical definition of civil society as a democratic and secular space which exists between the family and the state and represents the rights of the citizens.

There was a proliferation of such groups and their movements after the Emergency in 1977. 'Many of these consciously maintained a critical distance from the formal political arena, preferring to pursue a political strategy in the civil society domain'[5] (Mark Robinson, in Elliot 2003, 372). The main area of contestation was the state's policies and programmes which ignored

---

[3] For Marxists, the post-Independence bourgeois state is incapable of addressing the problems of the marginalized sections. It is the civil society which has played an important role in mobilizing such groups for their democratic rights against an impassive state. Referring to this realm as 'creative society', Mohanty concedes its role in making demands for a 'decentralized, responsive and participatory state' (Mahajan 2003, 183). Analysing in a different way are others like Rajni Kothari who considered the focus of the state on 'market efficiency', 'profitability', 'development' and 'national security' as an incorrect and a defective approach which sidelines the rights and liberty of the individual, undermining democracy (Kothari 1988, 2)

[4] For example, some groups such as the Rashtriya Swayamsevak Sangh (RSS) and the Vishva Hindu Parishad (VHP) have advocated the consolidation of a pan Hindu identity in India.

[5] Cited in the context of Narmada campaign, see Dwivedi 1998.

the interests of the poor and marginalized in favour of the rich and powerful. These include NBA against building of big dams on Narmada River which has led to displacement and loss of livelihood of thousands or Chipko campaign against the commercial felling of trees in the hill areas of Uttarakhand. Although these and similar movements have succeeded in making their voices heard in India as well as internationally, the mighty and powerful have had their way in most cases.

A large number of newer civil society groups have developed in urban areas from the 1990s onwards often led by educated middle classes holding the state-run organizations, municipal corporations and the like responsible for a variety of issues such as corruption, poor service delivery and lack of sanitation; fighting for their accountability to the public. The demands of these 'citizen action groups' are both local and national. They often have access to media and its various sources of publicity, thus making it difficult for the state machinery or political parties to ignore them (Mark Robinson, in Elliot 2003, 373).

Indegenous People's Rally, September 2016

Source: Media Collective
Photograph Courtesy: The Media Collective. Reproduced with Permission

Public Meeting on Non Performing Assets

Source: Media collective
Photograph Courtesy: The Media Collective. Reproduced with Permission

Student Protest in March 2017

Source: Media Collective
Photograph Courtesy: The Media Collective. Reproduced with Permission

SOME LANDMARK MOBILIZATIONS OF CIVIL SOCIETY GROUPS IN INDIA

Since the 1970s, a number of movements and mobilizations have been organized by civil society groups in the form of protests, satyagraha, strikes, agitations, social movements and so on. These collective actions have taken up issues of importance including both local and universal. These include women's rights, child rights, corruption, right to work, right to information, rights of backward 'classes, human rights, health and malnourishment, accountability in the bureaucracy and the political class, conserving environment, education for all and so on. These movements generally kept away from political parties and tried to remain apolitical.

It should be added that in the last few decades, the Supreme Court has allowed PILs (public interest litigations) on issues of public importance to be filed like 'The Vishaka writ petition' in 1992 and 'The Right To Food Case' in 2001. These and many other landmark cases have shown the importance of judicial activism and have often led to strengthening of civil society groups.

RIGHT TO INFORMATION (RTI) MOVEMENT

From the time of Independence, a major discrepancy had existed between the colonial laws which focused on secrecy of government operations and the Constitution of India which has enshrined in it an array of fundamental rights and liberties. The colonial laws such as the Indian Evidence Act (1872) and Official Secrets Act (1923) and the post independence provisions like the Central Civil Services Conduct Rules (1964) severely curtailed access to information on governmental matters for the common citizen. These laws had not only undermined the constitutional and democratic rights of the individual but had also prevented clean, accountable, transparent, corruption free and decentralized functioning of the Government. It was in response to this incongruity that a grass roots level movement started in the 1990s, the RTI Campaign (Venkatesu 2006).

PRECEDENTS TO THE MOVEMENT

There is no doubt that a number of factors were directly or indirectly responsible for creating the foundation for the RTI. The movement should be seen in the backdrop of the impact of the freedom movement; fundamental rights provided by the Constitution of India; the role of the Supreme Court in recognizing and protecting the right to freedom of speech and expression, as well as the part played by few politicians like V. P. Singh who advocated for RTI Act during his tenure as the prime minister. These are some of the important precedents which laid the foundation for the RTI movement of the 1990s, although the act did not become a reality then because of lack of support, absence of organizational structures and the like.

CONSTITUTIONAL PROVISIONS AND THE ROLE OF THE SUPREME COURT

Constitution does not provide for a definite RTI or for that matter a right to freedom of the press; but it is the provisions in the chapter on 'Fundamental Rights' that RTI has been read into.

> *These include Right to Equality Before the Law (Article 14); Right to Freedom and Expression (Article 19(1)(a)) and Right to Life and Personal Liberty (Article 21). The Right to Constitutional Remedies in Article 32, backs these, that is, the Right to approach the Supreme Court in case of infringement of any of these Rights. (Venkatesu 2006. 2)*

A number of judgments of the Supreme Court related to the Right to Freedom of Speech and Expression have brought into focus the need for a RTI, as a complementary right, a basic requirement of a democracy.

> *[I]n a government where all the agents of the public must be responsible for their conduct, there can be but few secrets. The people have a right to know every public act, everything that is done in a public way, by their public functionaries…. The responsibility of officials to explain or to justify their acts is the chief safeguard against oppression and corruption.*[6]

For over two decades, the apex court played an important role in laying the foundation for the RTI. The various decisions taken by the court were in the realm of the freedom of speech and expression like the petition contesting the government ban on newsprint. The campaign for the RTI began with a number of petitions submitted in the Supreme Court by the press under the provisions of the right to freedom of speech and expression. It is through these petitions that the concept of public's right to know started taking shape.

The grass roots level movement which led to the passing of the RTI Act started under the auspices of Rajasthan-based NGO, the Mazdoor Kisan Shakti Sangathan (hereafter MKSS), along with others like Parivarthan. The movement gained academic support by National Campaign for People's Rights to Information (NCPRI) and Commonwealth Human Rights Initiative (Venkatesu 2006). A major role, however, was played by MKSS.

MKSS

MKSS is a peasant–farmer combine which has been working in rural Rajasthan for over two decades. Its main thrust has been to organize campaigns around issues of importance through grass roots level mobilizations. They have also at times contested local elections. MKSS has been very active since 1990 and has achieved some success on matters such as minimum wages, right to food and right to work.

---

[6] Justice K. K. Mathew, Supreme Court of India: State of UP vs Rajnarain (AIR 1975 SC 865).

Their campaign for RTI started with public hearings or *Jan Sunwais*, a common method used by MKSS. It implies open democratic debate on public issues with NGOs, elected members of the panchayats, legislatures, government officials, representatives of media and so on. The common method has been to identify an issue and invite people accordingly. For instance, at one time, MKSS came to know of corruption in funds for drought relief and they organized a series of public hearings in which members of panchayati raj institutions, certain government officials and NGOs were invited and it was proved in front of the public how corruption had taken place. It was obvious that corruption happened due to lack of information and adherence to secrecy in records.

In addition to public hearings, MKSS organized dharnas in different parts of Rajasthan like Beawar in 1995, to push for their demand to put in force an administrative direct for citizen's RTI on local development funding. The dharna in Beawar had a massive impact on the local people who participated in large numbers in the various daily activities such as listening to speeches, singing and sloganeering. They also made financial contribution across classes from the very poor to the rich. While the dharna still continued in Beawar, the protest extended to Jaipur where as many as 70 people's organizations and many well-known respected citizens joined. The mainstream press to gave its support.

In the meanwhile, in October 1995, the Lal Bahadur Shastri Academy of Administration, Mussoorie, organized a national workshop on the issue of granting RTI. There was a widespread support among the participants.

It was in May 1996 that the government of Rajasthan announced its intention to set up a committee which would give, within two months, a definitive shape to the RTI. All along, the government insisted that the provision was coming through not because of the efforts of the civil society but because of government's own preference for creating a transparent system. However, even after a year, no orders were passed. This led to another dharna in Jaipur in May 1997. After 52 days of the dharna, the government announced that it had already given a notification on public's right to get photocopies of documents related to development work from local government bodies.

Although the government wanted to take the credit, it was very clear that the civil society groups like MKSS played a decisive role in getting citizens' an RTI. The step taken by the state government in Jaipur was a welcome step and it set a precedent for other states to follow suit. Due to demands made by the grassroots level groups, various state governments passed the RTI Act including Goa and Tamil Nadu in 1997, Karnataka (2000), Delhi (2001), Assam (2002), Maharashtra, Madhya Pradesh and Jammu and Kashmir (2003).

Introduction of the RTI Act at the level of states eventually paved the way for a national RTI Act, although efforts to have such an Act were being made from 1996 onwards when the NCPRI was set up. It comprised activists, retired civil servants, journalists, intellectuals, writers, lawyers, academicians and so on. Their aim was to get a national RTI Act passed. An international organization called—Common Wealth Human Rights Initiative also played an important role in pushing for the national-level act by supporting discussions and making recommendations.

It was in this environment of protest and pressure that the Press Council of India, chaired by Justice P. B. Sawant formulated a draft bill which was updated by the National Institute of Rural Development and submitted to the Government of India. However, it could not be presented in the Parliament due to multifarious reasons. Following this, the central government appointed a working group under H. D. Shourie which drafted 'The Freedom of Information Bill 1997'. Even this did not result in a legislation. It was in 2000 that the 'The Freedom of Information Bill 2000' was tabled in the Parliament. Even this did not become an Act.

It was in the year 2005 that the government at the Centre appointed a National Advisory Council which also included activists such as Aruna Roy and Jean Dreze who had worked all along to create an effective RTI Act and had been associated with NCPRI. Eventually, on 15 June 2005, the Parliament passed the bill and it was ratified by the President and the process for implementation started from 12 October 2005 onwards.

It is clear that a decisive role in the formation of the RTI Act was played by the civil society groups who continued to put pressure on governments at the state level and the centre. Once formed, the task of these organizations has been to work for its implementation. They have been active in creating awareness about the act among the masses, in encouraging them to take advantage of it and in preventing any proposed dilution of the Act by those in power. With threats or even at times, violence against RTI activists, their job is truly challenging.

THE ANTI-CORRUPTION MOVEMENT

Corruption limits the possibility of democratic governance and India, in-fact, is no exception. India is among the most corrupt countries of the world. The movement against corruption started in the 1960s when the first administrative reforms committee floated the idea of a Lokpal. The term Lokpal (Ombudsman) was coined in 1963 by L. M. Singhvi, a Member of Parliament during a debate. Subsequently, civil society activists like Aruna Roy were involved in the formulation of the anti-corruption law. There was a realization that an effective law could curb corruption among public functionaries and bring more accountability and transparency in their working. The Lokpal Bill was first introduced by advocate Shanti Bhushan in 1968 and was passed in 1969 by the fourth Lok Sabha. However, before it could be passed by the Rajya Sabha, the Lok Sabha was dissolved and the Bill lapsed. Following this, newer versions of the Bill were formulated in 1971, 1977, 1985, 1989, 1996, 1998, 2001, 2005 and 2008 but none of them were passed for one reason or the other.

Although the anti-corruption law has existed for a long time, corruption has increased manifold over the years. In 2010, a number of major cases of corruption came into the limelight. As a result, the Parliament decided to set up an independent body to tackle the many cases of political and bureaucratic corruption. In the same year, a draft Lokpal Bill (the Indian version of Ombudsman) was tabled in the Parliament. Activists and the civil society groups considered the Bill to be very mild which left the major political positions outside its purview such as that of the prime minister, cabinet ministers and members of Parliament.

This was the trigger for a major anti-corruption movement 'India Against Corruption' (IAC) led by Anna Hazare (Kisan Baburao Hazare), along with a group of activists such as Arvind Kejriwal, Prashant Bhushan, Yogendra Yadav, Kiran Bedi and Swami Agnivesh. The movement took place in two phases.

PHASE I

It started on 5 April 2011, when Anna Hazare and his team demanded the enactment of a long pending anti-corruption law, the 'Jan Lokpal Bill' (Citizen's Ombudsman Bill). They also demanded that civil society members must have a say in drafting the Bill. Anna Hazare used Gandhian means like indefinite fast to pressurize the government. 'The movement is considered to be a milestone in the constitutional history of India forcing the government to accept civil society's demand to have a say in drafting the stringent anti-corruption law, the Lokpal bill' (Singh and Sohoni 2016, 1). It got massive media support which helped in buttressing the movement. There was a huge public support, mostly from individuals and civil society groups, generally unconnected to political parties who came from all over India and gathered in Delhi to champion the cause.

Three days into the fast, the government agreed to include five members selected by Anna Hazare to be part of the drafting committee. The members, thus chosen were Anna Hazare himself, RTI activist Arvind Kejriwal, retired Supreme Court judge and Lokayukta of Karnataka at that time, Santosh Hegde as well as Prashant and Shanti Bhushan, both lawyers. The committee was to complete its work by 30 June 2011.

In an ultimatum given to the government on 8 June of the same year, Anna Hazare stated that the Jan Lokpal Bill should be passed by 15 August 2011. He threatened another hunger strike if it was not done. The government came up with an approved Bill in end July 2011, which kept the prime minister during his term in office, higher judiciary and the 'conduct of members of Parliament inside the Parliament' outside its purview. The drafting committee did not agree to the proposed Bill. Hence, the government tabled its own Bill in the Parliament in August of that year. IAC considered the Bill to be weak and would ridden with loopholes.

PHASE II

Following this development, Anna Hazare decided to start another protest and sought permission from the Delhi police for their chosen location (JP park). Police put up certain conditions which were unacceptable to IAC, calling it obstruction of their democratic rights. As a result, Anna Hazare and important team members were taken into preventive custody on the morning of 16 August 2011. There was a huge public protest which forced the government to release them by evening. However, Anna Hazare refused to leave the jail till a written, unconditional permission was given for the venue. In the meanwhile, he started his fast in the jail itself. Police had to keep him in jail for the night and the next day, permission was granted to the team Anna to hold their protest in the bigger Ramlila Maidan without any preconditions. The fast and agitation continued for the next 11 days. The government eventually responded by inviting a debate on the Bill in the Parliament on 27 August 2011. Anna Hazare ended his fast with the declaration that he was only suspending it temporarily and that it would only end when a strong Lokpal Bill is passed.

While on the one hand the team Anna was successful in pressurizing the government to work on a meaningful Lokpal Bill, cracks started developing within their own team. Santosh Hegde did not approve of Anna Hazare telling the Parliament what to do, giving timelines. Swami Agnivesh also gradually started distancing himself from the movement. Many others, including major political parties, had doubts about Anna Hazare's version of the Lokpal Bill. Some were apprehensive that this will give more powers to Lokpal in comparison to the Parliament. Others felt that it would be above the Constitution.

Just before the winter session of the Parliament in 2011, Anna Hazare fasted in Delhi for a day to press for his demand for a strong Bill and also criticized the proposals made by the parliamentary committee regarding the Bill. Following this, the proposed Bill was debated in the Parliament on 22 December 2011. Serious objections were made regarding inclusion of the prime minister, parliamentarians and judiciary under the Bill. Also it was labelled as unconstitutional. The government withdrew the Bill and reintroduced a revised version as 'the Lokpal and Lokayukta Bill 2011'. It was approved by Lok Sabha on 27 December 2011. But some opposition members found the revised version highly diluted and deeply flawed. The Bill was then referred to the Rajya Sabha where it got stalled amidst debate and objections and it could not be passed in the winter session. Meanwhile, Anna Hazare fasted for a day at Jantar Mantar on 25 March 2012 for a stronger Bill. Following this, he went on a five-week-long tour in Maharashtra to spread awareness on the issue and the need for a strong Bill.

Following this, on 25 July 2012, another indefinite fast was organized by Anna Hazare's fellow activists in the movement. Anna Hazare himself joined it on 29 July onwards and broke the fast on 3 August, with the pledge that the fight would go on. Some of the fellow activists announced the formation of a political party (Aam Aadmi Party or AAP) to fight for a transparent, corruption-free India.

It should be noted here that there were deep differences between Jan Lokpal Bill as proposed by Anna Hazare and his supporters and the government's various versions of Lokpal Bill on some crucial points. These include whether and when prime minister, higher judiciary, members of Parliament and all public servants could be investigated; whether the role of the Lokpal will be to take punitive action or just refer the matter to courts; whistleblower protection; whether NGOs would come under the Lokpal; removal of Lokpal functionaries and whether the anti-corruption wing of the CBI should be merged with the Lokpal.

While the government's version was seen by many as a diluted version, the Bill proposed by the civil society group was also criticized by many for being 'extra constitutional' and 'draconian' in nature. It was feared that such a Bill could subvert democratic process.[7]

It was in the December of 2013 that the Lokpal and Lokayukta Bill was finally passed in both houses of Parliament, in Lok Sabha on 17, and Rajya Sabha on 18. In keeping with their demand, a separate Whistleblowers Protection Act was passed in 2014. While the passing of the Lokpal Bill was a victory of sorts for IAC, it was clearly a different and diluted version of their Jan Lokpal Bill. In January of the same year, Delhi government led by an IAC member and Chief Minister Arvind Kejriwal prepared to introduce the Jan Lokpal Bill in the Delhi assembly but failed to do so following which he resigned as the chief minister.

THE PRESENT STATUS

The appointment of the Lokpal is to be done by the prime minister, Lok Sabha speaker, leader of the opposition, Chief justice of India and an eminent jurist nominated by the president. As no opposition party has at least 10 per cent of seats in the present Lok Sabha, there is no leader of opposition (this being as essential criteria for the appointment of leader of the opposition). There is now a proposal to amend the Lokpal Bill of 2013 to allow the leader of the largest opposition party to be part of the appointment committee. Hence, the Lokpal Bill was sent to the standing committee for review in 2016 leading to the Lokpal Amendment Act, 2016, a more diluted edition of the 2013 version. The status of this all-important Bill in 2018 is that a Lokpal has not yet been appointed and it is languishing in the corridors of power.

RIGHT TO FOOD CAMPAIGN (RTFC)

The RTFC began in April 2001, when a PIL on right to food was filed in the Supreme Court by People's Union for Civil Liberties (PUCL), an informal conglomerate of a number of civil

---

[7] Many from the political class and those outside it including civil society activists such as Arundhati Roy and Aruna Roy had reservations about the Bill.

society organizations, following reports of hunger deaths in Rajasthan while the government storehouses were brimming with food grain. Popularly known as the 'Right to Food Case', the petition questioned whether right to food was included under the Right to Life (Article 21) of the Constitution of India and demanded that the large food stocks with the government should be used with immediate effect to feed the hungry. In the beginning, the case was against the Government of India, six state governments and the Food Corporation of India (FCI) for insufficient drought relief. Later the scope of the case was expanded to include the larger issues of chronic hunger and malnutrition, and thus, all state governments came to be included in the petition. The petition highlights two areas of colossal neglect by the state—the public distribution system (PDS) and the drought relief work.

In a landmark judgment in November 2001, the Supreme Court ordered a complete implementation of PDS, made Midday Meal Scheme (MDM) obligatory (it was a voluntary scheme earlier) and ordered a better implementation of Integrated Child Development Services (ICDS).[8]

Over the years, the network has expanded to include organizations from different parts of the country involved in varied activities including organizations working for child rights, women's development and human rights organizations, those working for tribals or Dalits and so on. Such large numbers have come together because they believe that it is the fundamental right of every individual to be free from hunger and for this, the responsibility lies with the state. Coordination within this large network is done through a small secretariat and agenda is fixed through national conventions.

PUCL

PUCL was originally founded by Jaya Prakash Narayan and named as People's Union for Civil Liberties and Democratic Rights (PUCLDR) in 1976. It was conceived as an organization meant to defend civil liberties and human rights. It was renamed PUCL in 1980. Since then, it has emerged as voice of those on the margins of society.

In the course of this case, a number of important interim orders have been passed by the Supreme Court which have impacted the poor favourably. These include universalization of school midday meals; supplementary nutrition programme for children under six years, pregnant and lactating

---

[8] ICDS is a government programme in India launched on 2 October 1975 for providing food, preschool education and primary healthcare to children under six years of age and their mothers. ICDS was closed for some years but was later revived. In the tenth five year plan, it was linked to the anganwadi centres in rural areas and its scope was expanded to include gender inequality, immunization and referral services. ICDS operates under the Ministry of Women and Child Development.

mothers and adolescent girls and so on. Such interim orders have given legitimacy to the common man to approach the courts if these orders are not abided by the concerned authorities. For instance, if cooked midday meal is not provided to children in a primary school, the authorities can be taken to task under the Supreme Court orders. The immediate challenge is that they should be implemented in letter and spirit.

While the civil society groups lauded these orders, they felt that compliance with them would be a challenge. Hence, they started mobilizing people and organizations in large numbers for the implementation of these orders leading to formation of a major campaign which came to be known as RFC (Dreze 2002). Through discussions, a realization came that the right to food is directly connected to control of resources such as forests, land and water and the livelihood issues. Hence, the need to fight for a more people-oriented model of development based on equality. The campaign has since expanded its mandate to include implementation of legislation and schemes such as Mahatma Gandhi National Rural Employment Guarantee Act (MNREGA), ICDS, PDS and MDM. In addition, the campaign joins movements for forest right, land rights, forced displacement and so on.

NATIONAL LEGISLATION ON FOOD SECURITY

From 2009 onwards, the main agenda of RTFC was to get the government of the day to pass the National Food Security Act (NFSA). For the next four years, there were intense debates between the campaign members, the state, the political class and other stakeholders. The RTFC, in the meanwhile, drafted its own version of the Act titled 'Food Entitlement Act'. The proposed Act was a more comprehensive draft.

> *[It demanded a] decentralized procurement mechanism, a universal and expanded public distribution*
> *system including cereals, pulses, millets and oil, special provisions such as feeding programs for children,*
> *social security pensions for the aged and disabled, portability of entitlements for migrants and so on.*
> *The draft also listed broad principles related to coercive land acquisition, protecting small and marginal*
> *farmers, a moratorium on GM crops and so on. (RTFC 2009)*

Eventually, the NFSA, 2013 became a reality. However, this was a highly diluted version which mainly focused on distribution of subsidized food, a minimalist version.

The 'Right to Food case' ended on 10 February 2018 by an order of the Supreme Court. Referring to the passing of the NFSA, 2013 and the provisions there in, the Court said that there was nothing else left in the case. The Court, however, said that fresh petition could be filed under the NFSA for any grievances.

CONCLUSION

An overview of the concept of civil society, its various dimensions and its role in society, reveals its complex, highly variable and dynamic nature. Its various stated features like that of the third space between the state and the market or family; its opposition to the state; as a democratic secular rational space comprising informal relationships, networks and voluntary associations which champion the cause of the marginalized, have all been debated.

While at times civil society opposes the state, at other times it collaborates, overlaps or even merges with it. It may be fighting for the rights and dignity of the citizens, or on the other hand, may have narrower, parochial agendas. In the Indian context, the most secular, rational and democratic organizations are as much considered a part of civil society as are traditional, hierarchical, primordial organizations such as caste, ethnic or religious groups. Despite these complexities, there have been a number of landmark civil society mobilizations which have brought or have the promise to bring decisive changes in the lives of citizens of India such as the RTI, Right to Food and anti-corruption law.

POINTS FOR DISCUSSION

- The Western concept of civil society faces its deepest challenge in a traditional society like India where rights and dignity of the individual are undermined in the name of caste, kinship or religion. Comment.
- Will it be right to say that some of the most profound progressive changes in Indian society have been possible because of civil society mobilizations?
- How should democracies, in your opinion, respond to civil society movements that are autocratic in nature?

REFERENCES AND READINGS

Beteille, Andre. 2000. 'Civil Society and Its Institutions'. In *Civil Society and Democracy: A Reader*, edited by Carolyn M. Elliot, 191–200. New Delhi: Oxford University Press.

Chandoke, Neera. 1995. *State and Civil Society: Explorations in Political Theory*. New Delhi: SAGE Publications.

Rudolph, Susanne Hoeber. 2000. 'Civil Society and the Realm of Freedom'. *Economic and Political Weekly*, 35 (20): 1762–69.

Chaubey, N. P., Debabrata Panda and Girijesh Pant, eds. 2013. *People's Struggles and Movements for Equitable Society*. Allahabad: Indian Academy of Social Sciences.

Cohen, Jean, and Andrew Arato. 1992. *Political Theory and Civil Society*. Cambridge: MIT Press.

Dreze, J. 2002. 'The Right to Food: From Courts to the Streets'. Available at:www.righttofoodindia.org/links/articles_home.html (Accessed 25 March 2014).

Dwivedi, R. 1998. 'Resisting Dams and "Development": Contemporary Significance of the Campaign against Narmada Projects in India'. *European Journal of Development Research*, 10 (2): 135–83.

Elliot, Carolyn M. 2003. 'Civil Society and Democracy: A Comparative Review Essay'. In *Civil Society and Democracy: A Reader*, edited by Carolyn M. Elliot, 1–39. New Delhi: Oxford University Press.

Gramsci, Antonio. 1971. *Selections from Prison Notebooks*. Translated from Italian by Quintin Hoare and Geoffrey Nowell Smith. London: Lawrence and Wishart.

Gudavarthy, Ajay. 2013. *Politics of Post-Civil Society: Contemporary History of Political Movements in India*. New Delhi: SAGE Publications.

Jayal, Nirja Gopal. 2013. *Citizenship and Its Discontents: An Indian History*. Ranikhet: Permanent Black.

Jayaram, N. 2005. 'Civil Society: An Introduction to the Discourse'. In *Themes in Indian Sociology*. Vol. 7: *On Civil Society: Issues and Perspectives*, edited by N. Jayaram, 15–40. New Delhi: SAGE Publications.

Kothari, Rajni. 1988. *State against Democracy: In Search of Humane Governance*. Delhi: Ajanta Publishers.

Oommen, T. K. 2004. *Nation, Civil Society and Social Movements*. New Delhi: SAGE Publications.

Pelczynski, Z. A. 1988. 'Solidarity and the "Rebirth of Civil Society"'. In *Civil Society and the State: New Perspectives*, edited by John Keane, 361–80. London: Verso.

Putnam, Robert. 1993. *Making Democracy Work: Civic Traditions in Modern Italy*. Princeton, NJ: Princeton University Press.

RTFC. (n.d.) 'Foundation Statement'. Available at: www.righttofoodindia.org/foundation.html (Accessed 25 March 2014).

———. 2009. 'Food Entitlement Act, 2009—Draft of 12th September, 2009'. Available at: www.righttofoodindia.org/data/rtf_act_draft_charter_sept09.pdf (Accessed 25 March 2014).

Seligman, Adam. 1992. *The Idea of Civil Society*. New York, NY: Free Press.

Singh, Megha, and R. K. Sohoni. 2016. 'The Anti-Corruption Movement in India and the Lokpal'. *Imperial journal of Interdisciplinary Research (IJIR)*, 2 (4): 112–114.

Taylor, Charles. 1990. 'Modes of Civil Society'. *Public Culture*, 3 (1).

Venkatesu, E. 2006. 'Human Rights in the Era of Globalization'. Paper presented at National Seminar held in department of political science, University of Hyderabad, Hyderabad, November 3–4.

Index